Unlocking the Mysteries from Beyond

KRYON

Monika Muranyi

www.ariane-books.com

Published by: Ariane Books
1217, av. Bernard O., suite 101, Outremont, Quebec, Canada H2V 1V7
Phone: (1) 514-276-2949, Fax: (1) 514-276-4121
info@editions-ariane.com – www.editions-ariane.com

www.ariane-books.com – www.editions-ariane.com

Cover design: Deb DeLisi, Carl Lemyre
Interior design: Interscript

June 2015

ISBN: 978-2-89626-255-7 (pbk)
ISBN: 978-2-89626-256-4 (Pdf)
ISBN: 978-2-89626-257-1 (ebook)

Distributed by: New Leaf
401 Thornton Rd. Lithia Springs, GA 30122-1557
Phone: 770.948.7845 – Fax: 770.944.2313
domestic@newleaf-dist.com – foreign@newleaf-dist.com.
Printed in USA

This book
is dedicated to
all the mothers
everywhere: Gaia,
our Mother Earth;
The Pleiadians,
our spiritual mothers;
our biological mothers,
who birthed each
and every one of us;
and the many women
who have assumed
the role of mother
to the precious Souls
who needed one!

CONTENTS

ACKNOWLEDGEMENTS

This book is the third in the Kryon trilogy series that features a compilation of subject-driven information from Kryon's channelled messages given by Lee Carroll. My life, as well as thousands of others, has been deeply enhanced and transformed as a result of Lee's partnership with Kryon. Thank you, Lee, for saying yes to Kryon twenty-five years ago and for making it your life purpose to share these profound messages with the world. A special thank you, Lee, for guiding and mentoring me in the compilation of the Kryon trilogy series, and providing the insights and Human perspective of Kryon's messages. I have deeply enjoyed our many esoteric and thought-provoking conversations shared over the years.

I would like to express a heart-felt thank you to my exceptional editor, Lourana Howard, whose passion for Kryon is equaled by her passion for grammar and editing. I would be lost without her!

I wish to thank my publishers, Ariane Editions. Once again, I am blessed to be represented by a company with a high level of consciousness and a desire to help accelerate the great shift that is occurring on the planet.

My appreciation and gratitude goes out to the many readers of my previous two books who expressed their comments and thanks to me about my work. I am profoundly touched to hear about the positive effect that my books about the Kryon teachings have had. Each of us holds a unique resonance that interacts and affects others, our planet and the universe. Your own personal changes, self-empowerment and path to enlightenment are celebrated beyond imagination.

Finally, a big warm hug and loving embrace to you, dear reader, for choosing to read this book from amongst the many others that are available. It tells me a lot about who you are and I'd like to take this opportunity to thank you and wish you infinite blessings in your life.

FOREWORD

The frontiers of space beckon us with their mystique of vastness and spectacular undiscovered wonders. The oceans of the planet teem with mystery as well, since there is so much yet to be seen and revealed in its depths. History itself is being rediscovered, as we find out that civilization is far older than we thought. What we *don't know* is becoming a much larger issue than anyone ever thought!

However, nothing presents a larger area of discovery than the esoteric parts of the Human Being in this new Earth energy. The ones who are awakening the fullest to this concept, are *Old Souls*. The probability that you are an Old Soul is very high, since you are reading these words. Your interest in the energy today has brought you to this very page.

So, Old Soul, if you have picked up this book, and wondered about what's in it, we can tell you that the Human Soul is like an undiscovered country. We barely know what it is, or where it is, and the workings of it are a complete mystery. Kryon has even told us that it can't really be called "The Human Soul!" (We do anyway.)

There is a major shift happening on the planet, and it is beginning to change the very consciousness of humanity. We are moving out of the warring, survival mode, into a wiser place where we will begin to honor life more fully, and create a more benevolent society. It's a slow process, but 2015 is really the start of a new dispensation of time,

and this is also the basis for the calendars of the Ancients, all changing about now. The bottom line: The Soul is awakening, and beginning to show itself more fully.

*

* *

This particular book begins to examine everything that Kryon has given us within the last three years about the Human Soul. For your benefit, it has been assembled altogether in one place, which means that it's unique, and current for now. It's not just a revelation of the attributes of the Soul, but rather, it's a revelation about the entire Human Being.

What makes this book different than a normal Kryon book, is that there is commentary around the messages of Kryon. The author often gives explanation about the meanings of it all. This is her specialty, pulling scattered information together, so that messages given from all over the world, sometimes out of order, start to make some sense. In addition, Ms. Muranyi was often physically present when many of these channellings were given. This gives her the insight as to hidden unspoken things – sensed information, which Kryon often gives in live channelling, called "The Third Language."

As you read this book, it's important for it to make sense. Any doctor will tell you that you can't study just one organ in the body, even if that's going to be your specialty. You must understand what is known about the whole body, and all the chemistry that goes with it. So, there is much covered here that is what Kryon tells us is needed for us to understand the whole system better. Everything is intertwined in what Kryon has called, the "Soup of the Soul." This refers to the metaphor of the soup that he often gives: You can't study one ingredient in the soup, and understand the whole soup. It's the same with the Soul: Nothing stands alone, in this puzzle of multi-dimensional attributes.

The Soul is everywhere and nowhere, but the concepts of the Soul, as given by Kryon, can be graphed, taught, and studied. This requires that you be exposed to the latest Kryon teachings: "The Nine Attributes of the Human Being," as well as many recent channellings.

Kryon starts to open the jar of knowledge about exactly what the Soul is about, and why it's being seen as something more special than ever at this time in our consciousness evolution.

Is it possible that the Soul is far more than you thought? Can you communicate with it? Is it a part of you, or apart *from* you? Could it be that the Soul is split somehow, and that you don't carry the whole thing? If so, where is the rest of it? These are just some of the questions that are beginning to be answered by Kryon, and THIS is the book that brings it all together!

Lee Carroll

PREFACE

You have in your hands another book driven by the channelled messages from Kryon, as given for over twenty-five years by Lee Carroll, the original Kryon channeller. Kryon can be described as a loving entity who gives messages of peace and empowerment for humanity. Lee Carroll is the author of thirteen Kryon books and the co-author of *The Indigo Children*, *An Indigo Celebration* and *The Indigo Children Ten Years Later*. These books have been translated into over twenty-four languages.

All over the world Lee Carroll has presented many dynamic lectures that explain the Kryon teachings. If you are a devoted Kryon fan, you may already be familiar with the information presented here. Partial extracts of the channelled messages given by Kryon, that relate to our Human Soul, are rewritten here, with permission from Lee Carroll, so that others can discover these profound truths. The purpose of discovering these truths is to then apply them to our lives so that we become more balanced and peaceful in our countenance.

This book is the third in a Kryon trilogy series. The first book, *The Gaia Effect,* was a compilation of Kryon's messages and teachings about the relationship between humanity and Gaia. The second book, *The Human Akash,* was a compilation of Kryon's messages and teachings about our Akash (which encompasses all our past lives) and how we work with our own mastery. This third book is a compilation of Kryon's messages and teachings about the Human Soul. In addition, Kryon has provided some answers to over twenty questions relating to the topics within this book. The Kryon channels (used as excerpts in these books) are available as audio files from Lee Carroll's website: *www.kryon.com/freeaudio*

One of the main teachings from Kryon is that: *"You are bigger than you think!"* You are a piece of God and your Soul splits into many pieces and parts at birth. What does that mean? How can you (your Soul) be split apart and exist in many places simultaneously? Where does our Soul go when we die? When do we get our Soul? The answers (from Kryon) to these questions are very esoteric and extremely complex. The desire to know and understand these answers comes from a Human whom I call a seeker.

For a long time I was content and happy with life and wasn't seeking anything beyond my immediate day-to-day needs. I didn't want to get into anything that was remotely spiritual. Questions such as, *"What happens when we die?"* did not consume me. Neither did I have a burning desire to contemplate the meaning of life. Besides, I thought Monty Python did a brilliant rendition of defining "The Meaning of Life" in his 1983 British musical comedy film (smile). I preferred to study science, especially natural science, and spend my time in the beautiful outdoors of the Australian landscape. My learning was limited to tangible and physical things, such as our environment, plants and animals. I shied away from religion, psychology and anything that had abstract concepts.

I always had a sense and feeling that there was a bigger picture, but I didn't know what it was and I was definitely not interested in finding out. So, what changed? I did. I experienced a personal trauma that rocked my world as I knew it when my marriage suddenly ended. The subsequent heartache and grief that I experienced changed my perception of how I viewed the world. I began a quest to find answers to my questions about the Universe, and my personal place within it. I had given intent to "open the door," and my Higher-Self was there to greet me.

Your own unique experience and journey has led you to this book. It is no coincidence that your eyes are on this page and reading these words, and the entire Kryon entourage, along with your Higher-Self, is celebrating with so much love, joy and honor that you have chosen to be here now. I would like to thank you for giving intent to connect

with your Higher-Self (your Soul). It is my wish that the information within this book will change your perception and enrich your life.

There are a lot of subjects covered within this book. The title of each chapter is a guide to the type of information presented. If you are new to the Kryon work, be prepared to read about things that may seem unbelievable, but this is where Kryon encourages you to use your own discernment. Do we really have a Soul? Is it possible that there is a loving, benevolent energy that exists within the universe? Do guides and angels exist? What is your first intuitive thought to these questions? Many of you will have an instant response, while some of you may be unsure, but again, this is about your free choice.

Our family of humanity is evolving spiritually. Many individuals are awakening, and some find themselves drawn to the messages of Kryon. If you are new to the Kryon work, and especially if this is your first Kryon book, there may be some terms, such as Lemurian and Pleiadian, that are unfamiliar to you. You may be interested in reading my previous two books, *The Gaia Effect* and *The Human Akash,* to help you connect to the Kryon teachings and how they apply to your personal life.

Finally, I would like to invite you to read the additional chapters, that complement this book, which can be found on my website: *www.monikamuranyi.com* under the "Extras" tab. Due to publishing constraints, there is a page limit as to what can be physically printed. Yet, there is often more information to be conveyed. This is why you will also find additional chapters to *The Gaia Effect* and *The Human Akash* on my website. It is my absolute honor and pleasure to be able to share this with you for free.

Love and blessings,

Monika Muranyi

Chapter One

The Human Soul

Honestly, when I agreed to write a Kryon trilogy series, I had absolutely no idea what the subject and title of the third book would be. I never dreamed of being an author; I simply was on a quest to find out more about the relationship between humanity and our planet Earth, Gaia. For over two years, I searched for information about the energy grids of the planet, as described by Kryon. After continual frustration in not finding anything related to this subject, I woke up one morning, while living in Santiago, Chile, and mentally said, *"Okay, if I can't find the book, then I will write it!"* I had no idea how, but I simply began by compiling all of the Kryon channellings given about Gaia (my passion), and then received guidance from Lee Carroll on how to proceed. Having this collaboration with Lee was a clear sign that I was on the right track. Half-way through writing *The Gaia Effect,* it became obvious that the same approach was needed for the subject of the Human Akash.

When my manuscript was presented to a prospective publisher (Ariane Editions), it was accompanied by a note from Lee Carroll saying that I had begun research on another book that focused on the Akash. Imagine my surprise when Ariane Editions said they wanted to publish these two books as a special Kryon trilogy. While the news was

thrilling, I was also thrown into a panic, because I had no idea what the subject of the third book would be! However, there is a saying that my good friend, Dr. Amber Wolf, says: *"Spirit has a plan!"*

In 2014, Lee Carroll began presenting his new lecture series, describing the many places where your Soul exists. All of a sudden, it became obvious what the subject for the third book would be – the Human Soul. But how do you describe and explain the unexplainable? How do you write about multi-dimensional information in a linear format? The sheer magnitude of undertaking this project was a little daunting. Kind of like writing and describing the most exquisite sunset that you have ever seen to an audience that is blind and never had sight! Nevertheless, this is what Lee Carroll does every time he sits in the chair to channel Kryon. He takes quantum, conceptual information and translates it into linear language in real time. He is one of the best channellers I know, no doubt a result of twenty-five years practice.

Let's talk about Souls. The word *Soul* is used by humanity, even when there is no spiritual belief system involved. For example, it was very common for mariners of old to report how many *Souls* were on board, instead of how many humans were on board. Such a phrase is even used by humans who don't believe they have one! The word "Soul" has become common language and describes the *spiritual essence of a Human Being.* I think it is also worth mentioning that there is a genre of music, known as "Soul Music," that originated in the United States in the 1950s and early 1960s, combining elements of African-American gospel music, rhythm and blues, and often jazz. What do you know about music in general? Where do the lyrics and composition come from? Perhaps the term "Soul Music" can be applied to more than one genre (smile).

Describing and writing a book about the Human Soul is incredibly difficult for several reasons, but I think the major limitation, beyond the fact that there is really no such thing as a Human Soul, is our bias in linearity. Okay, I can hear you say, *"Wait a minute! Did you just say there is no such thing as a Human Soul?"* Well, yes I did, but let me explain. Kryon has told us that our Soul has also been on other planets of free choice, and so our Soul is not only a Human Soul, but it is a Soul that has been a Pleiadian, an Arcturian, an Orion, and more. The fact that you are reading this book and are interested in learning more about your Soul, strongly suggests that you are an Old Soul specialist. What does that mean? It means that you have been there, done that! I'll let Kryon explain:

Dear ones, when you were seeded as the Human Race, there were very few of you. The ones who were seeded, I will call "first Souls." These Souls were in the right place at the right time, to receive the duality from the Pleiadians. These who were seeded went through the Lemurian experience, and also the many changes that happened on the planet to follow. All this, so that they would arrive at a place where they might be listening today to this message.

You have become Old Souls, and you've had thousands of lifetimes in the hundred thousand years or so, which it took to get to this place. So far, so good? Now, let me review something that you haven't asked me yet: *"Dear Kryon, the ones who were here to receive the seeding – were they any different than any others? Perhaps there is some kind of a random pool of Soul selection that would have put them there during that profound time?"* A ha! I want to tell you, if you didn't already figure it out, that there is indeed a synchronicity here! No randomness involved.

If it is true, dear Human Being, that there is a system afoot, a system where the ones who were here first to receive the seeds, eventually become Old Souls, then where does that lead your logic? Might you ask if they were here by design, and somehow different? Indeed, these Souls had a special status: In order to be first, they had a special corporeal maturity that would let them become Old Souls, eventually. This represents many of you reading right now. Who were you, and where did you come from originally? Let me ask you: How is it that you received the Pleiadian seeding so easily? [Kryon laugh] What if I told you that you were created for this, and most of you arrived from the Seven Sisters to become humans! Did you ever think of that?

In Graduate Status, the Pleiadians were ready to go, and ready to seed the next planet, from the existing one. In other words, you were like seedlings, taken from existing crops in order to grow new crops. Some of you will understand exactly what I'm saying, and some of you will have no idea. But I just gave you an answer that is very profound. You are very special, and you're ready for this; selected for this. You wanted this, and there is no random selection of Souls from around the galaxy, who then come and be part of the first group of humanity. No. You were the ones who had been Old Souls before in other places, and would be Old Souls again. Your lineage of being an Old Soul in this universe is vast, and here you are yet again. So make it a good experience, as you did the last time, and stop wallowing in the minutia of how to do it.

Drop into the core of your Being and get on with it, Old Soul. Some of you know what I mean, and you know it isn't that hard. Go for it! It's time to talk this way, because in this new energy, some of you are having revelations of why you're here. There is no newcomer in this room. Do you understand what I'm saying? There is no newcomer here. I am Kryon, and I serve Old Souls! That's what I do. This is not the first time that I've come into a planet during the final stages of older energy, in order to encourage the Old Souls. I'm here to be next to you as you run the marathon of Old Soul-*dom*, and to try to give you glasses of water as you run. I'm careful not to touch you unless you ask for it, but I'm always ready to give you whatever answers you need. That's what we do!

We are ready for all of this, and we have seen it before. It's time you understood this, and know that it's not accidental. The system you are part of is one of help, benevolence, and love. It is powerful and we're ready to go. How about you? It's a good message, isn't it? It is profound, accurate, and true.

Kryon live channelling "The Truth about Spiritual Help"
Enhanced by Lee Carroll for this book
Given in Portland, Oregon – July 21, 2013.

Kryon has told us that our Soul is an eternal, multi-dimensional Soul soup of all that is and it is a part of the Creator that has no beginning and no end. When we (as a single individual Human Being) incarnate on Earth, we are suddenly pieces and parts of our multi-dimensional self, contained within ONE body. We therefore think we have ONE Soul, totally individual and separate, and then we think everyone else has their ONE Soul. Furthermore, many believe that our Souls go through training and there is some kind of hierarchy. What Kryon says is very controversial to the "one body, one Soul" belief. Kryon explains that once your Soul leaves your corporeal Human body, it becomes part of the soup of everyone's Soul and therefore, the notion of training, learning and a hierarchy is nonsensical. It is part of our Human bias of linearity and trying to humanize God.

The notion that we are not a single individual, but instead, we are a multi-dimensional soup of energy is an incredibly difficult concept to understand. To help us understand, Kryon revealed the nine attributes of the Human Being. This teaching from Kryon explains the mechanics involved with regard to the pieces and parts of our Soul, where they occur and how they all work together.

The Nine Attributes of the Human Being

The nine attributes of the Human Being were first defined during the Kryon Discovery Retreat given at Mt. Shasta in June, 2013. Prior to this, the information was given in small disparate pieces, cloaked in obscurity for the last decade. The reason was that Kryon was waiting for the appropriate time when we were ready to hear and receive the messages. The significance of Kryon revealing this information in 2013 is a reflection of the recalibration of Gaia and humanity. Kryon Book 13, *The Recalibration of Humanity: 2013 and Beyond*, provides details about the recalibration of humanity and unravels the history behind what is happening in our current events and news. Kryon also says that this is the beginning of the New Earth. It means that we are ready for a new consciousness to emerge on the planet, for Human nature to evolve and to discover even more of who we are.

Now, let me begin to explain the puzzle. These things are complex, and they do not necessarily fit together in a linear way as you might expect. All of these concepts, everything we are presenting, are accurate in their own way. They are translated into linearity for you, so that you can understand more about yourselves. The whole purpose of this channel is to expand the grandness of the Human evolutionary process.

You are beginning to grasp more of who you are, and some want a linear list, so we give one to you. Yet we warn you that after we have given it to you, it still may not satisfy you, or make much sense. Let me compare it to the Human meal that is prepared: You're looking at the cookbook, and you see it has all the ingredients, all the seasonings. You cook the meal and begin to consume it. Then you might ask, *"Where is the seasoning in this meal?"* The answer is that it is with each mouthful. It has imbued itself into the other ingredients, so that the meal is consumed as *one total thing*, yet as the cook, you saw it as many things.

So the *one thing* sits before me now, called the Human Being. However, I can still give you the ingredients, since I know how it was cooked. All the ingredients are still within you, just as they were in the cooked meal. I now wish to itemize them so that you can see something that you might not have seen before. All of the numbers I give you have energy. So when we speak of groups and numbers assigned to anything, they always represent metaphoric energies. Your perception of them has been explained in the past [numerology], so they have meanings that you already know, and will receive.

In the nine elements or energies of the Human Being, there are three groups of three. The *nine* represents completion, so we are giving you the complete Human Being. Let no one add to this, for it is complete. There may be those who will hear or read this message in the future, and say, *"Well, I would like to add some, for I think there are ten or twelve."* Dear ones, this system is complete as given, so if there is another energy or another perception that you believe belongs in the list, let it instead enhance one of the three groups of three.

It is difficult to explain what is next, for in a recipe, you would see that each single element is unique; however, in the three groups of three, there would appear to be repetitions. However, they are not really repetitions at all. Instead, they are simply descriptions of how the same item works differently within a different grouping set.

The Three Groups

The three groups are identified as the HUMAN group, the SOUL group and what we would call the SUPPORT (GAIA) group. All these are complementary to the Human. My partner may call them "attributes," which is simply to clarify the teaching.

THE HUMAN ATTRIBUTES - THE SOUL ATTRIBUTES - THE GAIA ATTRIBUTES

I would like to begin by explaining the simplest group first, and the one that is closest to you at the moment. I will explain the most complex one, second, and the most misunderstood, third. In the process of the explanation, I will tell you that there is a puzzle for you: The Higher-Self attribute is in all three groups! Now, this is a puzzle, because in a food recipe you do not have that happen, but in this recipe, you do. The best way to visualize this is to consider cooking three items completely, then mixing those three into still another one. There could, therefore, be salt in each of the three, before it got combined into the one.

The Higher-Self is identified, in each of the three groups, as belonging to that group. But when combined, it is still singular. That ought to tell you something about the Higher-Self. It is the only one element that seems to be repeated in all three groups.

The Higher-Self: What is it? It has been defined many, many times, so I cannot give you any one definition that is better than I have given you before. The true definition is dependent on how you are considering it. It varies depending on the category, so just consider it the *core source of your divinity*. If I could explain to you *who* you are now, and *who* you are when you are not on the planet, you still wouldn't understand. Because your perception of reality is limited only to what you have experienced; you can't understand what you have not seen yet. It is not in your consciousness to understand all these concepts yet, so my partner will linearize the teaching, as he steps through the things that I am giving him.

If I said the words to you, *core Creative Source*, what would be your perception? Would it be God? Would it be physics? Would it be both? These are the things that are often puzzles for the Human Being. So we are going to identify the nine energies for you, so that you will see not only the complexity, but the grandness of the Human. All along, we're giving you information about what is inside of you, not outside of you. More than anything else, we want you to understand that God is within, not without. The key to your enlightenment lies with self-understanding. Beyond definition is the fact that you are your own Creator. Now, as I step through these attributes, you will see a little bit more about why you do not sense all this immediately or intuitively.

The first thing I wish to tell you is that these nine elements split into three groups of three, representing the Human Being today. Also, the definitions I give today may change tomorrow, because you are evolving. Some of the aspects that I introduce may actually meld together later, for as the Human Being progresses in an evolutionary spiritual way, these elements start to shift. But remember, there will always be nine.

I will also add to this puzzle and give you some intellectual questions that I'll also answer for you, yet you still may not understand - and you are free not to understand. Listen: Dear ones, it is not necessary, when you consume the meal of the majesty of God, to understand how it works. It is not necessary for you, when you feel the love of God in your life, or receive a profound healing, to know the minutia of how it happened. Do you understand? As you enjoy a splendid meal, it's not necessary to know the full recipe. Do you understand? And if you do, then I can begin.

The Human Group

The simplest group to define is the HUMAN group. You relate to this, for it's the one you live with in 3D. (1) The Higher-Self in the Human Being, which resides in the DNA at the corporeal level, is number one. (2) Number two, as you might expect, is *Human consciousness*. Human consciousness is not apart from the Higher-Self, but it simply is one of the elements we wish to split apart because it is in 3D. Parts of Human consciousness are becoming multi-dimensional, and this is part of the evolutionary process that will change *who* you eventually become. (3) Number three is what we have called *Innate. Innate,* which is the "smart part" of the cellular body. It is the part that is accessed, at the moment, through that which you call *kinesiology*, *BodyTalk*, *tapping*, *de-coding*, and many other processes. All these processes cross the bridge between the corporeal three-dimensional consciousness, and that intelligence which *knows* what's going on at the cellular level in your body.

The three together create the Human Being walking in 3D. Now, as the Human evolves, these things not only will change, but two of them will get closer together. Now, we haven't given you an important premise yet in this teaching, so this is next: Right now, on this planet, the Human Being is operating at slightly less than 35 percent. You can say that this is the percent of your DNA that is active and working. This means that although you have 100 percent of everything you need within you, Human consciousness, by free choice, has only gotten to this lower percentage. This is what will be changing. Do you doubt this? If this were not true, then why do you search for the Higher-Self? Why should it be so elusive?

Your intellect and your consciousness together are always trying to figure out how to touch that part of you which is the Creative Source. That's separation, and it's not supposed to be that way. Things are not working as designed. You muscle-test to find out what the Innate of the body can tell you. You ask it many things: You ask it if it's all right to do this or that, and you ask it if something is going on within your body, which needs to be addressed. Does this fit in with logic, dear ones? What kind of system cannot access itself?

Now, listen: Your brain is separated from your internal molecular structure. You could sit in your chair right now and have a disease growing in your body, but *your brain* might be completely unaware of it. Your white cells could be rushing to a specific place to fight the disease. Alarm bells could be going off within your blood stream, yet your brain has no clue until you get a blood test. That's separation, and it should yell at you that your body is not working at full capacity, and that your brain is disconnected.

Now let me tell you about the evolving Human Being in this group. The Innate, along with Human consciousness, is going to start moving together. Each one of you can eventually become your own medical intuitive. This is evolution, and it represents DNA working at almost 44 percent. You will be aware of what is happening through intuition, and the bridge between those two attributes in the Human Group will start to come together. Also, within this group, the Higher-Self will begin to show itself. Now, what this means is that the Innate and Human consciousness will all begin to agree, and that is going to increase pineal awareness, and boost intuition. You are going to start being aware of a "bigger picture" of life itself.

You will begin to understand and accept that death has no sting. The ones who circle you right now, who have passed on and have come back for this moment, would agree. If they could vocally speak to you right now, they would shout it to you - that you are eternal! Do not fear that passage [death], because you're coming back sooner than you think.

The irony is this: Here you sit, wondering about the separation, trying to learn about it, yet when you come back, it's going to be more together than ever before, and you will awaken *remembering*. You won't remember what happened today, but instead, an overall intuitive remembrance of what has happened in all of your lives. That manifests itself as wisdom! That will manifest itself as a child who remembers how to read from previous life experience, and something not taught yet in this life. It manifests itself in a child who quickly remembers to walk, and is not taught or encouraged to do so; a child who remembers things which are practical, without experience or training. These things will come to the child automatically and instinctively, and it's about time! This will be the evidence that the spiritual part of the DNA is starting to increase its efficiency. That's group one, and that was easy.

Your Akash is tied to the Innate in this group, and will be the well of experience that this increased bridge awareness will draw upon. It's about time that you started to remember in a future life, what you have earned and lived in this one.

The Soul Group

Group two is the most complex and controversial for those who are spiritually minded. Humans tend to linearize all that is God, and compare it to all that is Human. It's difficult for you not to "humanize" God.

The three parts are: (1) The Higher-Self, (2) What you perceive as your guide set, and the third one, the most difficult to understand, (3) The part of your Soul that is always on the other side of the veil.

So let us again identify this SOUL group to you.

(1) The Higher-Self is part of each group of three, and part of the nine, three times. It's always there.

(2) Guides: Human Being, you want your guides, angels, or whatever you call them, to have more wisdom than you do. This is your logic. It may come as bad news to some of you, that they are actually part of YOU!

Guides must stand apart from you, in order to be your advisors on the planet. The guides are actually higher vibrational parts of your Soul, which stand apart from you. As you build your enlightenment, and as you are awakening to spiritual truth, it may appear that these guides actually change, but this is only a Human perception. We told you early in the Kryon work, that there is actually a time when they appear to leave. But what is actually happening, in your words, is that they technically *reboot* and come back during an emotional "dark night of the Soul." In this process, many of you sometimes "go to zero" emotionally, allowing for this rejuvenation process. Then you recover with more information and more wisdom, and with a different energy in your consciousness than you had before. However, you tend to humanize your guides, and you perceive them in linearity. When you awaken to new perceptions and more light, you see them and you think they are new. That's funny! They just changed clothes, dear ones! You changed, so they changed. They are you.

How can a Human Soul break apart and be in many places at the same time? Welcome to quantum energy! This is not difficult at all, and it's normal in a multi-dimensional state. But your 3D thinking limits this possibility, and you have trouble with it.

Start getting out of the box of your reality, into the box that gives allowance for things you don't understand.

The intellectual, linear mind wants to know everything, and it works overtime to compartmentalize and linearize all it sees: How do the guides communicate with each other? What if one argues? You've just humanized God yet again! This is what creates the mythology that my partner was talking about earlier. Do you really have to figure it all out? Well, don't. Understand the beauty of this system. It actually works without your being able to understand it. What a concept!

How many guides do you have? You might say, *"Three, of course."* This is a catalytic number in numerology. The catalyst is an energy that has the potential to change something else, while it remains the same. This is, then, the energy of the guides. They create wisdom and learning and healing and knowledge. They are also the ones who help with *Soul intuition*, and can see the overview of who you are in a much larger picture.

(3) The third one is the most misunderstood. Dear ones, can a piece of God, the Creative Source, really exist completely in a corporeal body, and walk the planet in purity? And the answer is "not without a system to temper it." This is because this pure divine energy cannot be sustained in a corporeal 3D body. The body would vanish, burn up, and explode! The Creative Source does not put itself on the planet as the full divine Creative Source. It splits apart, so when you come into the planet, only a portion of your Soul comes here. That's the portion that can be sustained in a corporeal body. The rest stays with the Creative Source.

We have spoken many times of the Hebrew prophet Elijah. This master was one of the only Human Beings in history who selected his own time to ascend. When he did it, his understudy, Elisha, took notes, and you can read the account in your scriptures. What I want you to see, is what happened when Elijah ascended: He turned into light! A vehicle appeared, to the eyes of Elisha, in the form of a chariot pulled by three white horses, and it took Elijah up into the sky. This apparent chariot received a name in Hebrew which means "to ride" – *Merkabah*. The point of this discussion is that nothing came to get him from the sky. He turned into light on the ground!

When he took the full power of who he was, he turned into light and vanished!

So understand this: Within this system, you can't carry all of your Soul, because it's just too much energy. Even the master Elijah couldn't do it. But the amount you do carry is inside of your multi-dimensional DNA. The other part is on the other side of the veil. So now there are two of you, so to speak. Are you confused yet? Let's talk about it: If part of you is on the other side of the veil, what is it doing? The answer ... helping YOU in a way that is unique.

If every single Human has parts of themselves on the other side, this becomes the "engine of synchronicity." This is how you meet the ones you didn't know you would meet, or have unexpected amazing things happen to you. There's a committee going on "upstairs" all the time, to help push you and steer you to those who you need to meet. You should hear them cheering up there when you, in three dimensions, meet the ones who you are supposed to meet, in order to do the things you are supposed to do! Do you understand? The portion of your Soul that is not in corporeal form is helping you in an *overhead* view, and steering you to benevolent things. Your intuition is the communication.

All of humanity has these attributes. Unenlightened humans have pieces and parts of themselves on the other side of the veil, just as you do. Do you understand this? So, an unenlightened Human Being can be a part of your life in a catalytic way, because part of them is also on the other side of the veil, with the mind of God. This is not easy for you to understand, but it helps to understand the phrase, "against all odds." For "odds" are based on a system of potentials and averages, and you are beating all of that. You see? It isn't against all odds, if it's part of the plan! This is the part of your Soul that creates synchronicity and changes your reality. For us, the idea is normal. It's a beautiful system, and it's sacred and magnificent. This is what co-creation is, and you're working with it all the time, yet you don't even know it that it's you with you.

It's time to trust what you don't understand. Most humans wish to stay in a "bubble of logic," for it is comfortable. Instead, why not come out of your comfortable shell and trust your God part? Why not come out of the bubble and acknowledge that pieces and parts of you are sacred enough that you can trust them? Their messages are the intuitive voice in your ear. *You*, helping *you*. Is that too much for you?

The Gaia Grid Group

The last three attributes represent the most misunderstood group. It's what we'll call the cooperative group of Gaia - the SUPPORT group, which is apart from the Human, but not really. We call it a grid since it surrounds you with support.

Let me set the stage: You're here in a beautiful place [Mt. Shasta] and you can feel what's in the mountain. However, are you aware that it's also in the trees, the grass, and in the beauty of the sky? You feel it everywhere! It's not just focused in the mountain, is it? It's in the lake, the water, and the air. There is a life-force around you that you may misunderstand. You are part of Gaia and Gaia is responsive to you.

We did a channelling on a mountaintop in the Andes last year [speaking of Mt. Aconcagua]: Kryon said: *"There are no mountain climbers who don't believe in God."* This is so. Just ask them about the majesty of Gaia, and how they feel God is there. There are those who are so married to nature, that they will journey to places just to be there alone, and absorb what is there. Little do they understand that they are in love with it, because they are part of it. So the third group, the cooperative group, is what we can also call the Gaia group.

The first part of this Gaia group is again, your Higher-Self. Now, how can your Higher-Self be part of Gaia? Again, the reason is because the Higher-Self is what ties together all three of these groups. In this group, the Higher-Self is represented by the magnetic grid of the planet. Does this sound familiar? Twenty-three years ago I introduced myself as the Magnetic Master. I explained how the magnetic grid is needed for life, and that I was here to help move it. Your compass can measure this grid, and it will tell you that since I arrived (and up through 2002), the magnetic grid has moved greatly, as I told you it would. All this was needed for your future.

You are part of the magnetic grid of the planet. Your DNA responds to it in ways that you don't know about yet, but it even explains why astrology works. Human consciousness is affected by the magnetic grid and the magnetic grid is affected by consciousness. The entire reason Kryon is here is because this grid now needs to be adjusted to allow for a higher consciousness of humanity to develop. This is beyond your knowledge or understanding at the moment, but I will enhance this entire concept in a later channelling for you.

The next is very misunderstood, and is called The Crystalline Grid – an esoteric invisible grid which is multi-dimensional, and which was placed at the same time that humans were seeded. Dear ones, this is a grid which holds and remembers Human vibration. What you experience as a Human, is never forgotten by the planet. It is a grid of remembered consciousness, influenced by Human action – a form of storage of Human remembrance.

This grid is the reason why you can stand in a battlefield that is 400 to 500 years old, and can still feel the energy of the battle. For what happened emotionally, is still there. All through the eons of history on this planet, the grid has seen and remembered what is the most dramatic for humans ... death, sorrow, and drama. The word "crystalline" is only a metaphor – an esoteric grid that "remembers" and stores vibration.

This grid is changing right now! We have told you that the evolution of the planet, especially right now, is starting to change the linearity or non-linearity of the actions of humanity. This grid is starting to be far more responsive to joy, laughter, and compassion. Death, war, and horror are beginning to take a back seat in the hierarchy of Human emotions. This is all part of the shift of consciousness on the planet, which my partner has spoken of many times as the prophesy of the planet's indigenous.

This begins the consciousness shift, which I had predicted in 1989, and which I told you was imminent. As this grid begins to remember differently, it will affect future generations. Children born in the future will sense this grid, as they walk upon the planet.

This grid is a "fast track" system to help the spiritual evolution of humanity. Can you see how this particular grid affects you, and all the things to come? For as you move into compassion and joy and love, you solve problems of integrity. These *stick* to the grid, and those who follow you will pick that up. Complex, it is, but it partners with the majesty of the Human Being.

That's eight of nine. Well, nine is very special and I cannot say much about it. However, I'll give it to you anyway. There is a cooperative energy in the mammal life of the planet. There has to be a balance, but I cannot tell you yet why or how. I can just tell you that your love of the cetaceans of this planet is well warranted. They are part of this grid system. I will also tell you something that I have channelled only once before: When the Pleiadians came here originally, with love and all appropriateness, as a graduate ascended race, they didn't just plant their divine seeds in Human Beings. They also changed the DNA of the cetaceans. That's why you're in love with these mammals. When some of you swim with the dolphins in the wild, and you get into the water, sometimes an entire pod of dolphins will alter course and come to you! Did you ever think of that? What is it that they are attracted to? What other animal on Earth does that? I'll let you think about that one.

There is more information coming, dear ones, and as this planet evolves, we will be able to tell you even more about the role that the cetaceans play. But you already know of their sacredness. You already know about the whales and the dolphins. The cetaceans are like a living library, and they are important to humanity. They hold an energy that is part of you. They are one of the nine, and that is our story for now.

I understand that this particular message creates more questions than answers. Can you get out of your bubble of logic and just be with it? Can you not ask for the minutia? It is not going to help you at all to know about it, any more than it will help you to understand the workings of the automatic transmission before you go to the store in your automobile. I want you to graduate into peace and neutrality, and move on to the next level, which is the appreciation for God inside, and the system that you helped put together. Dear ones, you are the planners. You are God. That is the message for this evening.

Go to this message again when you need to, and capture whatever part of it you need to. Through all of these things, see the beauty and the magnificence of what the Human Being is really about. Begin to plant the seeds of an ascended planet - for that's where it's going.

Kryon live channelling "The Nine Attributes of the Human Being"
Enhanced by Lee Carroll for this book
given in Mt. Shasta, California – June 21, 2013

How do you feel about what you just read? Is it possible that you exist in many places at once? If we exist everywhere at once, how does it work? Kryon's information about the nine attributes of a Human Being helps explain these deep mysteries. Even this explanation is not completely accurate, as it's impossible to quantify multi-dimensional energies. However, Kryon and Lee Carroll say it's the best they can do. If you've read Kryon Book 12, *The Twelve Layers of DNA*, you are aware that our DNA is described as having twelve layers – but don't count them! These DNA layers are like parts of a machine and the machine can only work when all the parts have been put into place and work together. The machine stops working when you take it apart. But, when you take the machine apart and look at all the parts on the floor and describe them, you gain a better understanding of the individual pieces that make the machine work. The same approach is used in describing the nine attributes.

The nine attributes of the Human Being are like a soup of energy, and once they are in the soup you can't go in and find the salt or anything else. But, before the soup is made, you can list the ingredients and individually identify and look at them. This is the best way that Lee Carroll and Kryon teach and explain this very complicated subject.

Let's first examine the numerology of the nine attributes. In Ancient Tibetan numerology, nine represents completion, and Kryon has clearly emphasized on several occasions that there are only nine attributes. There may be a tendency for others in the future to review this information and later say they have discovered twelve attributes of the Human Being. Kryon says, again, there are only nine! The nine attributes are complete – there are no more.

Within the nine attributes are three groups of three. If you take a look at the numerology of this statement you will find the number 33. What do you know about the number 33? Again, in Ancient Tibetan numerology, 33 is a master number and signifies Compassionate Action. In my first book, *The Gaia Effect*, I present a beautiful true story, narrated by Jorge Bianchi, about the 33 Miners' rescue in Chile, which is a wonderful example of Compassionate Action. The rescue of the 33 Miners is profoundly significant. This event was the first global compassionate event that celebrated life and joy instead of death and sorrow. What else do we know about 33? According to Kryon, it represents the percentage of DNA activation currently given by Gaia (planet Earth) via The Crystalline Grid.

Whoa! Does that sound too weird and spooky? In basic terms, it relates to how Kryon describes the way our DNA works. Your DNA contains the entire complement of everything you ever were, the knowledge of everything you ever had, including Pleiadian lifetimes; and it is only activated to the point at which the consciousness of the planet allows it to be activated. The consciousness of the planet is determined by humanity via the Magnetic Grid. Kryon has said that right now (2014), the consciousness of the planet is about 33 to 35 percent (reflecting the percentage of DNA that is working). This also explains why there are no definitions for the master numbers beyond 33. Although, given the number of times I keep seeing the number 44, I feel certain we may soon receive the knowledge of what this master number means (smile). In fact, during a Kryon channel, given in August 2014, Kryon hinted at what 44 might represent. (More on that in The Cetaceans section of Chapter Two: The Gaia Soul Group).

Okay, back to the three groups of three, in which, in Ancient Tibetan numerology, three represents a catalyst – the catalyzer of compassion. These three groups are: the Gaia Soul Group, the Human Soul Group and the Core Soul Group. While each group is explained in as much detail as possible, I'm also aware that Kryon will continue to add more information after publication of this book

in 2015. Don't be surprised if Kryon expands on these attributes in subsequent channels.

Questions for Kryon:

Humans experience many shifts and changes when they gain spiritual enlightenment, increase their awareness and raise their vibration. These changes raise the vibration of the planet. As each planet of free choice moves into ascension, what are the vibrational changes and experiences felt by other ascended beings on other planets? What are the changes and experiences felt by Spirit, if any? When Spirit and our guides celebrate our epiphanies, is there an energy change they feel? Does this change anything at the Great Central Sun? How does this fit into the bigger plan?

Answer:

This is the great question. You might even say, *"What is the meaning of life?"* The answer is *yes* and *yes*. At this stage of your development, you are babes in the woods. You only know what you know, and you are still wallowing in an undeveloped state. All ascended planets did this, and it is expected.

If you were able to ask an ancient cave dweller about plate tectonics, he wouldn't have a clue, but it's in his purview to learn, eventually. So the answers simply wouldn't mean much to you. So, like the cave dweller, I'll tell you that there is a system that is involved, elevated, and it connects all spiritual Souls together. The higher they evolve, the more they are connected. So yes, others know what's going on here, and even Spirit is involved. What happens here on Earth, indeed, affects the cosmos.

It's tough for you to believe that eventually there may be no more hatred or war, but these basic things are just humans, growing up and maturing into a whole different species. There will come a day when, perhaps, you see these words and smile, and remember a time when things were vastly different.

Some humans incarnate with psychic abilities in which they may have second sight, be a medical intuitive or have the ability to communicate with entities. My understanding is that these gifts are picked up from their Akash. At first glance, I would have thought these psychic abilities would give an advantage towards mastery and enlightenment. However, there are many occasions when I have observed those with these abilities to be unaware of the divinity within and sometimes they lack the ability to self-balance and, instead, spin in drama. Can you tell us more about what is happening in these instances?

Humans often make an assumption that great abilities are tied to spiritual awareness, and they are not. You have to look at these things apart from one another, and understand that the "marriage of mind, body, and Soul" is the key to great wisdom. Knowledge, and the gifts gleaned from knowledge, do not contain any wisdom at all.

Sometimes, there can even be readers, psychics, healers, and channellers who seem to be very aware of everything, but then as you get to know them, you realize that they really are not personally aware of the divinity that they might be using. So it's very confusing to many how such odd or unbalanced messages can come from such "spiritual people."

Look for balance first, then wisdom, and after that, look for gifts and knowledge. Watch for the "compassion" factor also, for an aware person is one who has empathy and compassion for others, and the wisdom to celebrate another person's victory.

Throughout history, there have been many notable creative geniuses whose lives tragically ended in suicide, or they became insane or unbalanced. Is there a greater propensity for creative geniuses to become unbalanced,

or is it the same free choice that all humans face, but we simply notice it more because of the popularity that creatives can achieve?

It's a very interesting premise isn't it – that very high creative humans might be unbalanced in certain ways? It's something we have never discussed with you, but the answer should make sense to you. Most of these *creatives* have come to give you art, music, and science. In other words, they are in a lineage of working many consecutive lives to do this. This would indicate to you that it's not an accident they are here. Yet, so often, "something" is missing, mentally.

Indeed, it's not that they are simply popular, and you notice them. Even the ones who are not popular are often unbalanced, as well. So the answer is, yes, it is so. There is a much greater propensity for unbalance. The reason: Except for a very few, these humans all arrive with the same level of low DNA efficiency that you do. At this writing, it's approximately 33 percent. Now, if they are gifted beyond what most humans are, you might say, they may have "used up a greater portion of their 33 percent with those gifts," and therefore, something else has to be diminished. This is the simplistic view, but it's the truth.

The result is often a personality disorder. The most common problem is unbalance of their reality, and they become self-destructive. This is common, but does not have to be the case with the newer energy of 2012 and beyond. For, there is now starting to be an evolution of DNA that will *see* this for what it is, and correct for it. It's about time you had "balanced" artists.

The nine attributes of a Human Being are made up of three groups of three. This describes the pieces and parts of our Soul that are split apart at birth. Are these attributes or energies the same for every humanoid race in the galaxy, such as the Pleiadians (who gave us

the seeds of divinity)? If so, does that also apply to the twelve layers of DNA?

This is the first question that actually asks to define the difference between "The Twelve Layers of DNA" and "The Nine Attributes of the Human." It has not been asked directly, but it should be addressed, so that the actual question is answered.

DNA: The Twelve Layers of DNA are unique to the Human Being. This is because your DNA is specific to a Human. It is true that the structure of DNA is universal, in that you can expect to find it in all life that you will eventually discover. However, you already see that your DNA is different from the animals. Therefore, you are aware that not all DNA is structured the same. The Pleiadians did not have Human DNA. They had Pleiadian DNA, and only a small amount of what we gave you in the DNA information would apply to them. They have their own layers with their own names and definitions.

The Nine Attributes: These are called "The Attributes of the Human" so you would know that they are unique to you. The Pleiadians had their attributes too, and there were also nine. But each race has their own evolution of spiritual consciousness, so the attributes change depending on where you are in the scheme of development.

HINT: Did I give you the Nine Attributes before 2012? Were they identical then? The answer is NO. There are always nine, but depending on your evolution, they change. You were only given them when it was certain you were going to stay.

NEW: The Pleiadians had their evolution also, but it was slightly different than yours. Their ancient cultures immediately recognized and used the energy of thought as a contributor to reality. Even now, your scientists roll their eyes when the idea of a "psychic" is given to them. But the Pleiadians had it as their reality. It was simply a different kind of evolution. They used it very early to hunt, controlling the animal's path.

What it meant was that they actually had a more difficult time passing the final marker than you did. It was because they had worked with "mind influence" from the beginning, and absolutely knew the power of the mind. The weak often had no chance when the strong were evil. Can you even imagine this? Take a moment and celebrate how they were able to get past this, and the difficulty they must have had.

So you might see that their "NINE" was very different than yours. One of your "sets of three" is the *Human Attributes*. One of those is the *Innate*, and the information on how you are slowly building the bridge from Innate to cellular consciousness within your body. But their "bridge" had always been built, due to their emphasis on the mind.

However, the Soul stands apart from DNA evolution, so the direct answer to your question is that the three parts of the Soul for the Pleiadians were the same. Their seed parents also had the same three. So, whereas many of the NINE are not the same from race to race, the Soul attributes have always stayed the same.

This, by the way, is why you are able to relate to them so well. For, spiritual communication is "Soul-based" and not "consciousness-based" or "DNA-based."

Chapter Two

The Gaia Soul Group

Isn't it interesting that Gaia is part of our Soul (smile). Prior to my spiritual awakening, I viewed the Earth as something separate to me and my consciousness. I had no understanding that Gaia, planet Earth, had a consciousness. As I awakened to the divinity within, I became aware of Gaia, and this new awareness helped me to remember the alliance we have with Mother Earth (something the indigenous know all about). As others awaken and remember their alliance with Gaia, it means that the Earth will start to matter in a way it didn't before. It creates a mature understanding of Gaia and her consciousness and the partnership that exists between Gaia and humans. Where does this alliance come from? Why do so many of us have such a deep connection with Gaia and all her magnificent creations? What are the mechanics that allow communication between humans and animals? The answers are explained by studying the Gaia Soul Group.

My first book, *The Gaia Effect*, was primarily written to provide comprehensive information about the three main energy grids of Gaia, as given by Kryon. These three grids are the Magnetic Grid, The Crystalline Grid and the Gaia Grid. The Crystalline Grid is a memory grid of Human action and compassion. The Gaia Grid is the life-force of Gaia and her plants and animals, which, of course, includes the whales and dolphins (cetaceans). The actual connection to Gaia is via the Magnetic Grid (the grid of communication), which is quantumly entangled with your Higher-Self through your DNA.

Before I continue discussion on the Gaia Soul Group, I want to emphasize a very important aspect. The entire reason the Earth has a consciousness, the Cave of Creation, and a Crystalline Grid, is because of the divinity that exists within humans. These attributes of Gaia were all created at the same time that humanity was seeded with divinity. Therefore, the Gaia system exists as a fast-track system for humanity. Because Gaia exists for you and works in cooperation with humanity, doesn't it make sense that pieces and parts of you have to reside within Gaia?

The three places where you exist in Gaia are:

- The Magnetic Grid (that part where your Higher-Self is in the Magnetic Grid) – Connection to Gaia.
- The Crystalline Grid (the pieces and parts of you within The Crystalline Grid) – Records and stores the memory of Human actions and represents the vibration of Gaia.
- The Cetaceans (the pieces and parts of you within the cetaceans) – Largely unknown. However, what Kryon has told us is that the DNA of cetaceans (whales and dolphins) was also changed at the same time as humanity's DNA was changed. The cetaceans are the Akashic Library for Gaia and humanity, and within them are time capsules waiting for activation and release.

The Magnetic Grid (Higher-Self)

The Magnetic Grid of Gaia, described in detail in *The Gaia Effect*, is the grid of communication, which is modified by Human consciousness (our Higher-Self). Kryon is known as the Magnetic Master and the opening statement of almost every Kryon live channelling begins:

Greetings, dear ones, I am Kryon of Magnetic Service.

Let's review the history of Kryon's partnership with Lee Carroll. Kryon arrived on the planet in 1989 as part of the grid changing entourage and the prediction in Kryon Book One, *The End Times*, was that the Magnetic Grid would shift more in the next ten years than it had in the last hundred years. By 2002, that is exactly what happened. Evidence of this great shift in the magnetics can be seen at airports, where some runways have been given entirely new runway compass headings. The great shift of the Magnetic Grid was a direct result of humanity's collective consciousness. What has Human consciousness to do with the Magnetic Grid? Everything!

The Magnetic Grid interfaces with both The Crystalline Grid and the Gaia Grid, and it is a delivery system to humanity. It is the grid of communication which "talks" to you through the quantum field that surrounds your DNA. The Magnetic Grid is enhanced by the heliosphere of the sun, which is the engine of astrology. Kryon has explained the mechanics of how astrology works and why we are susceptible to the movements of the planets:

The sun is the fulcrum of the solar system and the center of energy for life for you. There is a physical mechanism for the sending of information from the sun to the other planets and it's called the solar wind. This energy stream carries with it whatever pattern of multi-dimensional energy the sun has at that moment, and delivers it to whatever is in reach of the sun's magnetic field [the heliosphere]. It's always there, but it has cycles of intensity. Although science sees the solar wind as an energy player in the solar system, they have yet to see the multi-dimensional patterns it carries to the planets as this wind blasts out from the sun.

These patterns reflect the posturing of the sun as the other planets exhibit their tugs and pulls on it via gravity and magnetics (both are multi-dimensional energies). Therefore, these sun patterns change continuously as the planets provide new gravitational and magnetic situations to the sun.

When the solar wind, carrying this sun pattern, hits the Earth, it deposits the pattern upon the magnetic grid. The magnetic grid is dynamic (changes all the time), and is responsive to being constantly re-patterned. The grid lines of the planet alter the pattern slightly due to the fact that your grids aren't consistent and have greater and lesser areas of influence in different Earth locations.

Human DNA is sensitive to magnetics, since it is a magnetic engine itself. At birth, when the child is separated from the parent, there is a signal sent to the brain of the infant that says, "Your system is now active and on its own, apart from your mother." During that first breath of independent and unique life, the child's DNA receives the pattern from the magnetics of the Earth's grid, and takes on what you have come to call "astrological attributes."

Different places on the planet will carry the basic pattern, plus or minus what Earth's magnetic field has contributed due to geographic location. This explains why world-class astrology must take into consideration the location of birth. Astro*cartography is also based on this principle.

Astrology is the oldest science on the planet, and can be proven to be accurate. In addition, "generic" astrology is also a significant influence in Humanism**, from the cycles of the female's system, to the profound changes in Human behavior when the moon is full. You can't separate yourself from it, and those who don't believe in it might as well not believe in breathing, because it's that much of an influence on your life.

The new energy on the planet invites you to change your DNA. This is the teaching of Kryon. When you change your DNA, you're working with the very core of the pattern you had at birth, and so you're able to then work on some of the attributes of your astrological blueprint, and actually change it – even neutralize it. We told you all about that in 1989. Masters did this, and you're now coming into a time where your abilities are those of the masters. Look into your life and eliminate the things that are challenges and keep the attributes that support you. This is the true balanced Human Being.

You can change your sensitivity to attributes within your own individual astrology type, but the generic influences of the planets' and moon's movements will always affect you to some degree, since you're not an island apart from others. These would be things such as retrogrades and the moon's influence (as indicated). You might say, *"I'm no longer affected by retrogrades,"*

** Kryon's definition of Humanism is "typical behavior of humans."

and sit and smile all you want. Meanwhile, you still shouldn't sign contracts during that time, since all those around you are still affected. Think about it.

Kryon Q&A on astrology as given on the website: www.kryon.com

In summary, there is transference of information from the sun to the Earth, based upon what the planets are doing gravitationally, through the intersecting of the magnetic fields. When magnetic fields interact, inductance occurs, and it allows for energy exchange of information and amplification without a power source. The aurora borealis (the Northern Lights) and the aurora australis (the Southern Lights) are great examples of the intersecting magnetic fields of the sun and Earth. The quantum pattern from the sun is transferred to the Earth's magnetic field, which in turn is transferred to us. The Earth's magnetic field therefore postures and modifies our DNA and we cannot live without it.

> "The body does not exist outside a magnetic environment, and it never has – even from the embryo stage of a human's development. All biology on planet Earth is completely, entirely dependent on the Earth's natural magnetic fields. The Earth is our natal mother in more ways than we know. We are forever dependent upon our "Magnetic Mother." Only astronauts leave the Earth's magnetic field – albeit temporarily …
>
> … Space program managers and astronauts now understand that being out in space causes more issues with body functioning than just the loss of gravity. Research where the Earth's magnetic fields are suppressed is showing that big changes happen without the background field in which we have developed."

Source: http://drpawluk.com/education/geomagnetic-fields/

The communication flow that occurs between our DNA and the planet's magnetic field explains what scientists have observed. Scientists have found that the Earth's magnetic field becomes stronger and weaker with the profound events of humanity, such as the death of

Princess Diana, the 2004 Indian Ocean Tsunami, the event called 9/11 and the rescue of the 33 miners in Chile. Human consciousness is allied with Gaia and has been shown to change the Magnetic Grid, while the Magnetic Grid plays a great part in posturing the consciousness of humanity. That's the correlation. The significance of this is that the Magnetic Grid of the Earth:

- is needed for life;
- postures our DNA; and
- it actually moves with consciousness (it responds to compassionate events).

As the collective consciousness of humanity modifies and changes the Magnetic Grid, changes occur within our DNA which affects The Crystalline Grid. One shapes the other and vice versa (like a never-ending cycle). The significant changes that have occurred on the planet within the last few decades have recalibrated The Crystalline Grid, literally rewriting our past. This difficult concept is further explained in the next section (The Crystalline Grid). All of this means that:

The alliance and coherence between the Magnetic Grid and Human consciousness is directly responsible for the acceleration of spiritual evolution on the planet.

It is part of the system of benevolent design, helping us to move into ascension. There is something else you may not be aware of, and it has to do with our solar system:

These ideas are controversial, so listen carefully and I ask my partner to go slowly. I want him to present this accurately and with care so that there's no fear here.

If you were to visit the cosmos and talk to the intelligent life that is *out there* as it has been for millions of years before life on your planet, it would give you some different concepts to think about. How is time measured between different planetary cultural systems? Yours is tied to your sun and you use "years." This won't work for them. To create a meaningful time reference for all of you, you would need something that you all have in common, a consistency that you all share, and indeed there is one.

There is a consistency of the speed of all stars and solar systems as they move around the center of the galaxy. No matter where they are in the disk that surrounds the center, they all move at one exact speed. This is a galactic standard. Since it is a consistent speed and all stars experience it, this can be used as a time reference that you all understand. When one star system talks to another, they relate to what you have called *the cosmic year.* But since the word *year* is not in their vocabulary, they call it *revs,* which stands for *revolutions around the center.* That is a consistent time measure of how long it takes for your solar system to make one revolution around the center of your spiral galaxy. So all solar systems have this in common. How many revs do you think humanity has seen, dear Human Being? The answer is this: You haven't even had one! It takes approximately 230 million Earth years to go around one time [one rev].

Now, why I'm telling you is this: Because it means that as Human Beings on Earth, there are parts of space that you have never encountered before. Since you haven't even gone around one time, the complete "pathway" of your solar system is yet undiscovered by you, including what attributes in space might be there that you didn't expect. What if I told you you're starting to enter a very special "zone" now and that what you are going to experience has been prearranged all along? It's not predestined, dear ones, but was always there just in case you made it as a Human race. It was timed appropriately and perfectly, and it's for you.

In this new area of space, which your entire solar system is moving into, there is a different kind of physics represented by what scientists see as a kind of radiation that is new. Your solar system is now coming into this. (The actual fact of this is that you are coming out of a type of "cloud" that has been with you for eons, and now you are about to experience life without it.)

The first emotion or reaction to this might be fear, for this radiation will start to intersect the heliosphere first [the magnetic field of the sun]. The heliosphere of the sun is what intersects the magnetic field of planet Earth. Your magnetic field does several things for you. It shields you from those things that the sun puts out that may be harmful. But in addition, it is a communication process to your DNA and transfers whatever quantum aspects of the heliosphere right into the Human body via the field in your collective DNA.

Twenty-five years ago, we told you that the magnetic field was needed for your life on Earth, and now that is becoming scientific fact. The DNA molecule is not a quantum particle, dear ones, but it has quantum attributes. (It has a field that affects the spin of electrons in a quantum field). This scientific fact might tell you a little more about what might be hiding within this very special system. In your body, there, in what we would call an *entangled DNA field,* are hundreds of trillions of your DNA molecules, all *knowing* together as one. This field is called the Merkabah.

This new radiation, which your solar system is approaching, is designed to enhance your DNA. It is a fast-tracking system for your Human civilization, if you made it past the precession of the equinoxes - a set-up that all the Ancients spoke about and even your own religious doctrine referenced as a difficult or "end time." This is all on purpose and will create the potential of being able to evolve quicker and faster into a world without war. It will allow new invention, the ability to solve the unsolvable problems in 3D that you have right now, and more. That's the third one. Do not fear this, dear ones! There will be some scientists who will see it for what it is, and there will be others who will be alarmed. I want you to discern it when you see it and remember we told you about it here. Fear will disable your magnificence!

Kryon live channelling "The Fast-Track Systems"
given in Mt. Shasta, California – June 14, 2014

Question for Kryon:

Magnets have been used for healing since ancient times. Various products, such as magnetic underlays (to help with sleep) are readily available. However, previous channelled messages advised us to be cautious with the use of magnets. With the slow release of new ideas, inventions and information, will our understanding

of magnetic healing increase? Can you give advice for those who use magnetic therapy?

Answer:

The information you had previously, still stands: Treat magnetic healing as you do your drugs. If you need pills for a headache, would you take them all the time, even when you didn't have a headache? The answer is no. So use magnetics the same way, and do not simply expose yourself to magnetic fields because it seems like a good idea. It isn't ... not 100 percent of the time. Good magnetic therapists know that you use it when you need it. Then you stop.

The answer to your question is that when you are finally able to see and measure multi-dimensional fields (quantum fields), you will then have the full and complete picture of what is happening. Then you will be able to actually see in real time, the microscopic effects that a magnetic field has on cellular systems.

Then, and only then, will you be able to build "designer healing magnetics." For, without the ability to see the field, you have no idea what you are doing.

The Crystalline Grid

The Magnetic Grid is easily measured with a compass, and scientists can demonstrate a direct correlation between the Earth's magnetics and Human consciousness. The Crystalline Grid, however, is extremely esoteric and much more difficult to explain. It records and remembers Human action and emotion. The Crystalline Grid is, therefore, a spiritual grid that lays over the planet's surface and remembers everything we do and where we do it within the specific location that it occurred.

Human activity and vibration directly affects The Crystalline Grid. It is responsible for "remembering" Human consciousness. An example of how The Crystalline Grid "records" energetic attributes can be observed from the site of a battlefield. In parts of Europe, there are places that contain a long, repeated history of war after war. The energy of what occurred on a battlefield is recorded as an energetic *imprint*. There are many humans who walk upon a previous battlefield, which is now a beautiful grassy meadow, and they will feel the horror and death of the many warriors who died there. This is energy!

The Crystalline Grid also helps to explain some *hauntings*. The energy attributes of a dramatic Human emotion and activity are imprinted on The Crystalline Grid and these imprints are sometimes seen and felt by others. Hauntings, often believed to be paranormal activity, are often simply an energy recording on The Crystalline Grid, which repeats over and over. Those who measure "haunted areas" detect changes in magnetics, gravitation, light and time – all of which are multi-dimensional (and invisible) energies, and very real.

In certain places on Earth there are special overlapping energies between the three grids (Magnetic, Crystalline and Gaia) which create attributes of the land that humans can sense. There are two distinct ways that overlaps occur. The first specific overlap creates an amplification of The Crystalline Grid, and can be described as an energy *node* of Gaia. The second specific overlap cancels and voids The Crystalline Grid and can be described as an energy *null* of Gaia.

The energy *nodes* of Gaia are places of immense intensity, often in areas that are less accessible or desirable for human habitation. The indigenous of the Earth often built temples in these remote places. For many people, these places are called "power spots" or "sacred sites."

The energy *nulls* of Gaia are places that also feel wonderful, but it's too overwhelming to be in them for long periods of time. They represent pure Gaia energy, and are harder to live in because they are so intense. Nulls have odd magnetic field characteristics, making it difficult for life-force and balanced brain-synapse. The places on Earth where nulls exist are often uninhabited for that reason.

In physics, everything comes in pairs. This means that for every node on the planet there is a corresponding null. Each polarized pair (a node and null together) has a push-pull energy created by the three overlapping grids. What does this mean? Think of nodes and nulls working together to push new energy into the planet. Nodes are slowly taking away the things that are no longer needed by humanity, such as fear, war, and drama, while nulls are depositories of cosmic energy, where new information, ideas and invention are slowly being pushed to humanity via the grids. Humanity is on the cusp for new inventions and information that will redefine our understanding of biology and physics. I get so excited when I think about our future potentials and humanity's spiritual maturity.

For further explanation of the nodes and nulls of the planet, please visit my website: *http://monikamuranyi.com/extras/gaia-effect-extras/nodes-and-nulls/*

In summary, these pairs of nodes and nulls work together and modify the "remembrance" factor of The Crystalline Grid. The result is that there will be less remembrance of hatred and drama, and more remembrance of love and compassion. Remember the statement in the previous section, of how The Crystalline Grid is rewriting our past? It is due to the recalibration of humanity. The Crystalline Grid can't change what happened in history, but it's changing what it remembers, based upon the predominant energies being given to it. The Crystalline Grid has now become biased towards love. What is it that Lightworkers and Old Souls do best? They shine their light and love. So, if The Crystalline Grid is biased in love, it means that Lightworkers and Old Souls are having a greater impact. This is why less than one-half of one percent is needed to change the planet.

What is the other significance of a recalibrated crystalline grid? It means that when children are born, and interface with The Crystalline Grid, they receive a transference of energy which contains messages of what is important and what is not. In other words, children will be more apt to value love and compassion than fear and hate.

To conclude, the most important thing that Kryon wants us to know is that:

The Crystalline Grid (including the *nodes* and *nulls* of the planet) is a system of feedback and support for humanity, which was created and set up by our spiritual parents, the Pleiadians, to help fast-track Human evolution to ascension status.

Hopefully, you are now more aware of the role of the Magnetic and The Crystalline Grid. At the end of 2014, Kryon gave a profound channel called "The Energy of the Future," which puts it all together.

Below is a partial extract of that channel, but it is worth listening to the free audio on the Kryon website.

Number One: Locked into the Human body via your DNA is brilliance and mastery, working at approximately 34 percent.

Number Two: The magnetic grid of the planet postures everything to do with your DNA. It also has much to do with what you call Human nature, what you want and what you've created. It seems static, never changing, and has been seen as "the way it is." However, we will call it the *temporary lock* on DNA. You see, when your Human consciousness and spiritual maturity start to move in the next years, your DNA will start to change. This has nothing to do with chemistry, but everything to do with energy stored within it, and rewriting the data. New energies will unlock certain parts that have been locked, some of them being the very parts that I've just told you about at the beginning of this channelling - the things that are puzzling regarding healing and the Akash.

The Nodes and Nulls – Energies for the Future

Now, let's go a step further. Within the last two years, we told you about the opening of the nodes and the nulls, the time capsules of the planet that were waiting for this new energy. We told you who put them there and that the Creative Source itself is responsible. We told you that they have been there for more than 100,000 years, waiting to be opened if you would pass the marker, and you just did. They are opening slowly, and we have identified them and have matched up some of the pairs for you. [www.kryon.com/nodes] They're beginning to open.

What do they do? I'll tell you. They pour out information onto the Magnetic, Crystalline and Gaia grids - the three active interpersonal grids of this planet, the ones that interface between you and your consciousness. That's where their information goes. Isn't it interesting? The information does not go directly into your consciousness, but into the grids. Now, this allows for free choice, for it's not put into your mind. That would void free choice. Instead, it's put upon the grid. With free choice, any Human can ignore anything I'm saying and walk out of this room. He can say, *"The man in the chair is a fraud. The information is ridiculous; it's stupid!"*

At the same time, sitting next to this doubter will be someone who is being miraculously healed this day. That's the difference. Free choice to accept or reject things around you is the key to honoring your individual consciousness.

The New Approaching Energy of Space

If you could see multi-dimensional energies, and you had the ability to stand back and watch your solar system as it raced around the middle of the galaxy, you could see a ribbon of energy that you are currently intersecting. Right now, your solar system, you might say, has been in a bubble of protective energy since life began on this planet. This is an astronomical measurement and is known by science. It even has a name. So this is not esoteric. As this bubble dissipates and you move into a new area of space, this ribbon of energy that you are now intersecting is different. In fact, it represents higher energy, and some might even call it radiation.

As your solar system moves firmly into it, it's the first time that this has ever occurred with humans on the Earth. It takes millions of years for your solar system to make one revolution around the center. Therefore, you were not here the last time this took place. You are now sanctioned with the consciousness of the creative seed in you, and here comes the radiation, right on schedule. We have said this before and we have channelled this, for this is not new information. But now we put it together.

The first thing that this radiation intercepts is the largest thing in your solar system - your sun. The sun is a nuclear engine, and it has the most energy of your system. The new radiation interfaces with your sun and immediately the sun will change its energy. The sun will then blast this new information through the solar wind (the heliosphere of the sun) right to the Earth. It will immediately be intercepted by your magnetic grid, as normal, for your magnetic grid always intercepts any energy from the heliosphere. The heliosphere (the magnetic grid of the sun) overlaps the magnetic grid of the Earth, and the information transfer is complete through something called *inductance.* Now it's in your magnetic grid. As a review, remember that we have taught you that whatever attribute

is in your magnetic grid is then transmitted to your DNA. Connect the dots from a 25-year-old message: The new energy affects the sun. The sun gives the energy to your grid, and your grid gives it to your DNA. You are affected.
[www.newscientist.com]

The New "Message" from Space

Let me tell you what the message is that is being communicated: *Unlock to 44 percent!* This is the message: The Human race has passed the marker and is ready for the next step in evolution. I am talking about the Old Soul. You are the ones who will be first to get this message. It is you, and some of your "Old Soul" children, who are starting to feel and accept this!

Let me tell you in this lesson today that the first thing that this *unlocking* will begin to create is what we're going to call *Akashic acuity*. You're going to start remembering, and it's about time. Can you celebrate this? It's about time that when you're born you don't start from scratch, in the dark, and doing everything all over again. Instead, you remember!

I want to talk to some individuals who are listening to this and are in this room. Have your grandchildren had the audacity to tell you who they used to be? Don't raise your hand; I know you're here. They feel it, and they know it, and out of the mouths of these babes come the most profound information that this planet has ever heard! They know who they were! Some will point their fingers at you and say, *"Don't you remember? I was your mum in another life."* That's a bit disconcerting, isn't it?

I want you to remember one of the premises of incarnation, the one that we have given you over and over. You incarnate in family groups. There's a reason for this, so there is comfort and joy. It's so you don't have to learn the energy of each related person, all over again, each time. The energies of the family stay together and you can accomplish more that way. There's always a benevolent reason for these things. Every single attribute of the esoteric system of life, whether it's your grids or reincarnation, is benevolent. Did you hear that? It's a beautiful system, and not random. It's not about judgment; it's not about punishment. It is, instead,

about the love of God for you, and what I'm about to tell you is, what is changing is energy.

Akashic Acuity

So we have established that you are moving into this new radiation, and we have established that it intersects the sun. The sun blasts your magnetic field with it (via the solar wind) and the magnetic field talks to your DNA. Suddenly, there is the potential that some of your DNA is being unlocked. The attributes of unlocking Akashic acuity will help you to remember who you've been. Now, with this remembrance comes energy - not about who you were, but rather, it gives you the energy of what you did. I don't mean physically; I mean energetically and mentally. Old Souls carry with them experience. When you look into the eyes of a child, you're going to see wisdom just waiting to break out. Dear ones, these children are different. They are not going to go through what you did! They have a whole new set of issues, and most of their issues are trying to navigate the old issues you create for them!

There's something we brought up in a former channelling called the *wisdom factor.* Now, the wisdom factor is caused by Akashic acuity. After living Human life over and over, you start remembering the wisdom that you have gained through these past lifetimes. You don't necessarily remember who you were, but rather, the fact that you were at all and the experiences you had. Imagine a child coming into the planet knowing how to read? Imagine a child coming into the planet knowing not to touch something hot? Where did it come from? You're going to see more of this, and a feeling of "been there, done that."

Akashic acuity is *remembrance of experience during past lifetimes*. As the child grows, that remembrance becomes pure wisdom. As the child starts to awaken and the pineal opens, something else happens. The grid starts *talking* to the child through the DNA, and in the grid is also the information from the time capsules we spoke about in past channellings. The time capsules start feeding the planet with increased wisdom and knowledge. You don't have to reincarnate to awaken even further! Akashic acuity means suddenly humans know more than other children have in the past - much more.

Fast Tracking

This is the plan, and it's a fast-track system, an energy system for planetary ascension. It's going to take a long time to implement, dear ones, but it's beginning right now. You're going to see marginal evidence of this beginning to happen in 2015, 2016, 2017. You're going to see it slightly in many places. These energies take a long time to mature, and they're not all going to happen fast and instantaneous. Some of you are going to be convinced that the world is going through a dark place and you're all going with it. This is because you don't see the changes for what they are, and you don't understand what is really happening. We've said it before, that when you shine a lot of light in a dark place, the things that were always in the dark object. That's what you're seeing now, and you'll see more of it. These dark things were always there, but they just didn't have the light on them that you're placing on them now.

Kryon live channelling "The Energy of the Future"
given in Newport, California – December 7, 2014

Question for Kryon:

Information about the nodes and nulls of the planet, as well as the time capsules, was revealed after we had passed the 2012 marker. This is part of a fast-track system for the planet. Are there other benevolent systems for us that will be revealed when our consciousness is ready to receive them?

Answer:

Oh yes, and this will drive some of you crazy with intuitive anticipation. There is one more beautiful benevolent system for humanity, which lies in wait. It's the fast-track system for the next step. So, you might ask, *"What is the next step?"*

Again, each step of consciousness evolution is like a veil. You have to actually move through it in order to see what lies beyond. You can't anticipate it, since you don't have the consciousness yet to know what it is.

Have you ever told a 17-year-old that they need to just "calm down" and wait until they are about 26 before they take a certain action? You will often be met with this attitude: *"I'm as smart as you are ... perhaps even smarter. I know what I'm doing, and will do as I need."* Of course, when they get to be 26, they are mortified by their stupidity, and are embarrassed by what they said and did. But while they are 17, you can't even use logic to talk to them.

Humanity is the same. You are 17, and if I told you about 26, you wouldn't understand or believe it. It simply isn't in your consciousness yet.

The truth: The Whales of your planet are carrying the next fast-track time-capsules. Interested? Dear ones, love them and keep them safe.

The Cetaceans (Whales and Dolphins)

My previous two books, *The Gaia Effect* and *The Human Akash*, both discussed the cetaceans and their role on Earth. However, it is important to repeat some of this information here, because a piece and part of your Soul is linked with the cetaceans. The cetaceans are the living portions of the grid system, containing the history of the Earth's evolution and Akashic records. Their DNA was altered by the Pleiadians at the same time as humanity was seeded, giving us a very special connection with these mammals. What is this special connection? Kryon has told us that the DNA in humans and cetaceans are similar. Both are *built for quantum intuitive language recognition.* Kryon has revealed that the cetaceans:

... carry their own kind of time capsule or *template for future humanity,* and they have altered DNA that the Pleiadians gave them. Therefore, you might say, that they are "tuned" differently from any other animal on the planet.

Part of what they carry is "increased dimensionality." Warning: This is not something that is going to be widely understood, since it is not recognized yet. There simply is no teaching at this point about relative dimensionality. We will make it understandable in a very basic way. Imagine what evolved Human DNA will someday be like. *"Kryon, how can we know that?"* Just imagine what you think it might be like. Since you carry the template already, you will be accurate. Evolution is simply the process of activating templates that are already there. So it's in your consciousness to imagine it. But you knew that, didn't you?

Imagine thought transference, singing to someone through love and having them *hear* it [the love], sending a pure template to a sick template and having spontaneous remission. Do you follow me? These things are already in the DNA of humans, just waiting for the thousands of years it will take to bring them into reality.

Bringing them into reality must also be accompanied by a slight dimensional shift of consciousness across a barrier, a kind of elusive membrane between dimensions (something mentioned in earlier science channellings). The process for this coming shift is in data held in the cetacean time capsules, along with much more. In other words, these animals already have some of these very attributes, but they are whales and dolphins, not humans. So they are just carrying them around for eventual release to you, like a living, traveling, Pleiadian grid.

Quantumness is odd to you, since it does not follow your reality construct. For instance, there is no "place" where anything resides within a quantum system. In fact, something with quantum attributes has the potential to be "everywhere" at the same time. Since these cetacean time capsules carry these futuristic attributes, they have a quantum residual, a spill-over of energy into certain Human Beings who also have a spill-over of the same kind. These are humans born with DNA that is more ready to work into the *dimensional shift of the future.* All this is simply part of the biological evolutionary process. I have told you that some of the autistics are in this group – futurists, savants. However, for this discussion, suddenly the Human and the cetacean can "hear" each other!

Think of a music transmitter [radio station] that is slightly off of its frequency. Nobody can hear it because it moved off of the normal vibration place on the dial. Now think of a receiver that synchronistically is tuned slightly off center as well. Instead of a very clear music signal, now it has a very faint, hard to hear signal. But aha! Something else is being heard or sensed as well. It's the transmitter, which is also off, transmitting other music that is actually clearer and better. So both devices have to be slightly out of normal range to have this happen. You might say that both are moving into relative dimensionality. New information: **A specific dimensionality** [the description of a reality paradigm] **is relative to the perception of the dimension it is moving to.** See, I told you this would be hard ...

Kryon Question and Answer given in
The Human Akash, a Discovery of the Blueprint Within

... Human DNA is like a radio receiver for sound. Certain kinds of sounds, both audible and inaudible, can alter the instruction sets [the data] for DNA, and can send messages to Human consciousness. Certain kinds of sounds, audible and not, can send messages to the dolphins. You have this identical thing in common, and scientists will begin to see the correlation.

There'll come a day, dear ones, when you say, sing, or project the correct sounds to the cetaceans of Earth. They will see it as a structured language (even though it isn't to you), which they have been expecting. When this happens, there will be something they do which we will not tell you about yet. They are expecting you to do this. They "see" humans as family.

Meanwhile, they feel you when you are there, through the energy of a quantum intellect. Some ask, *"Kryon, what would happen if you looked at a monkey's DNA, a creature much like the Human? Would there be similarities?"* Yes. You would see the expected genomic development, Earth chemistry and similarities. But that's where it stops. Dear Human Being, there are only two kinds of DNA on the planet which are structured for quantum intellect: The Human Being and the cetacean. Finally, I give you this information: If you really looked at dolphin DNA closely, listen carefully ... you will also find that they are not from here. I will let that be what it is.

Kryon live channelling "Information about the Dolphins"
given in Cancun, Mexico – April 10, 2013

Kryon will often drop hints in the channelled messages and leave it up to us to explore and investigate further. I realize that, for many, the idea of humanity being "seeded" by the Pleiadians is like a script from a science fiction film. Now, we have the idea that whales and dolphins also had their DNA changed by an alien race! Not only that, but there are time capsules within them, waiting for release. That's about as much information as Kryon gives, telling us that we are not ready for the rest of the story (sigh). I think what Kryon means by that is the difficulty in explaining something to a society that has no concept of what it relates to, much like the difficulty of explaining the Internet to a society that lived 200 years ago.

However, the hints around the DNA of whales and dolphins left me curious. Imagine my surprise, when I discovered that typically, cetaceans have 22 pairs of chromosomes, giving them a total of 44! Wow – there's the master number I keep seeing lately – 44! Immediately after I discovered this, Kryon gave a channelled message that talked about the number 44:

Do you know what 44 percent of activated DNA is going to look like? What will be the definition of 44 in numerology? Long before the Tibetans tell you, I'll give you a hint: four is indeed a Gaia number and that is something to look at. Is this perhaps a link to Gaia that you haven't seen before? Let me ask you a question: Why are the cetaceans in the Gaia group? That's just a little hint. What are four and four added together? [8] Manifestation. What is it that you might manifest when you get to 44? I will tell you - Peace on Earth. That is the potential.

Kryon live channelling "Things are not always as they seem"
Enhanced by Lee Carroll for this book Given in Columbus, Ohio – August 24, 2014

I guess the complete secrets held by the cetaceans will reveal themselves when we are ready to understand them. In the meantime, it is important to recognize their role on Earth, and to focus our collective efforts to ensure that the oceans and seas are a safe haven for them. I am hopeful that there will come a day when the idea of killing whales and dolphins will no longer exist.

Questions for Kryon:

In general, hybrid species are rare and often infertile. However, fertile hybrids have been found to occur in the cetaceans – both in captivity and in the wild. Researchers say that since cetaceans have very similar numbers of chromosomes across species, they are able to produce viable hybrids more easily than other mammals. I feel that part of the answer is attributed to their DNA being altered by the Pleiadians. What can you tell us about this?

Answer:

Of course. You are absolutely right.

Know this: the ability of hybrids to survive is supposed to be based on a "life principle" which states: "Hybrid reproduction creates unhealthy and unpredictable offspring." Nature, in general, will then reject it and not allow it to continue through reproduction. This is nature at its best, and keeps survival at a more efficient level.

Whales have 44 chromosomes, and part of the reason they have more than you (almost double), is because of the seeding of the Pleiadians. These additional "codes" in their DNA represent programming that rejects the hybrid principle given above, and voids it out. There are also "codes" that hide the time capsules they carry. They need to survive ... at all costs.

Do not misinterpret this message to say that plants and animals with more chromosomes are better than you are. They simply carry information that is specific to their own purpose on the planet. Even some simple foods have a larger genome than you do. But what is in the DNA for YOU and the cetaceans has a multi-dimensional complement, which plants and animals do not.

Dr. David Busbee, of the University of Texas A&M, is researching how the dolphin DNA compares with Human DNA. He has discovered that the dolphin genome and the Human genome are basically the same. He claims that it's just that there are a few chromosomal rearrangements that have changed the way the genetic material is put together. Will his research discover the Pleiadian alteration of cetaceans' DNA? What can we learn from this type of research?

No, this researcher has only opened the door to a revolution ... that there is only one other animal on the planet who is a mirror of the Human. The whale (which includes dolphins).

There is a library contained in the whale, almost like a library in your physical grids. It's carried in the millions of chemical codes within the additional chromosomes of their DNA.

No current scientist will "discover" the Pleiadian connection. This is far-fetched to any scientific thinking at the moment, and even if they suspect it, they won't say it. It will come much later, when other things happen, and your science starts to acknowledge that there is intelligent life in your galaxy.

At first, however, there will be the strong proposition that certain life forms on the planet, including humans, did not evolve from anything on Earth. Most science will postulate the reason: *"Since there is no direct evolution connection to humans, meteors and comets brought DNA from somewhere else."* This is funny, since now they must agree that "somewhere else" exists with DNA! That will open another puzzle.

Dear ones, the rejection of other intelligent life in the galaxy will be funny to you some day. There is no judgment here, for there is really no reason for you to believe life is everywhere, since you have not seen it. However, there were hundreds of years when there was no such thing as germs, either. Now you know better, and your actions are different because of it. It was a different time then, wasn't it? This is what you will say some day about life in the galaxy.

The Gaia Grid

The Gaia Grid is also a part of the benevolent system created for humanity, but it exists outside of the nine attributes. However, it is very closely allied with Human consciousness through the Magnetic Grid, The Crystalline Grid, the Cave of Creation and the cetaceans. Gaia enhances whatever vibration humanity gives. Gaia is responsible for many things related to our planet Earth, such as creation and extinction of species. When humanity had a very low consciousness, Gaia allowed plagues and pandemics. A higher consciousness, therefore, means Gaia becomes active in reducing and stopping plagues and pandemics from occurring. Sound controversial? Very, but Kryon explains the mechanics of how it works:

We told you before that in your Human civilization, free choice has placed humanity at the crossroads of existence four times before on this planet. This is because the dark consciousness won those time periods. It's not that surprising either, since humanity was in survival mode all through these times and there was very little light from expanded spiritual thinking.

The Role of Gaia in Human Consciousness

One of those times might be frightening for you to know about, since it was a full cooperation with Gaia for your termination, and a pandemic almost wiped humanity off the map. A pandemic! Now, you say, *"What has that got to do with Human consciousness, Kryon?"* Pay attention, dear ones, because this is the day where the teaching was given by my partner, and he put together the Nine

Human Attributes. One of the attribute sets included three Gaia attributes and one of them was the consciousness of the planet. Gaia is related to Human consciousness!

Are you starting to connect the dots? You are connected to this planet in a profound and spiritual way. As goes humanity goes the planet's consciousness. Gaia, Mother Nature, whatever you want to call it, cooperates with Human consciousness. If you spend 1,000 years killing each other, then Gaia will do its best to cooperate with your desires! Gaia will look at Human consciousness and try to help with what you have shown you like to do! Did you know this role of Gaia with you? It's a partner with you, fast tracking what you give to it. You may wish to review what the indigenous of the planet still understand. Gaia is a partner!

Pandemic: Don't you find it odd that in the last 50 years, when you have a population of seven billion Human Beings, with up to 2,000 airplanes in the air at any given moment, going between almost every conceivable place, that there has not been a pandemic in your lifetime? There have been five starts of potential pandemics over the last 20 years, yet none became serious. Did any of you put this together? Dear ones, when the world was far less populated a few hundred years ago, with no mass travel to spread a virus, there were still millions wiped out by a pandemic. With the increased population and mass travel, there is far more danger today than before. It doesn't make sense, does it? What happened to stop it?

When you know humanity's relationship to Gaia, it makes sense. Gaia is a life-force that is your partner, watching you change the balance of light and dark and reflecting what humans want. It has polarity, too! Perhaps it's time to start your meditations with thanking your planet Earth for supporting you in the spirituality of your Akash, for always being with you, a life-force that is always present. The Ancients started their ceremonies in that way. Have you forgotten?

Ebola

Now, I've just set the stage for the next subject, haven't I? Ebola. Are you afraid yet? Gaia is a life-force that is a part of

Human consciousness. My partner put it on the screen today, so you could see the connections [during the lecture series]. Now it's time to connect the dots. Dear ones, Gaia is in the battle, too, for here comes something scary that you haven't had in your lifetime and you're afraid of it – the potential of a pandemic on the planet.

There's a very famous film that has some dialogue that my partner will quote. Some of you will know it and some of you won't, but here it is: *"Have a little fire, scarecrow?"* What are you afraid of? Darkness? Gaia is in the battle with you and is actively pursuing solutions through light. The energy of the planet is with you in this fight! The Ebola virus is a shock and a surprise. It is propelled by ignorance and fear, so it can flourish. Look at where it started and look at how it gets its ability to continue. It expands its fear and power easily with those who believe it's a curse, instead of those who understand the science.

Villages are filled with those who refuse to leave their family members, because they believe the disease is a curse! FEAR! Instead of understanding that they should be in isolation from the virus, the family dies together through ignorance and fear. This represents how darkness works. Are you going to become afraid, also? Dear ones, Ebola will be conquered. Know this and be at peace. Pray for light for those in the villages who are afraid, that they can know more about how to keep the spread of this disease and live to see their families.

You Are Changing History

You are the ones who have caused this change, dear ones. Congratulations for shining a light so bright that you've got darkness on the run. The proof of this is in everything I just told you. Against all odds, you've got a virus without a cure. Against all odds, you've got a barbarian movement that is as evil and dark as you could imagine and has seemingly organized overnight. Against all odds, this organization has multiple funding sources, financial distribution, and plenty of help to scare everyone around it. So frightening is it that there are coalitions between countries that would never get together and agree on anything, yet they are now at the table figuring out how to fight the darkness. That's evil!

Evil is not created through outside forces any more than light is created through outside forces. Light and dark is a balance that humanity has the ability to pull in either direction. Did you hear that? You can go as dark as you want or as light as you want, and you have always had that ability. This is the duality that you have seen through your history, forever. However, you are in a situation where you have now come out of a barbarian age – thousands of years of conquering and killing and war – and you've turned a corner.

Again, I say to you: Do not despair! Generate the light that you came in with and stand tall and out of fear. *"That's too simple, Kryon."* Oh really? How do you think this planet has turned this major corner, dear Lightworker? Old Soul, do you not understand that the light that you have is a multi-dimensional force? It is not linear. It is not the *amount* of it that is important. It's the intent of it and the truth of it. That is to say, a little goes a long way and Old Souls are extremely powerful in this department.

Kryon live channelling "Revelations of Darkness"
given in Philadelphia, Pennsylvania – October 11, 2014

I think the two key points from this channelled message is that evil energies are generated from humans and that Gaia responds to the vibration and consciousness of humanity. I want to discuss dark energies, as represented by evil spirits, demons, and other dark entities. Dark entities are seemingly able to interfere with humans, creating great fear and sometimes physical harm. In the previous channel, Kryon stated that the greatest evil power on Earth is found in the minds and intentions of humans. Humans are very capable of manifesting darkness, just as they hold the power to manifest light.

As a result, our planet has been open to evil, because Human consciousness has allowed it, created it, and made it real. Does it make sense to you that if Human consciousness can create demons, it can also dispel them? If so, then how? The answer, as given by Kryon, is to simply create light. Within each of us this can be accomplished

by loving ourselves and understanding the core essence of who we are [God]. The laws of conscious physics will not allow darkness in Human Beings who actively love themselves. Where there is light, no darkness can exist.

When you start to love yourself and increase your self-worth, your life begins to change. Evil cannot exist where there is light, and love represents the purity of the light of God within the Human Being. Thankfully, the collective consciousness of humanity is starting to increase in wisdom, intelligence and spiritual awareness. Actions that lack integrity are becoming noticed and are no longer acceptable. Slowly, humanity is changing and Human nature is beginning to change.

In generations to come, the negative things we see on our news today will take a back seat to the positive things. The idea of humans killing each other on purpose will be seen as barbaric and from a past age. It will be viewed as something that does not belong to modern humanity. Instead, humanity will begin to fall in love with itself and war will no longer be an option. One Human Being will see another Human Being and recognize the magnificence that is present in both. Tolerance will be the normal mode of existence, and the darkness that now allows for evil will be something relegated to a distant past.

Is there any proof of these grandiose ideas? Let's take a look at the correlation between Human consciousness and Gaia. The premise is that when humanity had a very low consciousness, Gaia allowed plagues and pandemics. The table below shows the top ten worst plagues in history:

	Name of Plague or Pandemic	**Year**	**Casualties**
1	The Black Death (also known as The Black Plague or Bubonic Plague)	1347-1351	Number of deaths estimated as 75 million people in Asia, Russia, Western Europe and North Africa.
2	The Third Pandemic	1855-1950s	More than 12 million people in India and China, spreading to all inhabited continents

	Name of Plague or Pandemic	Year	Casualties
3	Plague of Justinian	541-542 AD	Afflicted the Byzantine Empire and destroyed up to a quarter of the population in the Eastern Mediterranean.
4	Great Plague of London	1665-1666	Killed 75,000 to 100,000 people, up to a fifth of London's population.
5	American Plague	16th Century	Drastic drop in the population of the pre-European cultures within North, Central and South America.
6	Great Plague of Milan	1629-1631	Claimed the lives of 280,000 people in Italy.
7	Plague of Athens	430-427 BC	Approximately 75,000 to 100,000 people died, up to a quarter of the city's population.
8	Antonine Plague	165-180 AD	Total deaths in Roman Empire estimated at 5 million people.
9	Great Plague of Marseille	1720-1722	Killed 100,000 people in Marseille, France.
10	Moscow Plague and Riot	1771	At the peak of the plague, 20,000 people confirmed dead.

Source: http://listverse.com/2009/01/18/top-10-worst-plagues-in-history/

Did you notice the year of the plagues and pandemics in the table above? What do you know about the history of these times? Do you think there was a high or low consciousness? My understanding is that during these historic times, the consciousness was to separate and conquer. Many deaths occurred either through war, or for disobeying the ruler, whether it was king, queen or emperor. If it's true that Gaia has a consciousness which is hooked to humanity, what do you think was Gaia's interpretation of what humanity wanted? Could this have triggered large-scale plagues and pandemics? Kryon says that is exactly what happened (although I expect this answer to be controversial to many). Use your own discernment, but it sure does seem like more than a coincidence (wink).

Since the 1980s, a great shift has occurred on Earth. This shift has been prophesied by the Ancients, and heralds a new era in which the planet has a higher consciousness. If this is the case, why is it that various pandemics have arisen, such as HIV/AIDS, SARS (severe acute respiratory syndrome), Bird Flu (Avian influenza), Swine Flu (H1N1 influenza), and the Ebola virus, during this alleged new era of a higher consciousness? Let's analyze these pandemics. Many deaths resulted, and in some cases, continue to occur. But, if you calculate the potential number of deaths that could have occurred, compared with the actual number of deaths, I believe that the pandemics haven't spread to the degree that was predicted and anticipated. Part of this is due to a more sophisticated level of education and awareness in certain countries (who then help other countries who are ignorant about the disease). Do you think it's also possible that Gaia helped reduce the impact in some way? Again, I encourage you to use your own discernment to answer this question. I hope that pondering the answers to these questions may alter your perception about our planet's consciousness, Gaia.

Many of you are noticing that in this new energy (of 2013 and beyond), there is so much evidence of darkness on the planet. Kryon says it's the final battle between light and dark, and not surprisingly, Gaia is in the battle, too. Kryon admonishes us to stay out of fear. Fear and darkness cannot exist where there is light. That is why, dear Old Soul, your presence on the planet matters. You are far grander than you think. Everything you do blesses Gaia, and Gaia, in return, blesses you!

Questions for Kryon:

The cetaceans (whales and dolphins) are unique to the rest of Gaia's animals, having had their DNA altered by the Pleiadians. However, can you explain why there are some very special and unique animals, such as elephants, that share such a profound connection with humans? It seems as though elephants bond differently with humans than other animals that receive our love.

Answer:

The more intelligent an animal, the closer it will seem to you. Intelligence brings the opportunity for higher consciousness. The first things that develop beyond basic survival instincts are the things you see that are very Human: The Human attributes of love, compassion, and sacrifice. The elephant, the horse, and the pig (believe it or not), are some of the smartest common animals on the planet, and they have these attributes. Since you eat pigs, you don't want to think about it. But you don't eat elephants.

So the elephant "bond" is that they can love you, and love each other. They have shown compassion for each other, for situations, and have even sacrificed themselves for other elephants. The same is true of the horse, but they do not show it as clearly as the elephant. Elephants also mourn deeply. To you, it's very Human, so there is, indeed, the bond.

Does the higher consciousness of an ascended planet eliminate diseases, plagues and pandemics?

Yes. It's indirect, however. Higher consciousness of divine creatures is passed to the many grids of the planet, which include those in nature which carry and spread these things. The higher the consciousness, the less disease. So it's not about the ability to cure them as much as not catching them.

Hopefully, you can see how this correlation means that the grids are "alive" and they know who you are. They are here for you, and not for the planet. Many were placed by those who seeded the planet, and are not here by accident.

Right now, you have an enormous amount of humanity on the planet, and you have thousands of airplanes in the air at any given moment, traveling everywhere. Logic would tell you that this would be an actual breeding ground for pandemics ... the perfect biological storm. So I ask you, why isn't it happening? What happened to the plagues of the past that killed millions in just one city? It happened without huge populations and without air travel. This is counterintuitive to your reality and history! Perhaps there is another force at work to help out? Use common sense. When things are out of the paradigm of the way things are supposed to work, there are often reasons why.

Chapter Three

The Human Soul Group

The attributes within the Human Soul Group relate to your corporeal body, healing yourself, changing your DNA and mining your Akash. The three attributes within this group are:

- Human Consciousness (which drives Spiritual Evolution and the vibration of the planet).
- The Higher-Self (the Pineal and Intuition, which is the bridge with Innate).
- Innate (the Body Intelligence which is connected to your Akash (DNA) and the percentage that DNA is working).

Human Consciousness

Traditionally, the study of Human consciousness has been considered a matter for philosophical debate. For decades, any scientist crazy enough to start talking about Human consciousness within serious scientific circles risked their credentials being rescinded and forever labeled as someone who was a little deranged, or worse, an occultist. Thankfully, there is a growing number of renegade scientists who aren't afraid to tackle some of the big questions that relate to Human consciousness. There is even a Human Consciousness Project made up of an international consortium of multidisciplinary scientists and physicians. They are interested in researching the nature of consciousness and its relationship with the brain, as well as the neuronal processes that mediate and correspond to different facets of consciousness. Here is some information about their project:

> "Contrary to popular perception, death is not a specific moment, but a well-defined process. From a biological viewpoint, cardiac arrest is synonymous with clinical death. During a cardiac arrest, all three criteria of clinical death are present: the heart stops beating, the lungs stop working, and the brain ceases functioning. Subsequently, there is a period of time – which may last from a few seconds up to an hour or longer – in which emergency medical efforts may succeed in resuscitating the heart and reversing the dying process. The experiences that individuals undergo during this period of cardiac arrest provide a unique window of understanding into what we are all likely to experience during the dying process.
>
> In recent years, a number of scientific studies conducted by independent researchers have found that as many as 10-20 percent of individuals who undergo cardiac arrest report lucid, well-structured thought processes, reasoning, memories, and sometimes detailed recall of their cardiac arrest. What makes these experiences remarkable is that while studies of the brain during cardiac arrest have consistently [shown] that there is no brain activity during this period, these individuals have reported detailed perceptions that appear to indicate the presence of a high-level of consciousness in the absence of measurable brain activity.
>
> These studies appear to suggest that the human mind and consciousness may in fact function at a time when the clinical criteria of death are fully present and the brain has ceased functioning. If these smaller studies can be replicated and verified through the definitive, large-scale studies of the Human Consciousness Project, they may not only revolutionize the medical care of critically ill patients and the scientific study

of the mind and brain, but may also bear profound universal implications for our social understanding of death and the dying process."

Source: http://www.nourfoundation.com/events/Beyond-the-Mind-Body-Problem/The-Human-Consciousness-Project.html

It is very encouraging to learn about the existence of such projects. I especially love the idea of a revolution in medical care. Everything we do in the "now" is shaping the potentials of what is yet to come. The next hundred years, in particular, will bring a lot of new information, ideas and inventions. With it will come new understanding and awareness, including solutions to current problems that may seem unsolvable right now. Kryon has also given a prediction about how we may eventually view the subject of Human consciousness:

Human consciousness is complex. There will come a day when your science may consider Human consciousness as a branch of physics. This is because it does not follow the patterns of known linear physics or even the patterns of quantum physics. Consciousness is a synchronized energy that has structure. It has quantum patterning (as you will eventually find out), but it doesn't have a set of logic rules. Instead, it is biased by the Akash of the individual Human Being. It's complicated, and it's the only synchronized and coherent energy known to have its own agenda, its own personality and the ability to communicate. So it's the study of "living physics." Since Human consciousness carries with it attributes of the Soul, we can now substitute "Soul consciousness" as the same thing, for they are one and the same.

Kryon live channelling "Soul Communication – Part I"
given in San Antonio, Texas – February 22, 2014

Chances are, if you are reading this book, you already have a high level of consciousness. But what about some of the people you know? Do you sometimes get frustrated by others who appear to have a low level of consciousness? What is responsible for this difference?

How would you describe Human consciousness to others, especially when it's so difficult to research and measure? I think the reason for a low level of consciousness is a factor of many things that include: a programmed belief system; a limited three dimensional perception; the level of allowance a person has (with free choice); and the number of blocks and filters that prevent an elevation beyond survival mode. Here is how Kryon describes Human consciousness:

We wish to define, as best we can, Human consciousness. Now, this would not be the definition that you might read in your academia, for these are the things that *we* see. Human consciousness is divided into several parts, but we're only going to talk about two: Energies that are driven by two big parts of the Human. The first part is the synaptic brain. This is your *storehouse of experience.* The second is intuition, the multi-dimensional part that you believe is responsible for all creativity, sensitivity, and special perception. Consciousness is, therefore, a mixture of these two, through your free choice. It's a balance of those two, which creates a Human who, indeed, appears to others to be in control of their own life, and satisfied with themselves. When this is out of balance, either way, you get dysfunction.

When the Human Being has a consciousness that is only a product of the synaptic brain, there is no credibility of God in their lives, and no ability for them to have truly creative, intuitive thought. They are the intellectuals who constantly massage their egos by stating only what they know. This is dysfunctional to us, because the *God part* of them is always there, and always available. It would give them so much of an increased awareness and light to use it! But this is not seen, since the synaptic brain concentrates on survival, and part of survival in society is ego-driven. The more you know, the greater the perception of your importance. It is free choice for any Human to think any way they wish.

Then there's the other side of the situation, as well: Dysfunctional New Agers. I will call them *floaters*. They are so wrapped up in that which is esoteric, that they have no clue about real life situations, and the synaptic brain doesn't have a chance to work. They are illogical, filled with esoteric pride, elite in their ability to spiritually be above everyone else, wrapped up in their process, and no real help to anyone around them. Again, this imbalance is also ego-driven, and you have seen them as specialists in weirdness.

This is Human consciousness - a balance between that which represents synaptic survival, and that which represents the intuitive, creative energies. Now, where are you in this balance? That is how we must begin this channel.

Balance

If you are listening or reading this today, the chances are that you are aware of the divine part of you. The divine part of you is the mysterious part, the elusive part, but it's also as real as the synaptic brain. These two parts are linked strongly to your ability to actually *talk* to your body. If you are an intellectual reading this, and you are only trusting that which is logic (synapse) in your brain, you should stop now and go no further. The reason is because you will not have any success with what I'm about to tell you. Isn't it interesting that these two are linked so strongly, yet that is not apparent to most?

I want you to be aware of the divine inside, because that is the pathway of your communication, which is going to talk to INNATE (the smart body). We gave you information years ago, which told you that there would come a day on this planet when very healthy individuals might be seen in a far different way than they are today. Those with higher consciousness would be living much longer lives, yet there would be no obvious scientific reasons why. We told you that consciousness might eventually drive the very attribute of Human balance at a cellular and chemical way, and things such as diet and exercise would take a back seat to elevated consciousness.

The very attributes that keep you alive are going to start changing for the Human Being. You will not only start to have a greater awareness of the three-dimensional attributes of what your body needs, but also an awareness of what is going on inside your body. This is the bridge between the synaptic and the intuitive. So if you've come this far, and you can honestly say, *"I believe that there is a divine part of me,"* then we can continue. For the rest of this information will be given with the premise that you believe in what we are teaching.

The Linear Approach

Historically, as an enlightened creature, you live in your head. Everything that happens in your Human reality is perceived to come from your head. Your greatest intuitive and creative endeavors also seem to come from your head. The greatest poetry ever written, the greatest music ever composed, the greatest paintings - all started in your head. For most of humanity, the rest of your body seems to just "operate" by itself. You occasionally will look down at your body and say, *"I sure hope this thing keeps working!"* But that is your history and tradition. You don't think to yourself, *"I'm going to create good blood chemistry today."* NO. Instead you say, *"I sure hope my blood is not out of balance ... I have no idea."*

This scenario of "having no control over anything" is enhanced by watching those around you, who are catching diseases. Then the fear starts. The fear will create the hypochondriac who is afraid of everything, and who believes he is going to catch everything ... and by the way, they usually do! That's the Human body doing its best to "listen" to what it *hears* from consciousness, by the way. This should give you a hint of what's coming. That's the traditional thought - that you don't have any control.

Those who are spiritually minded, however, know more about the cellular structure of their body having a multi-dimensional, spiritual complement. They are ready to give instructions to their body, but what they do next is often interesting: Historically, the Human bias kicks in, and even those who would call themselves *enlightened* often start a totally linear process of verbal repetition and ceremony. This is very understandable, however, because it's all you have had in the past.

The New Age has been filled with processes that are supposed to let you talk to your cells, and these are filled with repetition and ceremony ... over and over. Some of the processes create ceremony for the cells, saying you have to go to a certain place in a certain temperature, or be in a certain energy of peace, or even face a certain direction. All this, and you might then have to do it several times. Indeed, you have been told the body wants some instructions, but what's missing here is that it's not responding to your 3D approach. The fact that you are trying to overwhelm it with this, is the Human bias.

Dear ones, it's time to de-mystify all of this. Barraging your body with ceremonial and verbal repetition is not the way to communicate to your divinity. These processes make an assumption that the body is stupid. It doesn't know anything about anything, and is completely and totally separated from your consciousness. It's clueless and needs all these 3D things to wake it up with sound, energy, and ceremony, and the more the better. I want to tell you the truth.

Scientifically, what follows is going to eventually be proven, and that proof is not going to be that far away. The cells of your body, especially what you would call *Innate,* is elegant and smart. It is beyond 3D, which explains why you can't diagnose yourself. It lives in a multi-dimensional space and responds to multi-dimensional instructions. Within that space, all your cells have something in common: We're going to give it a name: It's going to be C-A-L: *Cells Are Listening.*

Dear ones, this is how you were built. The divine, multi-dimensional complement within you is built into every cell of your body. No matter what kind of cells, they all have something in common. They are all connected to your DNA (which has the master blueprint), and every cell exists with one common attribute: *Every cell is neutral, waiting for instructions*, and the only *instructions* that they will *hear* and act upon are the ones given through the divine complement of Human consciousness. Did you hear that? Without this, they simply do the best they can in a linear world, which is often filled with fear, uncertainty, and chemical imbalance ... no master communication from YOU.

Let's talk about multi-dimensional communication for a moment. It's like every single cell had a telephone that is ready to be answered, if you only knew the number. If you could dial that number, you could talk to all of them at once. They would all pick up the phone and it would be you! That's built in, and it represents a system that doesn't respond to linear repetition. The communication with the cells of the body is a multi-dimensional communication, but your Human consciousness is also – it's part of the DNA field, and it's part of the Merkabah of your body. I'll tell you what an intuitive can do: Imagine a Human who can look at your Soul within the Merkabah field, and tell you whether or not you have activated any part of spiritual intent, or whether you are just playing the role.

What is pure intent? When you fall in love with someone and you look at them in the eyes, there's nothing like it. Do you feel God in that? Do you remember? Do you feel God in that? You do! But you're not even aware of it. Do you realize that this is why being in love is so amazing? It's because God is there. Do you realize that love is not a synaptic brain function? In fact, the brain is really frustrated that you are in love! It's saying:

"You know, you should eat better."
You say, *"Yeah but I'm in love."*
"Well you ought to have better reasoning."
"But I don't, because I'm in love."
"Why are you putting your shoes in the freezer?"
"Because I'm in love, I forgot!"

Now, when you look at someone and say, "*I love you*," that's pure intent. When you're in love, and you pour out your love to the other, you're entangled as one. There's nothing like it. Now, I want you to turn this inward: Consider that there is a divine part of you inside, who is *in love with the whole you*. It's always there, waiting for you to see it and say, "*I love you, too!*" And, by the way, it will know if you mean it or not.

If you're not in love with a person, the magic isn't there and the connection isn't there. The entanglement isn't there, and the phrase "I love you" become just words. It's not pure, and you don't have the right phone number to talk to the cells of your body. But when you fall in love with yourself, you are honoring the body to such a degree that you realize it's part of God's creation of you. Without this, there would be no enlightenment, no higher consciousness, nothing. It has to operate well, and it wants to. It wants to! Here is the opportunity.

Years ago, you saw the gurus of India being able to control the things that were supposed to be automatic in the body, yet they had control. They could slow their heart rates down and make their respiration extremely slow; they could take control of certain things within their body that nobody thought they could. They were talking to a part of their body that was listening and adjusting, and they knew how to do it. This is a very possible scenario and is not strange.

Kryon live channelling "Cellular Communication"
Enhanced by Lee Carroll for this book
Given in Delphi University, Georgia – April 12, 2014

There is something else very important to understand about Human consciousness that was mentioned earlier. It drives the vibration of the planet and is responsible for Spiritual Evolution. Human consciousness is entangled with the Magnetic Grid (part of the Earth's grid system), which shapes the future. Why is the vibration of our planet connected to it? Why would Human consciousness affect Spiritual Evolution? Kryon provides some insights to these questions, and not surprisingly, it is related to physics – the physics of consciousness:

What you describe as Human consciousness, isn't. It's just *consciousness*. It only belongs to the Human Being because you're Human and see it that way. You as a Human group generate an energy of consciousness, so you call it Human consciousness, but it's almost identical to the consciousness that the other planets have gone through. It's an energy that actually has substance [more to come on this]. Would you call physics, "Human physics?"

For you, consciousness is a life-produced awareness. Only life can create it. It represents individual and group thought-values and changes over time. The maturity cycle of planetary consciousness is almost identical from planet to planet, because the galaxy is made up of fractals of energy. From the smallest to the largest, fractals represent repetitive parts of the same thing. It's a beautiful idea, and what it means is that there is a common system of life throughout the galaxy and a commonality everywhere regarding the structure of it. This allows for the building blocks of life to be a DNA-like structure almost everywhere. In advanced life, DNA carries far more than chemical information, but everywhere, the same kinds of amino acid structures as you have in your body are common to all. We've seen this before. Doesn't this make sense to you, since you already have seen that the Universe started from one source, not many? Therefore, the source carried the fractals of what everything eventually became today.

You're a young civilization, dear ones, so young that it's difficult to even give you a perspective of how young you are. Your solar system, with your civilization as part of it, hasn't even orbited the galaxy one time yet! It has only moved a fraction of the distance of one revolution [rev]. It takes almost 200 million Earth years to travel around the center of the galaxy one time [one rev]. How does it make you feel to know that there are societies and civilizations on other worlds far from you who have been around three revs? The Pleiadians (your seed biology) - half a rev. This is just to show you how old some life is in this galaxy. Some of them visit you, but none of them, none of them are able to influence you to the degree that you can influence yourselves. The galaxy teems with life and you're well hidden, by the way. Until now.

We've seen planetary maturity happen before, so I want to give you a bigger picture. Your age as a Human on this planet starts to explain why the Earth has been through such a horrendous time. The history of Earth civilization looks ugly to you, doesn't it? Your past and your history are filled with survival energy: killing, ugly weaponry, mass destruction and no elegance or respect for life at all. Torture was common, and public execution was a sport. Dear ones, all those planets went through that! They all did, because civilization does this; it builds itself through time and growth. Part of growth doesn't always go the way of maturity. It has the ability to destroy itself, or the seeds of its knowledge, along the way. Sometimes that happens, and sometimes it does not. As you know, your Earth just passed a point where that was a possible scenario.

There comes a time when a Human child becomes self-aware. The ego takes over completely and all they think about is themselves. You can see it with the survival attributes on the playground at school. You can actually watch as some become bullies to survive and some do not. Some children never mature with their consciousness, and they remain bullies, even as adults. They fight and scrap all their lives. They never discover the elegance and the beauty that wisdom creates with maturity. They often die young.

Planetary consciousness and what you have called "Human nature" matures, or it doesn't. As you grow up as a civilization, you accumulate knowledge and experience. Eventually, a wisdom is created that produces new thinking about better ways to solve problems than the old survival techniques [war]. Through tolerance and cooperation, you have the opportunity to grow up and begin to work together, just like the process you experienced as children growing up.

You have to do this in order to move forward. Children don't know this, since they don't have the intellect to see it. They don't know what they haven't experienced yet, and as you know, some will never grow up, and their lives will reflect anger, violence and simple survival thinking all their lives. You truly get to see the whole system through the metaphor of your own children and how they mature.

As you bring up your children, they do the same things as civilizations do. They go through the terrible twos and the thrashing threes and the teenage years [gasp!] and then, hopefully, they'll grow up. I'm being simplistic and applying children's consciousness to Human civilization, but let me do it. The reason? You're still on the playground! You're still pushing each other around to see who is boss; you're still getting reactions; you're still in survival - until about 50 years ago, when it started to shift just a little. Now you've passed the marker where you could have destroyed yourselves and didn't. We have told you over and over what that timetable was and what the calendars of the Ancients told you. It also explained why I'm here - a true celebration of what you have done. Now, I want to go further than that in this particular channel.

The Unseen Energy of Consciousness

I want to talk to you about profound unseen energy, representing a profound unrecognized system.

There is a complement of energy that interests many of you. You can't see it, but you want to, because it touches you in ways that are fascinating. This unseen energy is responsible for what the new-agers and esoteric-minded sense first. Some are able to pick up energy in someone's auric field somehow. A real medical intuitive can actually intuit what is wrong with another Human. The field around you broadcasts sickness, health and joy. What is that energy? How does it work? For the science-minded among you, wouldn't you like to bottle it up, take it home, and analyze it? But you can't.

The very institute that puts this event together [referring to the Arlington Institute in West Virginia] is invested in these very energies - unseen energies that make a difference. What is it a reader reads or a psychic feels or a futurist can futurize? Where does this energy come from, and can you call it energy? Why is it so elusive? I'm going to tell you more in just a moment and a little bit more about this being a key to the future.

Again, a child would not know about the elegance of wisdom. A child does not think about how to put things together for the benefit of the children around them. A child who is ego-driven, who is only waking up to being self-aware, is only going to do what the child does that helps himself. The only equipment that the child has is basic emotion, and whatever else they need to create a solution in a very elementary way. The child will lash out, scream, pound, or push others in certain ways to get the things they want. If you gave this child a *plate of wisdom*, they would look at it and have no idea what it was. They'd throw it away as useless.

Humanity is at this crossroad. Survival consciousness is about to morph into a more mature way of thinking. This unseen energy has attributes you don't know anything about. If I gave you a plate of it, you might throw it away. You might not even be able to see it. The Lightworkers and Old Souls are discovering the change first. Everything about this unseen energy, which we call *the quantum consciousness of humanity*, is starting to enhance itself, so that it will be a little more obvious and far less elusive.

If I took you to another civilization right now, such as the Pleiadian or those from Orion or the Arcturians, you would not recognize anything. Like a child attending a poetry meeting, you would be so confused! Where are the toys? Why is this so boring? Why can't I understand what they are saying? When does the movie start? Are we there yet?

First of all, they don't have technology as you perceive it. How about that? Because physical machines that *do things* were thrown away long ago. They did that slowly, as they realized that the *physics of Human consciousness* could create anything they ever wanted. That's where it's going, dear ones, and you don't know what it is. You don't know what you don't know.

Now, we have given you some hints about it, so let's develop that. Human consciousness has no succinct definition, other than what I gave you at the beginning of this message, about an *energy of life*. But what if I told you that to other mature planets, it has a solid definition? Why? Because they can show it to you on a blackboard, to use a Human school metaphor. It's math! It has rules and it has physics! Not only that, it's not in 3D and does not follow any 3D rules. No wonder you can't understand this!

I could tell you all about it, but it wouldn't make any sense at all. Here is an example of the attributes that are puzzling to you: We have told you that less than one-half of one percent of humanity has to awaken in a certain way to then affect the entire planet. Now, that ought to tell you that Human consciousness is not 3D. How can something so small affect the whole? Less than one-half of one percent. It's not about how many of you there are, because that is "playground talk." Quantum energy is everywhere all the time and reacts to other quantum energy with the rules of quantum energy.

Listen, dear ones, there is a system, a confluence of systems that you don't know anything about yet. My explanation won't fall on *learned ears* yet. It won't be understandable to all of you, and that is why you may wish to read this again or put it in a time capsule.

How do you explain the Internet to someone who doesn't know about electricity yet? Where do you begin? How do you debate the elegant differences of specific race car engines to someone who hasn't had the wheel invented yet? This is the issue today. How do I tell you about what you have no concept of, yet you need to know about? So let me give you some building blocks and yet some more metaphors.

The Wisdom Barrier

There's something called the *wisdom barrier.* The wisdom barrier is what we have described as "what happens in the energy of Human consciousness when certain attributes occur that are not quantitative but that affect and even change this barrier." So it's not about *how much* or *how many.* Instead, it's about other things that will occur within the physics of consciousness that you don't yet know anything about. But these things must occur in a certain way, a distributed way, not a centralized way, in order to break this barrier. The wisdom barrier is not a wall or obstruction, but a barrier of energy that is waiting to be reached, like the sound barrier was waiting. When the wisdom barrier is reached, it breaks an old paradigm of consciousness, and nothing can be what it was.

When you broke the sound barrier, did you go home and say, *"That's nice! Let's continue to use old aircraft and old speeds from now on."* No! You could hardly wait to design aircraft that would go beyond it! Nothing remained the same, and you could not put the genie back in the bottle. Humanity has passed a point where it is no longer in survival mode. It has broken the wisdom barrier, and now it has gone into a mode that starts to build the process of getting along. You cannot easily go backwards into a less aware state.

It's a quantum attribute. Think about this – a wisdom that enhances the brains of all humanity to a point where most minds can agree on things that they never even realized before. All this, without actually having it taught to them. Did you hear that? Now, you didn't expect that. The barrier is broken and out comes "intuitive mature Human thought" for the entire planet.

It surrounds the Human Being in such a way, and Human civilization in such a way, that when a child is born, new maturity becomes second nature – the wisdom of getting along, of tolerance and how to solve puzzles, of Human with Human. It's called the wisdom barrier. Now, you're there! And it's not going to give you fireworks or sparks in the sky. There won't be a celebration, or toasts, or balloons, except on my side of the veil. All Old Souls are looking into the very essence of this barrier energy. You are peeking into what makes it work, and you're about to push the envelope that will affect all of humanity, not just Lightworkers and Old Souls. You're about to push the button on *physics you didn't know existed* – and it will take time.

The Missing Piece

Now, this is the part that I wanted to give you – the missing piece. How do I explain this? My partner, go very slow [speaking to Lee]. Humanity explains things only from what it knows, not from what it doesn't know. Here's an example: Perhaps scientists look into space and they find attributes they cannot explain. The attributes do not seem to be Newtonian science, but Newtonian physics is the gold standard of motion everywhere, so the Human Being struggles to find formulas that will put the unexplained into Newtonian boxes. Welcome to dark matter! You're going to laugh later at the box you were in. Now, we've told you this before, but this is the Human propensity for logic, and it's very understandable. Take what is known, observe what is unknown, and try to place the unknown into the boxes of the known, even if they are convoluted boxes and even if they don't make sense. Even if they're mysterious! Instead of actively looking for missing laws of physics, go with what you know.

Well, let me tell you that one of the biggest pieces of fractal information is the one you're missing. Why would you separate the known energy of consciousness from the world of physics? Energy has fractals, too, and from the little to the big, they all

work together. Atomic structure creates energy! Consciousness is energy and has quantum laws. The missing piece of understanding or realization is the *physics of consciousness.*

Listen to me: How does humanity define consciousness? *"Well,"* they might say, *"consciousness is a concept, and it describes the self-aware state of a Human Being. It cannot be measured, since it is only a concept."* No it isn't! How do you like this statement? *Gravity is a concept that describes why you drop stuff. It can't be measured, since it's just a concept.* You know better! Gravity is invisible energy that can be calculated and is quantum energy. Magnetism is invisible, measurable and is quantum energy. Consciousness is the same. It is physics, and you should get used to this, because that is one of the next areas of physics that will pull you through the hole from 3D to multi-dimensional. What you think of as a concept (consciousness) is not. You are unaware that there are rules of consciousness, and that it is a part of quantum physics.

There are rules, postulates, math, graphs and solutions. There are beautiful attributes, as yet unknown, of the physics of consciousness. When you start to see this, it will begin to explain what is going to happen and the way of the future. But at the moment, you don't see it that way. The missing piece is *the knowledge that you can track and measure consciousness, that you can plot it, even outside of humanity*. It's beautiful! Imagine not having the elegance of Newtonian rules and wondering about how the motion of things in the solar system worked - you don't have to. Newton brought it together. His math now allows you to launch a rocket and meet up years later with an asteroid that can't be seen with the Human eye! It's pure math and predictable, and this creates some beautiful potentials.

The technology that you have and work with on this planet that is so beautiful and helpful is brought to you by the knowledge of the physics that you know. There is action and reaction; push this and that will happen. When you understand the laws of physics, you can make your lives better and, indeed, you have.

Right now, humanity understands and uses the four basic laws of physics. We have told you that there are six, but even without the last two, you are aware of how to use the first four. It has changed humanity. Beautiful! Now, what if I told you that that same scenario exists in consciousness?

There are laws of consciousness that are just like the laws of physics, in that they are causal (changing one thing causes another to change). But in the quantum world, these *laws* of consciousness motion are not linear, so they create different kinds of reactions. Now, my partner, it gets harder [speaking again to Lee directly]. I'm showing things to my partner right now and he can't verbalize them. So I'm going to say, just do your best. He sees the emotion of it: OMG!

New Kinds of Laws of Physics

If you knew the physics of consciousness, you could build a better world. Listen to these attributes: First of all, consciousness does not travel from place to place; it does not travel in a straight direction; it does not travel! Consciousness is not in one place, going to another; consciousness does not expand. It does not get bigger or smaller. Consciousness just IS. The consciousness of physics is just like the attributes of 3D physics, in that it just sits there, ready to be enhanced or not, based upon other laws around it. When certain rules or laws are applied, then other laws all change together. Consciousness is the glue of life existence. If there were a formula for life, this is it.

Let me tell you about a couple of factors that can apply to consciousness to effect change. One is called the *benevolence factor.* Did you know that, as the physics of consciousness is explored, and the wisdom factor is applied (gained by passing the wisdom barrier), what happens next is an *exponential understanding and application of the rules of consciousness that creates a factor that generates benevolent action*. Oh, that's convoluted, my partner! Can you say that better? [Lee shakes his head].

Let me tell you this way: Right now on this planet, there's a struggle between energy forces. Because of the consciousness that you have developed and the "laws" that you have put in place through the physics of consciousness, a struggle has arisen right now of many things on this planet that we've never talked about. Is there evil on the planet? Yes. Are there entities dedicated to coming in and messing with you? Yes. Is that shocking? And why would that be? At a time of passing into the potential of higher consciousness, why would that be? Dear ones, it's because with what you have created in the physics of consciousness and with the rules that have been applied, you are pushing on low consciousness in a way that forces it to get out of the way! Remember, it's in 3D survival mode. So what do you think it's going to do? Fight! Did you get that?

When the rules of physics are applied in certain situations, you can control what happens. This is the beauty of knowing 3D physics. However, it's the same with consciousness. When you reach a point of understanding of the physics of consciousness, how it works, the mechanics of it, the distribution of it and *the spiral delivery of it,* you shut the door to older energies. Certain entities that have visited this planet in the past can't visit anymore. Did you hear that? They can't get in! Physics creates a barrier and they can't get in. There are dark energies and ideas of darkness that would want to come in and play with your consciousness. Some call that evil. It affects humans, and those humans work with it. It helps them gain power and control, and there is no elegance in how they obtain it. But that door is being closed! Evil, as you know it, will start to diminish. Evil is an energy that is sucked up by certain humans. Then those humans truly become evil, and it's their choice. That's old consciousness. That's the best explanation we have for what is going to happen in the future.

The Pleiadians are jumping up and down right now, because they know what has happened here. It's almost an exponential evolution, if you want it to be. One thing leads to another and it builds on itself. Eventually, you won't have to start over every single time you're born, as my partner described earlier today. Spiritual evolution begins, and you start to come into the planet with knowledge of the factors that you learn today and you build upon them in your next life. If I could use a term, it would be *born wise.*

Later on, when the physics is revealed to you, you will understand about devices that can work with consciousness.

After all, it's just physics. What you won't think of is that they won't necessarily be machines, but rather, biological assists. But you're not going to have them for a while. *"How many generations are required, Kryon?"* I'm not going to tell you. The reason is that I don't want to give you a set-up that will spoil the party. Every single planet has had its own time cycle regarding the speed of their own evolution.

"How does it work? How fast does it work? When will it start?" It has already started! You are at the wisdom barrier and have broken through. Once you are at the wisdom barrier, I would like to tell you that the track record of all the planets who have reached this place are the same. They've all moved forward, every single one. It's like the collective consciousness of the whole planet was involved. It's like you threw a switch and no amount of dark energy could stop it. Oh, it will try! I've told you that before. Humans who are invested in old ways, like the kids on the playground, don't want to grow up. They'll kick and yell and bully. They know that light will change everything and they haven't got a chance to work as they did before.

This is what we are talking about. The benevolence factor and the wisdom barrier all work within the laws of consciousness physics in ways that you will, indeed, figure out. You will end up creating an increased DNA percentage activation, and this will increase generation after generation. Eventually, you will have a Human Being who can manipulate matter and seemingly create things out of nothing. Why is that so special? It's just physics! Doesn't it make sense that a multi-dimensional physics would be able to control a lower kind of physics? The highest kind of physics is consciousness, and this physics can control 3D physics any day.

Peace on Earth? Oh, that's easy. That's the beginning. That's planting the seeds, and it's a certainty. Look at your news. It's not going to look like it does now forever. That's just for today. Peace on Earth is not the end goal - hardly! When you grow up and you're an adult, you stop throwing stones at each other on the playground. You stop! That's normal. Then you begin having more elegant ideas. Peace on the planet is just the beginning, and then it gets good.

This is what we see. I've never said these things in this way before. I wanted you to hear the full story. What do you think will happen to a civilization without war that could create anything it wanted physically, so it was never hungry? What would it be like to live three or four times as long as you do now, and have good health through all of it? What would a civilization be like that could put themselves into a quantum state if they wanted to and be "anywhere?" This exists! Think of where you were 1,000 years ago. Now consider civilizations in the galaxy that are a million Earth years older! Is this too hard to speculate? It's just physics!

What if I told you that these civilizations have no central control - did you hear that? Have you ever heard of a manager-less corporation? It's like that. You would say, *"That can't work."* Oh, yes it can! It can when everyone is connected to such an extent that they agree with the obvious and know their jobs. It's intuitive and natural. For you? Impossible. That's what you're headed for. There will be no such thing as world government. That's so 3D! Instead, there will be a *world consciousness agreement.* You'll simply "know better." How about that? What happens to a group of adults who go to a party for the first time and they've never met each other? What do they do? Do they throw rocks at each other? No. There's a consciousness at the party where they get together and they talk to each other, eat great food, and have fun. Who told them those rules? Did they rehearse for that? No! It just came with maturity and knowing better. What about a planet that had just that? They're born into a situation where they *know better.* That's the wisdom factor, and that's the barrier that you're crossing.

Eventually, you will throw away any system that you ever thought you needed, especially the ones that organize you into groups to do things. It will be second nature and you'll all *know together.* Too good to be true? Ask a Pleiadian. Ask those from Orion or ask those from Arcturus. Ask any past planet of free choice, because they are all looking at you right now. This room is filled with them, and they are nodding their heads and saying, *"Right on! Right on, Right on!"*

The beauty of this message is that it doesn't matter if you believe it today or not, for you will be experiencing it on this planet. You just wait; you'll be there. You are the ones who are going to create the very essence of these predictions.

Kryon live channelling "The Physics of Consciousness" given in Berkeley Springs, West Virginia – June 29, 2014

What is your perception of what you just read? If consciousness is a part of physics, an energy that responds to belief and intent, is it possible that you have control of your reality? I believe that it is, and to help explain, I'd like to discuss something known as the bell-shaped curve. The term "bell-shaped curve" comes from the fact that a graph depicts the most common type of distribution for a variable, known as normal distribution. It is used in statistics and gives us probabilities such as, four in ten people will get cancer and average life expectancy is 80 years. Kryon has said that this is the way everything works, if left alone, where you come into life and you have no control over anything, hoping that everything will work. This is the way things work unless there is an outside force. That outside force has to do with your belief and consciousness. It means that you can create your own reality, and steer your life in the direction that you want, because consciousness is energy (the outside force).

Have you ever had someone say to you, *"Gee, you're lucky!"* or perhaps, someone you know always lands on their feet, no matter what the circumstance. I call this the "lucky you" factor, which can be explained by understanding synchronicity. Synchronicity and co-creation are part of the systems of benevolent design – available to all of us. The difficulty for most people is that their beliefs often prevent them from seeing the structure of synchronicity. Very few actually believe that we can influence outside forces to manifest our reality. If you have never heard about "synchronicity" or "co-creation," I invite you to read a free chapter called "Co-creating Your Reality" under the Extras tab on my website: *www.monikamuranyi.com*

Questions for Kryon:

You have said, "As goes Human consciousness, so goes humanity." Lightworkers and Old Souls are all over the globe, yet there are distinct differences with countries and cultures on the planet. Each place has a different level of consciousness, as demonstrated by many countries that lack basic human rights. Many also allow and tolerate abhorrent abuse towards women and children. Can you explain the reason as to why this polarity occurs?

Answer:

The answer is something you already know. The phrase, "All humans are created equal," doesn't mean what you think. It means that each Human is created with the same spiritual aspect. Each Human has an equal part of God. No matter what, each of you can access the Higher-Self, and awaken to spiritual concepts, no matter where you are, or what your culture ... created equal.

Common sense, however, tells you that where you are born will be the guide to if you have better chances of free thinking or health, or gender equality. The planet is a cauldron of mixed consciousness, and yes, there are better and worse places for the potentials of high consciousness, or the ability to send and hold light. So, being an Old Soul doesn't give you an "edge" to where you are born.

The distribution of Old Souls on the planet is not random, but it's also fair. They are everywhere, and some have greater challenges, because they asked for that before they got here. Old Souls also tend to "clump" in groups (more later from another question).

Do you now understand why I'm telling Old Souls in "better" places to awaken and go to work? It is no accident that you are reading this. You might be far more able to hold light than someone else. Did you realize that this was the plan all along? There are no accidents.

I have observed that countries and communities that have an abundance of resources, generally get along better. Those that lack resources are more apt to remain in a survival consciousness. In previous channels, there are hints about potentials in which we can create resources, such as fresh water, food and free energy. I think this will provide a starting point for countries and communities to begin a process of spiritual evolution. However, it still remains free choice and is only a potential. Can you tell us more about the dynamics of how this works?

This is something that is actually happening, which is going to change society ... all of it. But it's not what you think. It's due to the "free choice" of the past, that created the potential of the "advanced invention" of the future. It's an attribute of a new Earth, as we have told you.

Countries who have resources are no different than what happens when people are "born into money." They socialize and form cliques with others who have money, go to their clubs, restaurants ... and often never even talk to those without abundance. It's basic Human nature.

But what would happen with the "resource intensive" countries when their resources are no longer needed? The answer is that they will change. The world will change. If a country is rich with oil, what will happen when others no longer need oil? If a country is rich with the ability to grow food, and technology comes along to grow an abundance of food anywhere, what happens then?

Countries rich in resources will slowly lose their ability to stay rich, and the whole balance will start to become more equal. Small neighborhoods can create energy off the grid, or create fresh water, or grow food. It will be the elimination of any kind of centralized grid. It's a paradigm changer, and an equalizer that never happened before. The very attributes that kept countries poor, or easily controlled, will be eliminated.

Use common sense. Do you see how these things will change everything?

Higher-Self (Pineal and Intuition)

The Higher-Self within the Human Soul Group is represented by the pineal and intuition. The pineal gland (also called the pineal body, conarium, or epiphysis cerebri) is a small endocrine gland located in the epithalamus, near the center of the brain, between the two hemispheres. It produces melatonin, a hormone that affects sleep patterns and circadian rhythms. The pineal has often been linked with an esoteric concept known as "The Third Eye," which is a metaphor for higher consciousness and a symbol of enlightenment.

> "What's fascinating is that the interior of the pineal gland actually has retinal tissue composed of rods and cones (photoreceptors) inside its interior lining just like the eye, and is even wired into the visual cortex in the brain. 'The photoreceptors of the retina strongly resemble the cells of the pineal gland.' Dr. David Klein, Science Daily. It even has vitreous fluid in it like an eye does."

Source: http://www.spiritscienceandmetaphysics.com/proof-that-the-pineal-gland-is-literally-a-3rd-eye

Kryon says the pineal is the quantum part of the brain that combines with our brain synapse and is the bridge to our intuition, which is currently working at around 35 percent. According to Kryon, when the DNA starts to work at a higher percentage, these connections are going to improve, and the intuitive mind will work better with the intellectual mind and the emotional mind, creating greater balance within the Human. This is the mechanism that moves humans out of a survival consciousness.

Dr. Todd Ovokaitys is a long-time associate of Lee Carroll, and is a Kryon Team member. In 2001, Dr. Todd began remembering an ancient and sacred practice of toning that activated the pineal gland

and created profoundly expansive experiences. Dr. Todd began to teach others these Pineal Tones, which, when sung with intent, have a multi-dimensional overtone structure that creates light within the DNA field. Singing the Pineal Tones creates a quantum field for health and extended life and activates the coherence of the pineal gland to serve as a quantum transmitter. Kryon delivered a vast amount of information about the Pineal Tones, following one of Dr. Todd's Pineal Tone workshops.

The information that Kryon gives about the tones is what I call extreme high science and esoteric to the max! None of it is provable, but the ones who sing the tones are aware that something special is going on. There are also many others on the planet who use toning, chanting, sounds and music to activate the pineal.

Let us first speak of Pineal Toning. Let us take it apart, and then let's put it together. Let us see why it is what it is, and let's identify what it does, what it's for, and let's discuss what it's going to do.

But first, I take you back to Lemuria ... for some of you were there, not all, but many who are here. *Yawee* is the high priest. [Dr. Todd]. He is not the one who would lead you in spiritual ceremony back then. Yawee is instead, the Spin Master. And they named him that, because he seemed to know a lot about atomic structure. The atomic structure that he knew about was about the spin of electrons, and the spin of electrons seemed to be germane to something he also was able to create: longer life. The spin of electrons actually created something else which we will get to in a moment. He was a specialist in quantum DNA.

Now, back in Lemuria, they didn't know about DNA; they didn't know about biology; they had no microscopes; they had no tools like this at all. It's a misnomer that humans think that back then the Ancients had all the tools and somehow these were lost. They did not have any modern instruments. Instead, they had something you don't have today, but which you are re-learning: They had *quantum intuition*. This is to say, they could see things because they were there, but not in 3D. They were entangled with science, that is to say, the physics before them, they knew all about intuitively ... *doesn't everybody?* They were entangled! [being

part of]. It was a confluence, you might say, of consciousness and physics. They knew how things worked.

Yawee was one step better. He was the "priest of life." He lived three lifetimes longer than any normal Lemurian lived; he knew how it worked. Although it was so long ago, all of the things that he knew that were given to him, he practiced. This included the quantum intuition of being able to "see the spin" and actually generate in his mind, a picture of the double helix. All this has been imbued into his Akash.

Now, we should just stop there a moment and say this is the way it works, Human Being: No matter what you've done, no matter who you are or what you've described as a past life, whatever you've learned becomes imbued into the Akash and it stays there. Some of you can retrieve it if you choose, for it never goes away. Lifetime after lifetime after lifetime it lays there, ready, to actually be received again, and used by you. You earned it.

Yawee is here today in the form of Dr. Todd Ovokaitys, and in this new energy, before he ever came into the planet, he knew it was his turn to, once again. If humanity came forward with an energy that was high enough, once again, he would do what he had done before in Lemuria. For it was built into his Akash, and ready to regenerate.

You might ask the question, "*What about all those lifetimes and years between then and now? Who was he and what did he do?*" So again, I will give you this: He was always medical, always. He wasn't always a trained doctor, but always medical. This is the overlay in his Akash, and this has always been his passion. Yawee came back this time and created a situation where school was not difficult. He excelled greatly in all of the things that he touched [was interested in], to get to the place where he is now.

Some years ago, in my partner's meetings, Yawee started to *tone*. My partner had no idea what it was. I, Kryon, jumped up and down, for it was happening, it was happening! My partner had no idea what to make of funny strange sounds that sounded like an airplane coming from Dr. Todd's mouth.

[Laughter]

"What is this?" I wondered? *"Why now?"* He named it ***Pineal Toning***.

So let's study it.

Kryon: Yawee, you're here, is that affirmative?

Dr. Todd: (Affirmative nod)

Kryon: What does the pineal gland actually do?

Dr. Todd: The pineal is a receptor that integrates the daylight impulses into a signal that then integrates the rhythms of the body both daily and over great periods of time.

Kryon: How medical of you! So why would you call it Pineal Toning if it's quantum? That seems non-biological.

Dr. Todd: The focus on the pineal in this context is the notion of the so-called master cell of the pineal, which is what I began to observe when looking for the solution to remove the so-called eighth dimensional filter, blocking eight of the higher strands.

Kryon: What happens when you remove the filter?

Dr. Todd: It is the metaphorically lifting of the veil itself.

Kryon: And if the veil is lifted?

Dr. Todd: If the veil is lifted, the otherwise dormant strands come into function first, and then the rest of them come into coherence.

Kryon: Aha! There is the word we were after! [coherence] Yawee knew something and so do you. You haven't used that word, because I'm not sure that you know what it really does. The metaphysical quantum coherence of the pineal energy creates a quantum transmitter ... you knew that?

Dr. Todd: Yes ... It is from the concept that the DNA is always transmitting and receiving.

Kryon: Metaphysically, what is the pineal called?

Dr. Todd: It has been called the gland associated with the crown chakra and enlightenment and has been called the blooming of the thousand petals lotus.

Kryon: So here we are with all the hints you needed. Notice that Yawee starts with the pineal tones in 3D in order to create that for you which is healing and extending life. One at a time they come to him and he presents them to you. Yawee is building a foundation for something grander and greater, which has now come to fruition.

Knowing intuitively from the past, he now slowly picks up those things from his Akash that are building a *toning house,* block by block. But he doesn't even know the shape of it yet, or even where the door is. Still, he's pulling in the building blocks, one at a time ... the things which he needs and remembers intuitively, one at a time, layer after layer after layer.

Okay, back to the transmitter, in a moment, don't go away.

The pineal tone is that which is multi-dimensional, but which is only *hearable* by biological Human awareness in 3D. Now, my partner didn't do a very good job of that translation, so I'll give him another chance ... [Kryon telling Lee to give it another shot] These are new concepts, and my partner needs to go slowly here.

If you have an iceberg, the metaphor is that the tip which shows itself above the water is in 3D. But the major part of it under the water is metaphorically quantum [in other dimensions]. Let's call that iceberg a pineal tone. But you have to remember what we have told you before: You are only aware of the tone in 3D ... the small tip of the iceberg. Therefore, you could say that the tone really is being created with two parts for you: (1) the part which expresses sound in the air, that which is the throat chakra, and which is what you call a transmission of sound ... and (2) The multi-dimensional part which is not seen, and which does something you didn't expect.

Combined with divine Human consciousness, the multi-dimensional part of the pineal tone creates *quantum communication*. And there it is again, information from the moment I ever showed up as Kryon ... when I told you about the power of intent. The toning will not work unless both parts are engaged [the 3D and the multi D] and in a crowd like this, you know that; for as you tone, you shut your eyes. You then take the meditation posture, and you feel that which it does to your body. Each tone has a purpose, each tone was developed for health, and Yawee has given you information as to what it does. You feel it! But it's doing something else you didn't expect ... it communicates in a way that will shock you.

Last year I gave Yawee a project, and now it blossoms and now it blooms and he is working it. The tones enhance humanity and they extend life if they are used properly, but there is more. If we were to start describing this ... my partner, go slow ... [admonishment to Lee that something is coming he has never heard before] it is about frequency modulation of multi-dimensional pair sets. More than that. Much more than that. The pineal tones are to be used, eventually in pairs. That is to say, one is supposed to beat against the other ... one is sung with the other at equal volume and intensity.

Then what you have is (1) that sound in the air, which is the tip of the iceberg, plus (2) a quantum consciousness of one group creating something which we will call a vibrational sonority, which is specific to the tone pairs. When paired with what it should be paired with, which is what Yawee knows best, it will create something you only suspected. The two of them together do something that one of them cannot. It's far more than just the 3D complement of *open fifths*. Much more. Now my partner, go slow.

In physics, you know something about 3D broadcast of signals. What you know is that there are certain kinds of broadcasting, whether it is in the air for audio or video, or even that which you hear right now ... being broadcast from this microphone to a receiver at the other room. [Lee is using a wireless microphone] In elementary terms, there is often what we would call a *carrier*, which is like a magnetic *bed* that the actual audio signal can lay in. There is no sound to you without the carrier. So this wireless broadcast you are hearing really requires two parts: part one, the carrier; part two, the signal.

Now you know why you are doing it in pairs, Yawee. There is something going on here that absolutely requires the catalytic confluence of the pairing of the tones. What is going on is that when you combine them correctly, they talk to [activate] the pineal. The pineal becomes a *quantum transmitter* that is entangled with the galaxy [becomes one with the galaxy].That means that you are going to transmit something so that it can be received everywhere at once, no matter what the distance involved ... a very quantum attribute.

It's interesting about the DNA molecule, isn't it? Let me ask Yawee, the Spin Master: Do you believe it is significant that the DNA molecule can actually choose to spin atoms in a certain direction?

Dr. Todd: That is a rather extraordinary new scientific realization, information.

Kryon: Well, why do they call you the Spin Master, if you don't know it?

Dr. Todd: It takes a little while to remember everything.

[Laughter]

Kryon: Here's the point. Altogether, you have remembered you're building a house that requires a foundation to be perfect, and when the house is complete, it will be perfect. So intuitively, the Spin Master knows that DNA controls the spin of electrons in certain situations. The spin direction of electrons are necessary for you to build frequencies that you need for the quantum transmitter. The frequencies are not even describable in your physics because they are at a quantum atomic level [multi-dimensional in nature]. There have been few who have measured the frequencies of atomic structure. The spin directions within the atom sets up that which can be altered by DNA. It's almost like programming a receiver. This begins to explain why DNA responds to the pineal tones. But there is much more.

This is not going to be available for your understanding, but I'm going to say it anyway, because I'm giving it to my partner now: If you live in a black and white world and you look at atomic structure, which is in color, you only see that the nucleus is extremely far from even the first layer of spinning electrons. There is only empty space ... and it doesn't make sense to any of you. The black and white viewer sees empty space. But let me tell you, that in that empty space there's something blue which you can't see [a metaphor Kryon is setting up that is unknown by science yet, but will be seen as relating to *blue* later] and that *something* is an attribute of multi-dimensional physics that has not yet been discovered. That something [in the empty space] is that which is responsible for the frequency modulation of the atomic spin itself. The *blue* can be *tuned* by spinning the atomic structure in a different way. If you could see in color [using this metaphor], it would glow! Therefore, are you getting the picture? The "empty space" is the greater attribute of the atom, and (ready?) you can manipulate it!

So now you have two tones being sung together, which are starting then to alter atomic structure, and it is addressing the pineal to do that. The pineal is then activated and it starts to transmit. Now ... what is it going to be transmitting in pairs that it didn't with a single tone? These are interesting things, are they not?

In Lemuria, once a year, on December 21 [the solstice], Human Beings got together and they sang the 12 sets of pineal tones. They activated all of that which is in the pineal from all of them, and you had hundreds of Human quantum transmitters all going at once. Each one of them from a Human Being, put together something that one Human Being could not do ... a mass consciousness quantum signal. And the signal was sent through the galaxy for anyone to hear, but, dear ones, there was only one set of **ears** listening. These were the seed planters, the seven sisters, the Pleiadians.

You might say, it was calling home [Kryon smile]. And once a year the Lemurians, remembering those elders who planted the seeds of enlightenment on Earth, and who lived among them from the start, were giving a message to the home planet. It was a thank you for all of the years of their teachings, a thank you for planting the seeds that you and I know today as the divinity within your DNA. Once a year, this message went out to say, "*We are well and thankful for all you did.*" The message was, "*We are here, and we know who you are. We love you. We thank you for giving us these elders who still walk among us.*"

Kryon live channelling "Lemurian Choir Rehearsal Seminar"
given in Sedona, Arizona – June 14, 2011

According to Kryon that message (of the Lemurian Choir) stopped approximately 26,000 years ago. On December 21, 2012, Dr. Todd, along with 900 participants, sang the Pineal Tones in specific paired combinations. This Lemurian Choir, at Maui, Hawaii, created a mass consciousness quantum signal that was sent through the galaxy as a "thank you" message to our spiritual parents, the Pleiadians. Kryon described Dr. Todd's memory of the tones as "shockingly accurate" and this event *turned the key in the "lock"* representing humanity's choice to recalibrate The Crystalline Grid with compassion. Turning the key in the lock stimulated the 12 "time capsules" in the planet, enabling them, and preparing them to be opened and activated. This event was also the catalyst for Kryon to reveal information about the nodes and nulls of the planet.

The nodes and nulls of the planet represent *time capsules* and they are part of the Gaia system that was created by the Pleiadians. It is also part of a fast-track system of awakening, and the Pineal Tone choirs led by Dr. Todd play an integral role. The 2012 Lemurian Choir *enabled* all of the 12 time capsules and *opened* the first one. Since then, further events and choirs have *identified* and *opened* other time capsules until, finally, the required percentage of time capsules were opened in 2014, and they began to broadcast the continual stream of transmissions coming from the Great Central Sun. Think of the nodes and nulls as receptors where they have antennas that can pick up signals and then broadcast them to humanity.

Just like the Gaia system, the spiritual pineal system is a fast-track system of awakening, representing the communication to the other side of the veil. Kryon tell us even more about what the pineal is:

The pineal is the portal to your Higher-Self and it uses intuition – Innate – to talk to you. The pineal helps you to know you're *in touch.* Now, listen for a minute: How many of you know you're in touch? Often the answer is, *"Well, Kryon, sometimes I feel in touch with Spirit and sometimes I don't. Sometimes I'm in a bad mood and I'm not quite as in touch."* How would you just like to be 24/7 connected all the time? Then when you're in a bad mood, instead of the brain taking over and the heart racing with uncertainty and fear, instead you have "coherent" thought and the communication stays wide open. How do you think the masters dealt with stress? How would you like to deal with it in the same way? What I want to tell you is there is a fast-track system through the pineal of the Human body that is ready to make DNA work better and, in that process, there is more stability for you. We are going to call this the *self-balance factor.* The Human Being will be able to self-balance instantly and immediately, no matter what the situation. They will be able to analyze and stay centered. This is evolution. This is a spiritual system, dear ones, because the invisible force called *God* sees your belief and it starts to alter things, based upon what you have given it. Does this sound like the theme of the day? It's in every single part of nature.

Kryon live channelling "The Fast-Track Systems"
given in Mt. Shasta, California – June 14, 2014

The role of the pineal is to act as a portal to your Higher-Self. The spiritual components of the pineal and intuition are very elusive. How would you describe intuition? When you receive an intuitive thought, what does it feel like? The Merriam-Webster dictionary defines intuition as:

- a natural ability or power that makes it possible to know something without any proof or evidence: a feeling that guides a person to act a certain way without fully understanding why
- something that is known or understood without proof or evidence
- quick and ready insight
- immediate apprehension or cognition
- knowledge or conviction gained by intuition
- the power or faculty of attaining to direct knowledge or cognition without evident rational thought and inference

Source: http://www.merriam-webster.com/dictionary/intuition

Most intuitive thoughts happen in a fleeting, elusive way, such that sometimes it's difficult to even describe what that first intuitive thought was. Some of us are better at using intuition than others, and then there are many who have no idea or understanding about their own intuitive ability. Perhaps this is because an attribute of intuition is that it does not come from synaptic thought. Your brain is a beautiful super-computer, giving you past experiences that helps you to survive in future times. If you touch a hot stove and burn your finger, chances are you are unlikely to do that again, because your brain gives you signals every time you see a hot stove, not to touch it! All of these past experiences are amplified and applied in relationships, business, the workplace and everything else. You live a life of balance, based upon what your brain is telling you is there or not there to help you.

All of a sudden, *whoosh*, in comes an intuitive thought and you cannot understand it clearly, nor can you remember what the message was. Kryon has emphasized that intuitive thought does not mirror synaptic brain function. Many find this statement controversial, saying that the brain has to be part of intuition. It is, but it is not the origin. The information from Kryon indicates that our intuition comes from a marriage between the pineal, the intuitive part of the brain, and synaptic thought. This marriage creates a whole Human Being that has moved out of a survival consciousness.

Humanity will start developing intuitive thought as a result of the planetary shift in consciousness. Intuition is like an antenna that is able to receive broadcasts of universal wisdom and knowledge. This helps to explain why many individuals in different geographical locations develop new technologies and inventions at the same time. For example, the Wright Brothers are famous for being the first ones to fly an airplane, but there were many others who were already working on the concept of building an airplane.

Kryon has defined intuition in the following way:

Let us look for a moment at what those who study the brain say about intuition. It's extremely hard to define. Some have said that it's *random thoughts created by the brain at random times*. It presents itself randomly through the intellect and the logic. That's about as good as it gets.

Main Human consciousness has four attributes: Intellect, logic, emotion, and intuition. These represent the full gambit of Human thought and action. Psychologists love to trace your thought groups and put them in these boxes. An intellectual person will make certain types of decisions based on intellectual thought, and an emotional person will make certain kinds of decisions that are entirely driven by feelings. The ultra-logical person will only do things that are filled with solutions based only on logic. So where does intuition fit in? The answer is that it really doesn't fit in much, until now. You'll have to look at what intuition is, and where it comes from, and how you feel about it ...

... What is it supposed to do? How is it manufactured in your body? Why don't you believe in it when it happens? Let us start looking at where it comes from. This will not be a shock to some of you, for intuitive thought is a product of the pineal gland. The pineal gland, which represents the third eye to many cultures, is that part of your consciousness portal that responds to your Higher-Self. The small little thoughts that you might receive, which some of you might dismiss, are intuitive action. These thoughts may come and go so fast you're not even certain what they were about. They arrive through the pineal portal, through your Higher-Self.

As the Human Beings begin to recalibrate the cellular structure that we talked about, the very DNA of their bodies responds to the new instructions from an evolving consciousness. Those who seek truth, and those who are awakening to light, start to have an increased portal size in the pineal. The communication to the Higher-Self widens, and intuitive thought starts to take precedence over logic and emotion. This, dear ones, starts to draw the line between you and others around you. For intuitive thought does not look like it makes sense, when examined by logic.

If you decide to change your life's path because you had a momentary intuitive thought, those around you may say, *"Wait a minute! This doesn't make any sense. Have you studied it? Is it logical? What does the intellectual mind say about it?"* Your answer is that it doesn't matter because, *"My intuitive thoughts come from that place where I am God."* Now you start understanding why the puzzle widens for the Lightworker. You're starting to get messages from your God-self. Now listen, dear Human Being, this is not a judgment. But you have a tremendous tendency to ignore your intuition, or even to admit you have it. So let us look at how it works.

If intuition is mostly multi-dimensional, it is not going to be linear in communication to you. Let me take you into the mind of an artist who is writing a piece of music. Now, here's what that artist can never explain to you: The composition that he is writing happened all at once in his brain. All of the phrases, the melody, and those things that bridge from one part to another is not happening as the ear will eventually hear it. Instead, it's all happening in a split second, presented all at once to the brain. Then the artist proceeds to translate all this by writing this elusive intuitive idea down as structured musical notation.

What music composition touches your Soul? Perhaps it even brings a tear to your eye and touches your heart? I'll tell you something, this amazing music may be profound when you hear it in linear time, but it all came as a flash to the composer, yet it has the power to touch you inside. This is channelling!

An artist knows about quantum intuition. The one who puts the colors on the canvas is not experimenting and erasing as they go. The master's artwork you see in the galleries was not a result of them experimenting with color. They knew exactly what to do. They got it all in less than a second, as intuition. The painting, in all of its beauty, was in their mind long before they started with a brush. We've said it before, that the sculptor takes a rock and removes what doesn't belong there, in order to create what he already knew was there. It was all created in a split second.

Now, carry this into your life. There is a new process, a new paradigm where intuitive thought has to be felt, known, and recognized. The more you do this, the better you get. However, why is it that you don't believe your own intuitive thoughts? It's interesting, is it not, how emotions and intellect respond to authority? But intuition is not even a player in that scenario. Instead, you have to get out of the 3D world and start letting intuition be a player that is equal to the others. If you can do that, both the intellect and the emotion will line up and unify and will make sense.

Let us say you have some intuitive Human Beings guided by quantum intuition. If you start asking them how it feels, they will give you very balanced answers about their intuitive thought. The intellect, which manufactures the logic, will now make sense, because it has become subservient to the intuition. Emotionally, they also feel balanced, not fearful ...

... Let's do a test. Intuition comes and goes so quickly that you don't believe it. So, here is the test. I'm going to ask you to dismiss everything that you've ever learned, and intuit answers. When I give you a question, I want you to feel the intuitive thought that happens around it. First impressions are the way of this. Use the first intuitive thought that you have and when you do this, it is a revelation to your own mind. Intuition is not hooked to your 3D thoughts, so when you start to recognize it, it starts to reveal what you really think. The portal to the Higher-Self does not lie to you. It's going to give you the truth every time. It's how you accept it that is the puzzle. If it fights with what you've been trained, then the three-dimensional part of you has won.

So let's sit for a moment. Some of these questions are easy, and some may not be. I'll ask a question and I want you to grab the first intuitive thought you have, not what you've been told, and not what your parents told you, or that society has pressed upon you. You're totally alone in this, with your own thoughts. What are your answers to these questions?

Question: Is God real?

Feel it. Did you feel it? Oh, that's an easy one. You wouldn't be here otherwise. You wouldn't be in this group otherwise, would you? So you know the answer to that. It was your first intuitive flash: *"Of course, absolutely."* But your intellect and logic knows there is no proof. So why were you so certain? Because your life experience with an invisible God has supplied you with all you need, to say yes. It was, therefore, your first intuitive thought, and you recognized it.

Now, watch what happens if we start asking you to define God. For the intuition starts to fight with the intellect and the emotion.

Now it gets harder.

Question: Is it possible to talk to God?

First intuitive flash. Go with it! Can you have a conversation with the Creator? Yes or no? Now, this starts to interfere with your training, doesn't it. Do you feel the slight conflict?

Question: Is God inside you?

You're getting pretty good at this. I know who's here, and I am purposely giving you intuitive lessons on things you already know. This is to exercise the *intuitive muscle,* so that you know what it feels like. No question I'm asking is provable, however, so the intellect cannot authoritatively give you good information about it. It can only give an opinion based on your training ... that you're a fool, or that it's not logical, or that you're being too emotional. Those are not proofs or dis-proofs. Those are judgments! This, dear one, starts to identify the duality of the Human Being. Is God inside you? Use your intuition. Don't get an opinion from your brain.

My partner gave an answer earlier today that was from me, and not him. Some of you picked it up, and even he was uncertain as to why he said it. He told you that Human Beings have a tendency to judge themselves. This is the fight between divine intuitive thought and emotion and intellect. The intellect will say, *"Well, you got an intuitive thought and it didn't last very long, did it? Therefore, it was just a mini-dream and didn't mean anything. It wasn't even logical. You can't even figure out what your intuition said, so stop thinking about invisible stuff and come back to Earth."* Your own consciousness has made a judgment based on opinion, not a conclusion.

Is God real? Does God talk to you? Yes. If you can strengthen the intuitive muscle in the brain, you can make intuitive thought clearer and last longer.

Answer this question: Picture yourself in the forest or the jungle, or perhaps in the wilderness. You're completely and totally alone, and there is no other Human for hundreds of kilometers and there you stand.

Now, answer the question: Does nature know you're there? Are you just an observer, or are you participating in nature by being there? Almost everyone here knows the answer, and it is that you sit and bathe in *being known* and that you're not alone. The very leaves on the trees greet you. The air that you take into your lungs knows who you are, and the dirt of the Earth knows the size of your shoe. There is tremendous communication! Now, prove it.

Where is the intellect and the emotional body when you need to prove it? It can't be proven, yet the Lightworker doesn't hesitate with intuitive truth. So you have placed the emphasis and power on intuitive thought, and you don't have to use the other to verify anything. You "Know" at the intuitive level, and you let the intellect and the emotion come along later. In this case, you know truth with intuitive thought first. These are examples to help you see what good intuitive answers feel like, so you can start using intuition for the hard questions of life.

Kryon live channelling "The Letter I in the word Kundalini"
given in Cusco, Peru – October 31, 2012

One of the best ways we can develop our intuition is to practice. Kryon says we need to acknowledge it, work with it, exercise it and use it. Intuitive instructions are being broadcast all the time as part of the benevolent system that supports us. In the previous channel, Kryon posed some questions to allow your intuition to respond. I have a few more questions for you.

What is your intuitive thought about the information presented within this book? What brings your eyes to this page? Who are the people in your life? Do you recognize any of them as Akashic participants in your history? Do you believe that there is a God inside which is a part of your corporeal self? If you do, you are among all of the masters on the planet who said the same thing. If God is inside, where is the connection? Where is God, Spirit or the Creative Source? Kryon answers this last question in the following way:

Greetings, dear ones, I am Kryon of Magnetic Service. Sometimes there's a question about God, and the question is this: *"God, where are you, really? Where do you live? If we're going to worship and pray and meditate, we need at least the concept of where you are."*

These are all reasonable questions for a Human to ask, for it reflects concepts in your own reality. We talk about the *Great Central*

Source, but it is not a *place*. In a multi-dimensional reality, there is no such thing as a *place*. It's because you are in a three dimensional corporeal state, that this is confusing. Kryon is not in a place, either. We are a concept of *cognized reality*, and the quantum physicist knows what I'm talking about. For in a quantum state, reality is variable, and consciousness plays a large part in it. An atheist will tell you that God is not real. In a way, they are right. For their consciousness does not include a cognition that would allow God to exist. In a certain way, they are actually creating a Godless existence.

We continue to speak of things you call *quantum,* but that does not refer to an atomic particle. Rather, it is your esoteric word which means "multi-dimensional." Quantum is the word we use which simply means "a reality where dimensionality is total and complete." It's a reality where *all dimensions* are represented, and where nothing is missing. It's not a place; it's a concept. Where are we, you ask? Conceptually, everywhere. The Great Central Source is everywhere, and it's only called *central* because it is seemingly at the center of everything. We're in you, and you are in us.

So consciousness is also a concept. If I ask, *"Where is the consciousness of humanity?"* what would you say? It's difficult, because there's no place where it exists, unless you wish to localize it to Earth. Consciousness is everywhere. Where is love? Is it centralized, or could it be everywhere? Why am I giving these examples? It's because I want you to be comfortable with the presence of God. As you increase your belief, you increase the reality of God in your life.

Today, you have gone through the story of Michael Thomas and the Seven Angels. It represents the channelled book, *The Journey Home. [Speaking of the seminar before this channelling]*. This book is filled with things that mean other things, and Human life is the same. Many times, life lessons in 3D actually stem from the concepts of love. Many things that you may not think make sense, are actually working within the consciousness of love. They make sense in a way that you have not yet seen. I want you to trust this and take it a step at a time.

Do you feel God in you? Intellectual, don't try to localize it or assign it to a place. Think with me: There's nothing like that first contact with a mother and her child. Mum, the first time you saw that child and your eyes met theirs in the birthing room, did your heart leap for joy? So I want to ask you, *"Where was love? Was it in you, or in the child, or did it come from somewhere else?"* I'll tell you where it was: it was in the natural essence of the Universe. Can you sense that? I want you to understand that you are starting to develop multi-dimensional concepts within your lives, and you're going to start applying them. With this, there's going to have to be trust. Love comes from tapping into the Great Central Source, and feeling what is there.

The *Journey Home* book speaks about that. Is it possible that you can create your own reality? Is it possible that you can go back and pull from your Akash? The Akash is the energy of everything you've learned. Is it possible that you can drop karma, simply through your free choice to do so? Is it possible that your personality itself can change? Can you rewrite who you think you are? The answers to all these: *"Yes, it is your right to do so."* These all represent multi-dimensional tasks, and are things where you can't ask *how* or *why*, not yet. They just *are*.

When you walk from place to place, you experience gravity. Are you intellectually possessed to know why it exists in order for you to take a step? No. You have no choice but to participate with it. It is what it is. You deal with it with every step, but you don't analyze it, and you don't have to know how or why. But you feel it, don't you? You always know it's there. Why is the love of God so different for you? It follows you around and you are always participating in it. Did you know that it is with every single Human? It's with all of you with the same beauty and strength, waiting for free choice of a Human to see it or not. Did you know that the Angels surround you with love?

Some of you sit in the dark because you either don't think you're worthy, or because you don't think you deserve it. Can you see love? No. Can you see magnetism? No. Can you see gravity? No. There are things that are unseen, which are powerful – and the love of God is one. Our hands are always outstretched to you, inviting you to put your own face on that which you consider God. You need to understand your part in all this. Start standing tall and seeing a new reality.

Yesterday we started the meeting, and we asked the question, *"Who are you?"* Now, we are at the end of the second day, the channellings are done, the lectures are finished, and the study of the book is complete. You're about to stand and leave. Did anything happen to you? Was it just a nice two days, or was there more? How many are willing to take the hand of God and start discovering the grandness inside?

Listen: Every single one of you is unique. Some of you beg us to know how to do the spiritual things we have discussed. *"Just give us the steps, Kryon. Please, just give us the list of what to do."* Dear ones, it is time for you to see the truth: There are no steps, and there is no list. There can't be! Within the uniqueness of each of you is your own custom learning. You will discover what to do next *for you*, when you start giving intent. It's not that hard. Can you soften your heart and be open enough to say, *"Dear God, I have no idea what to do next, but would you take my hand and show me? Give me synchronicity, and give me signals and signs. I'll pay attention; I won't try to figure it out. I want the love and that's good enough for me."*

This is the first step, dear ones. It also might be the last step, because from now on, you will start to change your reality. God knows your heart. God knows when you're pretending, and God knows if you're just trying it out. I want you to know that, before you give permission to change. Many will leave this place and they'll say, *"Well, I understood a little of it, but I really just wasn't ready."* If that's you, I have a message for you: God is patient. When you're ready, we are. When you're ready, we are.

Kryon live channelling "Who you really are"
Enhanced by Lee Carroll for this book
Given in Basel, Switzerland – September 7, 2014

There is a benevolent system of love and support that is waiting for you to connect to through your intuition and intelligence (spiritual logic). Kryon has told us that in this system are guides, angels, helpers, the grids of the planet, and the Higher-Self, which are all part of a system of awakening. That means you truly have the ability (with free choice) to change your life. The physics of consciousness will create whatever you decide. Perhaps this helps to explain the phrase "you are what you think you are!"

Questions for Kryon:

The pineal gland is thought to secrete a chemical knows as DMT (Dimethyltryptamine), also called "The Spirit Molecule." Currently it is only a hypothesis that the pineal releases DMT during dreaming, during spiritual and mystical experiences, and during the time of death. DMT is also found across the planet in plants and animals, and many humans have ingested this chemical compound and experienced powerful hallucinations. Can you tell us more about this?

Answer:

Dimethyltryptamine (DMT) is a "feel good" chemical to the body. You might say, it's part of a chemical family member of serotonin and melatonin. There is much of this in the Human body, and not just from the Pineal. Tryptophan is also related, and is a standard amino acid - a low-level aspect of the same kind of chemistry, given to you for the same reasons.

The truth is that you are looking into simple body chemistry that is not that unusual or special. Indeed, it is also in plants, for some of the same reasons (for their well-being).

A body in good health, joyful, and peaceful, is releasing these chemicals in a very balanced way. Do you think that a balanced, peaceful Human Being is a miracle? No. It's one who has the Innate working with the chemistry in ways that release and balance this chemistry and help to add years to Human life. Your system needs this for profound peace, joy, laughter, and love. This chemistry also plays a part in spiritual release, and meditation.

Older energy often blocks these chemicals, since "survival" consciousness has no use for it. Do you know people who are simply not compassionate at all? Are they troubled all the time? They are out of balance in their own way. Now you start to understand how you can actually work with Innate, and re-wire how your body works. The new energy will allow much greater release of these chemicals, and bring you into a more balanced "New Human."

When isolated, and experienced in ways that are not normal, these chemicals will create hallucinogenic, out of balance, temporary feelings. It does not enhance the Pineal to throw it out of balance. Your brain may think so, but it knows better, later. This is no different than a "night on the town." When it's over, you know better.

Let Innate release these things naturally, permanently, and appropriately. Isn't this spiritual common sense?

Having experienced unseen energies as an EMF practitioner, and also during the channelled messages, I felt a connection to my core, Higher-Self and the Creative Source. However, humans who have blocks and filters that keep them in survival mode would have great difficulty in understanding this experience. In attempting to describe the experience to some, it may appear as though I was mentally unbalanced and hallucinating. Can you explain the differences between a Lightworker connecting with the God within, compared to a Human who has a chemical imbalance that gives them hallucinations?

This is not difficult at all to explain. One is natural and balanced, and one is not. However, to a medical professional, compassionate actions can seem unbalanced, if they have not seen it before. If professionals are used to survival reactions, then you could even be considered insane if you don't follow "normal" reactions. Example:

It's normal to experience fear and anxiety in certain emergency situations. These are "normal" survival scenarios. But what if you were mature enough to void fear, and move towards a more logical place during this same emergency? You would not flee, or run around, or yell or scream. Instead, you might be still, and think yourself through the issues, and then move slowly, without emotion, towards a solution. Others around you would say you "froze," and were out of balance ... perhaps insane. But the truth is that you were simply more mature. Getting rid of the survival blocks creates a far more peaceful Human.

Innate (Body Intelligence)

In basic terms, Innate is the bridge that connects with the intelligent part of the body, and I'm not talking about the brain. *"You mean our body has intelligence outside of the brain?"* Absolutely it does! It's the part of the body that talks to us when we use muscle testing. Kryon has even called it the second brain. Every Human Being on the planet has their own body intelligence, called Innate, but just like intuition, your Higher-Self and your Akash, it is extremely elusive. There is still a missing bridge of clear communication. However, this gap is narrowing, because we have passed the 2012 marker. Kryon has also greatly enhanced our understanding about this remarkable attribute that exists within us:

Innate has been described in the past as the *smart part of your cells.* Now, that might indicate that there's also a *non-smart* part, but let us say that it's a more ignorant part, and believe it or not, that ignorant part is your brain. Now, the brain perceives many things, and it's a most excellent calculator. It's the best memory and relational computational instrument on the Earth today. Everything that you have experienced is in your brain. It tempers how you behave, what you do, how you act, what you believe, and how you perceive things. But let me tell you where it falls short. It doesn't know anything about what's going on within your cells or your emotional body. It may send signals to operate your body, but it is blind to what happens after that. It is also easily confused.

Your Brain Is Not "In the Loop"

You can intellectualize this for a very long time, yet you will never find out from your brain how your cells are doing. Do you have an allergy to something that your body has not experienced yet? Perhaps it is a food you have never tasted or a chemical you have not seen. How would you know? As you begin to eat the food, or ingest the chemical, shouldn't the brain yell, "*Don't do that! You are allergic to it! You will pay the price!*" But it does not. It is not connected to cellular structure. But the Innate is.

The Innate is the smart corporeal body. It knows everything about your overall system. It actually is as smart as your brain, but in a different way. So, what can a Human Being do to find out if he/she is allergic to something? Let's say, that is you; so you can ask your brain, but it has no idea. So instead, you place the food or chemistry in your hand and *muscle-test* it. That is called kinesiology, a big word for something very simple. Muscle-testing is using the body's *Innate* to give you a "yes or no" signal about something it knows about, but that your brain does not.

So, in the process of kinesiology, do you understand that you have acknowledged that there is a part of your body system that knows more than your brain? Indeed, this is a process that has been used for centuries, and it's very accurate.

This Innate knows a lot more than what you are allergic to, my friend. It is also tuned in completely to the quantum parts of your DNA that know everything about your spiritual and cellular evolvement. Innate handshakes with your Higher-Self at all the *three Human group levels*, and that is difficult to describe. If you put this information in a circle chart, you can draw the lines between the groups and you'd see what I mean. It's your smart body, and it's connected to everything.

Let me ask you a question, dear one: Don't you find it odd that there are certain kinds of diseases that can lurk within your cells, that can attack you, yet you only know it through your discomfort or through your death! What kind of brain do you have that would not tell you about this? You never have the signal through your brain about any of it except discomfort and pain! But Innate knows about it the moment it happens. Innate knows when it entered your body. As your white blood cells go to the places they need to fight, your entire immune system goes into alert! Yet you have no idea about it, since your brain is just doing what it always does – it computes and remembers. But, in this case, it does a very poor job helping you survive.

About Innate

What is Innate? Where is it? This is difficult to explain. We told you, dear Human Being, that the elusive Akash information is not in your brain, either. You cannot go to your brain to find out who you used to be in a past life. The Innate is the same. It's not in your brain, but instead, it's in every cell of your body and every molecule of your DNA. The difference between Innate and the Akash is that Innate is *on top (a linear concept for you)*, and it is always broadcasting, always there. If you know how to listen to it and where it is, you can tune in. Muscle-testing is one way of knowing, a very basic way. Some of you also know that Innate responds to acupuncture. Did you know that? Your brain does not.

The Merkabah – Innate's Quantum Field

Innate is aware of all things at the cellular level and is broadcasting all the time. It broadcasts so well that it flows into that which you call the Merkabah of the body. Now, the Merkabah is a quantum field around your body that pulses very strongly with esoteric information, including corporeal health. Many have the ability to see and read this field.

A medical intuitive can stand before you in various degrees of success and *read* the messages from your Innate. This intuitive person does not have to muscle-test to know you've got something going on within your cells. They can *see it* or *sense it* within the field around your body. Now, you may have thought that a medical intuitive is looking at your liver or your heart, doing some kind of analysis. That's very linear thinking and is not what is happening. That's your box of belief working overtime. Instead, the medical intuitives are sensing the quantum energy within your field that your Innate is broadcasting about your health, of what's going on in the chemistry, and of what might be developing inside you. It's different than you thought, isn't it? That's the Innate and that's only one of the things that Innate does ...

The Next Step

One of the attributes of the future Human Being is to build a bridge between your Human consciousness and your Innate. This is one of the three things in the cellular parts of the nine attributes lesson, the Human energies part. This needs to be a bridge of new tools so you no longer have to muscle-test. In fact, you can become your own medical intuitive. Doesn't this make sense? So, when a virus or bacteria invades your body – something your brain can't warn you about – you will *know it* anyway! This bridge will begin to complete the Human Being's evolution and is a logical next step for longer life. I know this makes sense to you. You should be able to sense these things when they occur, rather than going to a doctor for tests. Going to a doctor for tests is not a bad thing, but it should validate what you know is happening and not be the discovery of it.

The Second Brain

Innate does so many things for you! Some of you are starting to get a bigger picture of where I'm going with this discussion. Here is a concept that we've not really broached before. We're going to give it a name, but please do not misunderstand it. You only have one word for your intelligent control center, and the word is called *brain*. So we are going to give you a concept that the Innate is your *second brain*. It doesn't function like your first one at all, but it is smart and it is intelligent and it knows what you need. Sometimes, it can even replace a function that your logical brain normally does.

Let me show you what I mean. Here is a puzzle, a conundrum of medicine: When an accident happens that severs your spinal cord completely, it leaves you with no feeling or muscle function from the [neck] down. This is because the signals from the brain to your muscles are no longer able to be sent. The pathway for those signals is severed. You then spend the rest of your life in a chair, perhaps even being fed by others. But the puzzle is that there are some things within you that continue to function anyway. One of them is your heart. Another is digestion. Many of these things continue to work, even though you are told that your brain, the central nervous system, the organ that sends all the signals to make things work, had its signals severed. The conduit where the signals are sent within the spine is broken. So what keeps all these organs below the neck going?

Your heart depends upon signals from the brain to function. It needs the electrical pulses sent from specific parts of the brain, creating a synchronized rhythm, in order for the heart to beat. Yet the brain is disconnected, and the heart keeps its rhythm. How can that work? Now I'll tell you: The Innate takes over and continues the signal. It's always there, for the Merkabah is body-wide, not centralized in one place, as your brain is. The organs will continue to function, but the pathway to the muscles is gone. Even reproduction can still happen! The heart keeps going and digestion continues, and all without connection to the brain.

Innate is smart! It's a second brain. Medical science is often puzzled over this, and I just gave you the answer. So Innate is the intelligence in your body that is smarter about cellular things than your brain. Now I want to wrap this all up.

What are you supposed to do with all this information? I want you to get in touch with Innate. It's the *heart connection,* dear ones. The Higher-Self, Innate and Human consciousness are the three Human energies that need to meld - Human consciousness, Higher-Self and Innate.

When DNA starts to work at a higher efficiency, there are bridges that start to be built between these things. You'll start to feel them when you recognize and sense truth. When you start to have discernment and cognize things for what they are, you stop looking around for answers. You are far more self-contained, and your answers are often the same as those around you who have the same discernment engine. All this now comes from within, instead of an outside source.

Kryon live channelling "The Mysterious Innate"
given in Gaithersburg, Maryland – August 31, 2013

For some of you, the above channel is a review of information you already knew. Regardless of your level of knowledge, most of us desire better communication with Innate. How can we become better at listening to our own cellular structure? Do you have health concerns? Perhaps you have an injury, illness, or disease? Maybe you would simply like to feel more life-force and vitality flowing through your veins? Wouldn't it be great to hit upon a solution that will help us overcome our challenges? Well, this is exactly what Kryon has said Innate can help us with.

Earlier, in the section on Human consciousness, Kryon gave us an entirely new premise. It was how you can get in touch with the divine part of you, which creates a pathway to communicate with your cells. In 2014, Kryon gave a new acronym – CAL (Cells Are Listening). Your cells are with you from birth, so they are continuously listening to what you want. They are waiting for Human consciousness to give them instructions. But how do we do this?

Some individuals use methods such as talking out loud to the cellular structure with specific demands of what is desired. Often, there is a regimented protocol as to how many times the statements are said, and great importance to make sure it is said every day. Kryon says this is applying a linear Human attribute to a multi-dimensional system that is beyond anything we can imagine, because Innate doesn't respond to monotonous repetition. *"Wait a minute, what about the use of affirmations? Kryon said they were powerful!"* Yes, affirmations are powerful; so let me explain the difference. It has to do with intent.

Have you ever had someone tell you they are sorry, but you didn't feel the energy behind their words? Equally, there can be someone who says they love you, but their actions show otherwise. So a set of statements that you say repeatedly to your cells on a regular basis, in the hope that something will change, is not likely to be received by Innate. Especially when said with doubt and the emotions of anxiety, frustration and impatience accompany the statement, because the issue or problem is still present. In contrast, an affirmation that you have created yourself, using words that make you feel empowered, and said with intent, can help you to change your life. Especially when the emotion you feel is a euphoric joy and happiness of already experiencing the outcome of what you desire (using your imagination to experience the feelings of "already done").

Kryon has said that when you speak affirmations out loud with a conscious intent, you hear it with your ears, and your body understands what you are doing. Statements of intent carry energy, and words in the air have frequencies that Innate (your intelligent body consciousness) understands. Whatever you consciously tell your body with intent, Innate listens and starts to cooperate with what you are doing. Innate is also waiting for your actions to signal the change. For example, if you desire to increase your fitness, your intent is markedly improved when you begin to exercise in whatever way you can.

Affirmations should say ***what you have***, not the desire to have it. If you desire love in your life, the affirmation becomes: *I am love.* If you desire good health, the affirmation is: *I am healthy*. Use words such as *I am* or *I have.* Never used words such as *I desire* or *I want.* Affirmations are statements of truth, not wishful thinking. If you have trouble creating affirmations, begin with the things you are grateful for. As your gratitude increases, you attract more things to be thankful for.

As I am writing this book, I am also in the process of exploring the potential of creating an "Affirmations App" for smart phone and tablet devices. Kryon has often given us messages and intentions to say aloud, which inspired me to write affirmative statements. If you are interested in these Kryon-inspired affirmations, please check my website regularly for details. At this stage, I'm not sure when or how it will be created, but I keep stating the following affirmation: *I give thanks for the perfect app, created by the perfect team, giving perfect satisfaction to all!*

Kryon tells us the real secret is for you to create your own affirmations that are specific to you. Innate is far more likely to take notice of what you have consciously chosen to say, than repeating someone else's words. However, as a starting point, using affirmations from others can help you get started. There are numerous websites that feature affirmations, including one by international author Louise L. Hay. Louise is regarded as one of the founders of the self-help movement and has implemented her teachings within her own life. After being diagnosed with cancer, she decided to follow an intensive program of affirmations, visualization, nutritional cleansing and psychotherapy instead of drugs and surgery. Within six months, she was completely healed of cancer.

I consider Louise Hay to be one of the leading experts in affirmations. She has directed her wisdom and knowledge in the creation of an Affirmation Meditations app found at: *www.supermindapps.com* This Affirmation Meditations App features Louise's most effective "power thoughts" delivered through a "whole body" learning process that combines: deep relaxation (with animated meditation exercises), advanced brainwave technology, multi-sensory learning (seeing, hearing, speaking and typing), and multi-modal input (in which Louise says the affirmation in both the first and second person). Why am I telling you about Louise's app when my intention is to create my own? I believe each of us should find the tools and techniques that help us the best. This is why I'm happy to promote the work of others. We all have something to contribute, so there isn't any competition; it is simply a matter of having choices (smile).

In relation to choices, when I first started to awaken spiritually, I found a wonderful book written by Florence Scovel Shinn (it was much later that I discovered the work of Louise Hay). Florence was a truly remarkable woman, born in 1871, who understood the power of words, said with intent. She has written many books, including *Your Word is Your Wand* and *The Power of the Spoken Word,* first published in 1928 and 1944 respectively. You can find out more about Florence at the following website: *http://www.florence-scovel-shinn.com/*

My absolute favorite affirmation from Florence is:

All that is mine by Divine Right is now released and reaches me in great avalanches of abundance, under grace in miraculous ways.

Not everyone reading this affirmation will have the same powerful feeling that these words invoke within me, which is why I encourage you to create your own. No one understands you more than you – and you have an entire entourage that represents you within the realm of your guides, Innate, your Higher-Self and your Soul. Use words that create a strong, positive emotion within you. Have fun experimenting, and then stand back and watch the amazing results!

Okay, back to Innate and some more information from Kryon:

You're getting ready to talk to a system that hasn't heard from you before, not really, not like this. There is a new energy,

Lightworker, on this planet. Old Soul, listen to me: Your toolset is being enhanced, and that's why you're listening to this. You can do this, dear one. I wouldn't be giving you something you cannot accomplish.

The Rules of "Talking" to Your Cells

When you start to get in touch with your cells, they're going to react. I'll give you that information in just a moment. I just want you to look at this in linearity. Every one of you has had a best friend. Perhaps it's your partner in life, or perhaps an old friend. But it's someone you can just sit with and talk to, and there are no rules. You can say anything you want to, and you can pour your heart out to them and they will listen. They can do the same with you, and that's a best friend.

I want to ask you something: Let's say you're going to be with this best friend for three days. So this is day one: You get up the next morning, you sit together at the table, and you begin to discuss things. You tell them everything! The next day you do the same, and the next day you do the same – the same information, over and over. How do you think that's going to work? It doesn't! How do you think your friend will take it? They are bored!

This doesn't work with your cells, either. Do you understand what I'm saying? Your cells are you. What would *you* say to *you*? Would you repeat things you already knew? Then why would you do it with your cells? Your cells are listening – C-A-L. They've been listening since you were born, waiting for the time when you would awaken to the possibility that you could actually speak to them. So do it, and do it as a best friend.

What would be something you would say to your cells, and how would you approach this? First of all, I want to tell you that they understand your language. They're part of you. Talk to them any way you want to. Do it out loud, through thought, through writing, through music – any way you want to. It doesn't matter, because you have their number. Dear ones, the key is love. You have got to love your cellular structure enough, so you can say, "*I love you*," and they all know you do. It can't be simpler, yet it can't be harder for some of you. Sit for a moment. What would you say? What would happen?

When the body starts to listen to you, there are processes involved. Let me tell you what they are, and I will give you an example of the communication. I want you to know some things. When you start talking to your cellular structure, and you have the number right [the example of the phone number], the first thing that's going to happen is massive amounts of chills. You're going to know you're getting through, dear one! Chills are the cells of your body celebrating. Celebrating! The Innate, the smart body, whatever you want to call it, is part of you, and it's having a party. Did you hear that? You've got communication!

Although this is all metaphoric and perhaps silly sounding, I'm going to tell you, this is what happens! The body has joy. Those of you involved with health, do you know what it feels like to be healthy? Your entire body is rejoicing with every step, with every breath. That's the Innate, celebrating. All these years, and it has been listening, hoping you would communicate, because without direction, it just does what it can, in the dark. You know that, don't you? Your entire health simply goes on "automatic" without direction, and "automatic" often brings unbalance. Without instructions, your body is simply going to follow that which is average, and will do its own thing. With instructions, however, you control it. Is this logical to you?

Time is Still the Key

The first thing your body does with communication is to celebrate. The next thing it does is *start to work*. Depending upon the things that you are communicating to your cellular structure, it needs time to work with it. Whether it is for health or for healing, or for youthing, no matter what it is, you've got to give it some time.

There is a practicality here that you must understand, because these things are only going to be accomplished through 3D cell division, which you call rejuvenation. Your body is built to rejuvenate itself. Most of the organs in the body, including the skin, rejuvenate themselves within different time frames. Over a period of time you get entirely new cells. This is how you stay alive. However, when you start talking to your cellular structure, those instructions are going into the data in DNA, and these things are going to be implemented within the next rejuvenation cycle. So you're not going to get results tomorrow. Doesn't that make sense? So you will start to feel it over time, and the things that you are working on and asking for, will slowly start to show themselves. What you really are doing, through your Innate, is reprogramming the DNA. Science will tell you that your DNA stays the same from birth. The chemistry may look the same, but the esoteric instructions within the DNA are being reprogrammed. You are indeed changing it!

The last thing I want to tell you about, you may not be ready for. When you start talking to your cells, the Innate knows if your consciousness is benevolent or not. It knows what you want. However, it's only going to give you what you need, and not what you want. There will be automatic systems that will go into place, improving other parts of your body that you never asked to have improved. You're going to start a process of extended life. Healing and balance will start to occur in areas that your consciousness has no idea about, but which your Innate knows all about. You have just awakened the bridge between Human consciousness and cellular structure. It's easy, but you've got to fall in love with yourself, understand that the smart body knows what you do not, and give permission for your instructions to work the way Innate directs.

Imagine for a moment sitting alone, and you're going to make first contact. It doesn't matter how old you are, how young you are, but you are realizing that you really are in love with the divine part of you. Perhaps you can even visualize the face of God within you. You can see your eternal-ness in every cell of your body, and you realize that you have a cellular structure that is waiting to hear from you. C-A-L.

Slowly, you begin. Then you realize that you've got their number – you can feel it! Chills begin, because they picked up the telephone, and now they're really listening. For the first time, you can say: *"We know each other and I love you! I'm sorry it took so long for me to figure it out. I want you to go into the processes that you know about, which I don't. I want you to come together in a benevolence that would create health and a long lasting Human Being ... me! I want you to talk to me in whatever ways you can, so that I can recognize you. I want to hold your hand and you hold mine, for the rest of my life. If there's any inappropriateness and any imbalances chemically in my body, I want it to go away through time and appropriate action. I realize I may have habits that are aging me, and I want them to change. I realize that I have a very bad height-to-weight ratio." [Laughter]* Want me to explain that? I'm being benevolent and kind.

"Dear cellular structure, I want my metabolism to echo my magnificence. Help me to be at the right size for the greatest health. Change what is needed, and pull on the Akash if you need to, in remembrance of who I used to be. Change my diet preferences, if need be. Let my body crave what it needs, and not what I want or it is used to. Bring me to a place of balanced divinity, and I promise I will talk to you every day, because I love you."

Then ... don't hang up the phone, don't ever hang up the phone.

If you want to analyze this channelling, you'll realize that your consciousness never told the body about any specifics. This is because the Innate knows what to do. It's just waiting for the call. You're asking for balance, and Innate knows what to do. The smart part of your body can even get in touch with your Akash. It can pull on the right parts for health, for change, for dropping habits that are harmful to you. These can be as simple as eating too much, or eating the wrong thing for your enhanced metabolism. You can't help it, because it's a habit, but that can change very, very quickly.

Within a couple of cycles of cellular rejuvenation, Innate can create actual differences in what you *want* to eat, so that there's no hunger. It has pulled a *you* from the past that didn't have the habits that you have today. That is the power waiting for you. C-A-L.

Lastly, how does it make you feel, Old Soul, to know that you've got a friend inside? It's a friend to the extent that, with it, you can put years and years onto your life. All of this is in appropriateness, within a plan that you've laid out for Earth. It involves who you're going to be next time - and when you're supposed to come and go. It's about staying healthy while you're here, something that is way outside of the bell-shaped curve, and that's what you can do.

The channel today is given in a very sacred place to create new tools for you, because it's time.

Kryon live channelling "Cellular Communication"
Enhanced by Lee Carroll for this book
Given in Delphi University, Georgia – April 12, 2014

Don't you find the information about Innate amazing? Well, get ready for more! The next channel will take you to a new level. The reason is, because Kryon gives us startling information about Innate being programmed for spiritual survival. Whatever does that mean, and why are we only learning about it now? Think of it this way: Innate knows every past life you have ever had and is hooked to the energy of your Akash. For thousands of lifetimes, reincarnation was the engine of spiritual growth, and karma was created to "push humans" one way or another. Karma was needed mainly in an older Earth energy as a way to move the energy of the planet vibrationally, higher or lower. As humanity worked the karma they had been given, with total free choice, it provided the catalyst for change.

Karma is about situations with other humans, unfinished business, and a system in interaction. Karmic energy pushes you to do things. It's about the group around you, your place in it, and the emotional energies that are developed from that energy. It is the unfulfilled energetic puzzles that often drive us to do things. Karma is an old *energy driving system* that did its job well with a lower vibration humanity, but it is no longer needed in our new energy.

When you drop your karma, you are releasing an old controlling energy and moving to one where you are free to better help the planet with your light. This is your free choice, and it is driven by your intent. Those who are coming in with new attributes of pure spiritual intent, begin to understand that they don't need past-life karma to complicate their new energy decisions. Part of this karma-dropping process understands that becoming multi-dimensional means blending the past, present and future (potential) into a new reality called "the now." This leaves no room for "past karmic instruction sets" within the DNA. Our DNA is evolving spiritually.

In the old energy, karma pushed you to places to do things and meet people. In the new energy, you don't need karma to push you anywhere, because you are able to put yourself exactly where you are meant to be. These new understandings bring a level of responsibility – a total responsibility for all that is around you. No more playing the role of a victim and no more "accidents." This is called "co-creation," and is the spiritual evolution being given to all of us.

All of this means we now have the scenario where Innate, our smart body, is operating in the new energy of 2013 and beyond. A word of caution: Kryon tells us that the recalibration into this new energy is not automatic, especially for Innate. That means we need to reprogram Innate, and thankfully, Kryon is able to tell us how:

This evening I wish to expose a very important system to you, in ways we have not before. We're going to call this information, *"The beginning of information about Innate."* We have given channels before, and one of them was called, *The Mysterious Innate.* In addition, we have given you some of the attributes about your own body, and tonight we wish to enhance that even more.

The Magnificent Innate

Dear ones, I want to tell you about a process in your body, not only mysterious because it's not in 3D, but elusive enough that you can't really define it. Yet it belongs to you so well, that it is actually *you*. You might ask, *"How can something be inside me, Kryon, that I don't really know about?"* The answer I give yet again, is that your DNA is not working at full capacity yet, and that this is the subject. Your consciousness is not yet synchronized to the reality of certain kinds of things at work within your body. But these realizations are coming to you eventually, and the recalibration of humanity includes an evolved Spirit within you, and we're going to talk a little bit more about that in this channelling.

Let us first identify Innate: What makes Innate so mysterious is that it is not a brain function. It is also, perhaps, one of the only systems in the body that is not centralized. This is difficult for you to conceive of. This system has not been discovered, so it is also not yet defined in medical science. Yet it has been seen over and over.

What you have in DNA is very difficult to explain. The trillions of DNA molecules in your body are all in communication with each other, all the time. It has to be the way of it, if you consider what DNA does. How does your body know which kind of cell it needs, and where it needs it? It is Innate that is responsible for all that, at your birth. The DNA, you might say, is truly an *esoteric central control*. It is the field around the trillions of pieces of DNA that knows itself as *one entity*. All the DNA together work as one system through this field, and that one system is called *Innate*. So, you might say, that it is the combination of all the DNA molecules in your body together, seen as one thing - which you call the *smart body* – Innate. It is decentralized. There is no single organ or gland of the body that is responsible for Innate. Every single part of the body is involved in this smart body system.

As elusive as it is, you know how to find body solutions through Innate, and you often use muscle testing, or kinesiology. There are many ways - tapping, BodyTalk, de-coding, and more. All of these systems give you what we would call *smart body feedback*. This is done, very successfully, in order to find out what the smart body wants to tell you. Those who facilitate these processes absolutely know that they are talking to the "smart field" in the body. This field is representing the DNA as a whole, not an organ or a gland, and not the brain.

Innate is a Smart Back-up System

So the first thing we want to tell you about Innate, is that it is a body-wide system that "knows" more than anything that your nervous system or brain system could ever know. Innate is everywhere. It's in your toenail and in your hair. Innate is everywhere DNA is, in any form that DNA exists. It's unique, and it's you.

Now, I've told you that medical science has seen this over and over, but they don't understand it. Let me give you an example: When a Human Being has the spinal cord severed in an accident, it is severed forever. We have talked about this before, and we said to you, *"Isn't it odd that the spinal nerves don't reconnect and grow back?"* Everything else in the body is programmed to regenerate, yet the cells in this area do not regenerate well. A severed limb can do it, but the nerves in the spinal cord don't reconnect. We've also told you there will be a time when it does regenerate, and that this is all part of the *evolved Human* that is coming. But let us talk about the way that it is now.

Picture this: Let us say that you know, or have seen, a paraplegic [or quadriplegic]. Here is a man or woman in a chair, who can move nothing but his or her head. Now, does it make sense to you, that most of the nerves are severed in the spinal cord that allow any movement at all, yet the things in the body that depend on the brain's severed signals, continue to work? The heart muscles continue to beat; even though you're told that the heart's beat-timing is sent from the brain, for the signals to be in the right pattern.

Science has an answer to this for the heart (below), **however**, digestion also continues, reproduction continues, and most of the body functions below the neck are un-interrupted. Yet the brain is not sending signals anymore. How do you explain it? Medical science actually has a pretty good explanation for the heart, since they see it all the time. They tell you that the heart can be autonomous, that it makes itself beat through special cells in the sinoatrial node. This is their description of Innate! They also are seeing a profound back-up system at work.

It's a back-up system within the DNA field that keeps you alive. The DNA field of your body actually connects with the brain, and the signals are still sent in a quantum way [wireless]. The sinoatrial node is a nerve antenna that continues to "pick up" the brain's transmissions through the field. It's so good at this, that even if the brain is dead, it "remembers" the pattern for a while, like a battery back-up. This is the power of Innate.

Remember that your quantum DNA field is in connection with the full body, all the time, even though the spinal cord is severed. The brain continues to send the signals, the DNA field receives them, and sends them to the heart muscles, to the digestive processes - everything but the muscles in other areas. I ask you to look carefully at this oddity of the body through spinal injury, and you'll know that I'm right. This is so you have real-world proof of this phenomenon.

Innate, the smart body, will keep you alive even if the wires to the brain are severed. Innate is smart, much more than what you will call the survival organ - the brain. The brain is a massive computer of survival and existence. It gives you the ability to be here. But it's not that smart. It can't even tell you if you have a horrible disease in your blood. But Innate can.

The Singularity of Innate

It's time for you to think of your DNA as one thing, not trillions of things. Science does not even acknowledge that DNA can communicate with itself, yet it has to, in order for your body to sort things out the way it does. The beauty of what we are teaching is this: The corporeal body, the one that the brain controls, is beginning to build a bridge to Innate. This bridge is going to be through intuition, and will eventually create a time when you will be your own medical intuitive! You will not only know what is going on within your body, but you will also have a much higher understanding of the energy of your Akash.

Innate has its own kind of programming. It is programmed for something that you should know about, since, with this new energy, it's time to rewrite that program.

Survival Programming

Whereas the Human brain is programmed for corporeal survival, Innate is programmed for spiritual survival. You might ask, *"What is the difference?"* Corporeal survival is your ability to get away from the tiger chasing you, and find food and shelter. It gives you the logic to figure out these things, and to stay alive. Spiritual survival is a very different thing, and it's very esoteric.

It's a much larger kind of survival. It pushes humanity's spiritual evolution, and provides a higher working level of your DNA. Let me explain:

Innate knows what the Ancients knew: It knows the grand plan; remember, it's connected to the Higher-Self. It knows how long humanity has on this planet, before it will no longer be able to make a decision toward planetary graduation. Innate knows that; your DNA knows that. What is the prime directive of Innate? It is to do everything it can for you, giving you multiple chances at free choice, allowing an awakening to take place; therefore, allowing humanity to go across the bridge of survival, and move into an ascended planet status. That is the prime directive.

Spiritual survival represents the potential evolution of Earth, and everything is designed around that. Innate is designed to push you forward in any way possible within the free choice system, into spiritual awareness. That is what Innate is for. Do you see the grand plan in all this? You have a built-in guidance system to help you navigate your potential.

In this process, Innate also crosses the bridge with corporeal chemistry in very different ways. Innate is responsible for spontaneous remission. Now you know where that comes from. Did you really think that came out of the brain? How can a Human have a disease disappear overnight? How is it possible that the corporeal body can cleanse itself of something so unbalanced overnight? How can tissue grow in a greatly accelerated rate to cause healing, almost overnight? I have just given you things that hospitals have seen over and over. They have x-rayed them and verified them and chemically tested them. There is no way, they might say, that this could *normally* happen. For those who are spiritual, it has to be a miracle! For the science minded, it remains unexplainable. The beauty of this is that it is, indeed, explainable: It's the miracle of Innate! It's your own body keeping you alive. It's a profound, miraculous back-up system.

That's the power that you have. When Innate finally starts to build the bridge to the corporeal self, the Human Being, as you know it today, will disappear. The one who takes its place will have a much longer life, be able to repair itself, and even grow limbs back. This is how it was designed, dear ones, and this should start to make sense to you.

Innate's Old Energy Programming

Now that you know what Innate is, let's talk about Innate's programming from the past: In Kryon Book One [1993], I spoke about something that Innate is responsible for. I said, *"It's time to drop your karma."* Karma is energy carried with you as a result of past-life experience, pulled forward through the veil into a reincarnated body. It is an energy of *unfinished business.* That's karma. It's real, and it was needed in an older energy.

It's in the DNA, and Innate governs it. So when I told you to drop your karma, I told you that you must *talk to your body*, and *talk to your cells.* When you do that, say, *"I am done with the energy of the past. I drop my old karma. I move forward."* These were the first instructions you ever had from me about a process that crosses the bridge from the corporeal self, to the Innate. We told you to use *pure intent.*

Cellular Shift Is Not Automatic

Pure intent addresses your cells in a way that is so pure, that the body sees it as truth, and acts upon it. That is how karma is dropped. It sees you as the boss (as it should), and acts. Now, I want you to see what was not stated all those years ago, that it's now time to reveal. I want this to make sense to you, so we first present the logic for it: Whatever programming the body has, it is totally governed by free choice. You have the choice to obey your brain's survival instructions or not. You have the free choice to believe that this message is real or not. Therefore, the esoteric choices in this new energy are not going to come automatically from your body. Free choice means you are required to use your divine consciousness to direct Innate to move into the new energy. Does it make sense to you that, as you come into a new energy as an Old Soul, where karma is no longer needed, Innate would drop it by itself? The answer is no. Innate waits for direction, and your consciousness shift isn't programmed into your DNA. That is what free choice is all about.

Now listen, for this is the teaching of the day. Innate, as smart as it is, will continue as before, until it gets its new instruction. You have got to reprogram Innate, because it has an old energy bias. It has been working with you the same way as long as you've been a Human. It was designed to do certain things in a certain way, and it's time to change that. Your consciousness is the key to change this. It always was, and always will be. Your free choice is needed to deprogram what I will call the *instruction sets of Innate*. So dropping your karma was the first new energy instruction I ever gave you, and now there is another one.

Reprogram the Innate in your body right now! This reprogramming is through your free conscious intent, and it's not hard. Your consciousness, through pure intent, is the King of body change. You've always known you can change your chemistry, and heal your body, so talking to Innate is the key. Now it gets more complicated. I'll tell you what the old program is, in a moment.

The Power of You

How would you like to trigger your own spontaneous remission? Think about that. You can do this, for it's the next step, dear ones. Talking to a cellular structure and controlling your chemistry is one thing. Controlling Innate is another. With this, you are beginning the next evolutionary step.

In a recent channelling, we told you that affirmations are important. Affirmations are not repetitive phrases of meaningless consequence, and I know you understand the difference. If you've memorized things that people told you to memorize, and mindlessly repeat them over and over a certain number of times, nobody is listening. This is not seen by Spirit as anything but verbose conversation with yourself. That's it. Consciousness that is focused, is done with pure intent: you have to *mean it*. Affirmations, especially the ones you create yourself out of your own consciousness, represent the highest form of pure intent. These are energy instructions to your body on a regular time schedule, on purpose, almost like you have an appointment with Innate. It's personal.

Here is the way it works: You must talk to Innate as your best friend, as you would a Human Being sitting in front of you. Consider, you're going to have a conversation with your best friend. Would you then just repeat things over and over? The answer is no. Instead, you'd give a good friend the credibility of intelligence to listen and understand. That is the credibility you must have with Innate. Innate is your smart body and it's time for you to reprogram what it thinks is your spiritual survival. This is because Innate has not crossed that marker of energy with you. Your consciousness has crossed into this new energy, not your old original cellular structure. Recalibration, dear ones, is not automatic.

Old Soul, there are a few things you should understand. Do you find it interesting that Innate knows all about your past lives, but you don't? How is that for an efficient system? Would you like to know more? What energy is it that you have had in a past life, which you have earned, that you could use again today? We've talked about this. Mining the Akash is done through free choice of consciousness, and talking to your Innate. Muscle testing, tapping, BodyTalk, affirmations, decoding - whatever you can do that circumvents the corporeal logic of the Human brain, constitutes working with Innate. You have got to think differently in your reality, to fully realize this potential. You are used to quantity, repetition, and other linear concepts, in order to change things within you. Not anymore.

Homeopathy also counts on Innate, for it to work! Did you know that? The entire area of homeopathy is an Innate function. A tincture sends a signal to the smart body to make the changes, which the tincture has given the pattern for. That's the reason that homeopathy remedies work. They're designed specifically to send a signal to Innate. Do they work? Oh, yes! You see, there's a whole concept of healing and survival within you, which lurks in a place that we're asking you to connect to. If you connect to Innate, you can start finding out about who you used to be, and who you are today. Innate will give you what you need to know, because it's smart. You can ask Innate who you were in a past life, and it will not tell you, unless it's important for your spiritual survival.

So now let us talk about what you have to reprogram, which is the biggest issue of Innate.

Reprogramming Your Body

Number one: Drop your karma. We say it again, that is number one. What is it that continues to push you around, dear ones, which is the Achilles Heel of your personality? What is it that is there, that you just don't understand? I'll tell you, it's the energy of the past, and it's not needed for the future. Get rid of it. Innate will do what you tell it to. If it sees it as spiritual logic, it will cooperate, because with this channel, Innate is listening along with you! It knows what you know, and you are the consciousness trigger to change your own Innate.

Number two: Change the prime directive of Innate: What is it that Innate is built to do, which makes no sense at all? I'm going to tell you right now, and it's one of the largest revelations to date: Dear ones, there is a system called reincarnation that is the engine, at the moment, for spiritual advancement on the planet. Example: You live a lifetime; you learn certain things; and you pass on. You are reborn into the planet, and within your DNA and Akash, is the wisdom you carried from the past life. Each life gives you more wisdom, and you have the free choice to use it or not. But it comes in with you at birth, as a new potential.

An Old Soul carries far more esoteric wisdom than a new Soul does. You understand this so far? You, as an Old Soul, have *been there and done that*. Have you see newbies on the planet? They can't make heads or tails out of anything! Every single lifetime builds a library of wisdom, as you sit in the chair today. You know you're an Old Soul. Now guess what Innate does with that?

Innate's Old Program

Here is what Innate has learned to do, which the old system required. Are you ready? *Death*. In order for you to graduate, pick up the wisdom and move forward into a higher spiritual consciousness in the next life, you need a short and productive life. Then you reincarnate with that wisdom. The faster the learning cycles are, the higher potential there is for the planet to awaken into a higher vibration – Spiritual Evolution. Are you starting to see where this is going? Innate, by design, will give you short lifetimes! What a system! It's important that you see the sense in this. In an older consciousness, this became the "engine of enlightenment." The recycling of Old Souls was the key. Let them have experience and wisdom. Then recycle them back into the planet so that the wisdom could be used.

It's important to remember that the "old energy" didn't really allow for present-life wisdom to be realized (used) by the grids of the planet. This was only accomplished through rebirth, and from DNA only working at about one third its potential.

Suddenly, in 2012, you passed the marker [as measured by the precession of the equinoxes], and you've come to a place in consciousness that the ancient prophecies all told you about. Dear ones, that's why I'm here! You have the ability, for the first time, to do what we saw was possible, twenty-five years ago when I arrived. Your DNA is starting to evolve.

I want all of you to start telling Innate that you don't need to go through the transition of death, to pass on the wisdom you have. There is a new process now, and it's different than any you have had in the past: Not only can your present wisdom pass into the grids of the planet today, but everything you have learned from the beginning can be applied, too. Your full Akashic wisdom and learning is suddenly accessible in real time to the energy of the Earth.

You don't need to reincarnate quickly anymore. Instead, you can do it by remaining here, as your DNA starts to increase in efficiency. By the time you get to 36 percent (do the numerology), the process is complete. You will then have the ability to stay – a very long time! Dear ones, Innate doesn't know that. For thousands of years, it has been progressing this planet's potential spiritual growth, by giving short lifetimes. Innate needs to know this, and you are the ones to tell it. Longer lifetimes are the key to the planet's evolution!

Doesn't it make sense, dear ones, logically, that you could accomplish more on this planet if you don't have to be reborn and have to grow up all over again? Stay!

Other Reasons to Drop the Karma

Some of you carry around what we would call a *near death experience* potential. This is a time, imprinted into your Karmic energy, when there was a potential for your death. This potential exists as a synchronicity that pushes you right into what Innate thinks you need! Innate's reasoning is that it's time for completion of life, because you need to be reborn and get on with it. This is the only process Innate has ever known, to carry the wisdom over the veil into the planet again.

However, now, as you start to touch the Higher-Self within this new energy, you can bring the wisdom into your current lifetime. This has been our teaching for many years. Some of you can be brought to your knees through profound life experience, and come out with a completely different personality! It's almost like a rebirth while alive! This has actually happened to some who are listening to this right now! Let me ask you, *who* were you 15 years ago? Are you really the same person? Do you think the same way, or do the same things? Think about what happened.

There are many on this Earth who will say, *"This is silly. You are born one way and stay that way."* But this is simply old traditional thinking. You can reprogram almost everything in your body! Many of you know that you've changed your entire personality, perhaps even your Human nature! You've even changed your corporeal structure. There are those reading this who have stopped aging, and that's what this is about - proof that these things are real.

The key to stopping the aging process as you know it today, is reprogramming the Innate. Your body is designed to age you, even against common sense! Your cellular body was designed to rejuvenate, and it isn't doing it well. Do you understand? It is the job of Innate to change this, but it needs the signal to do that. This is free choice, and you are the only one who can do it - not a facilitator or a healer – not a channeller. YOU need to learn how to communicate with Innate.

Tell Innate: "*I no longer have to die to create spiritual growth*." You can do this almost any way you want. Learn how to build affirmations that are positive. Get in touch with the body through whatever process that comes your way. You are ready to communicate to the *smart body*.

Now ... the beauty of this is the following: You don't have to convince Innate of anything. It knows! It has been waiting for the call! As soon as it sees the progress that you have made in your consciousness, it's a done deal. Did you hear that? Innate knows who you are! After all, it's the *smart body*. But it doesn't know until you make the call.

Innate is ready to cooperate as soon as it sees the new and evolved avenue of spiritual evolution. The result of this is that you may live a lot longer. Some say, *"I'm not certain I want that!"* If you say that, then you are buying into an old paradigm: Age equals health problems. It doesn't have to! So that's the next thing: Stay healthy as you *don't age*. [Kryon smile] Youthing is not complicated! Is it possible it's filled with love? Yes. Is it new? Yes. It's also smart enough to work well.

Dear ones, I just gave you an attribute that I have never been able to give humanity, and you heard it for the first time tonight. For this information to be given, you had to cross the 2012 energy, past 2013, into 2014. It's time you knew the truth: You are in control of so much more than you have been taught. That's how powerful you are. You're going to see it, and then you're going to believe it. Indeed, you are all unique, and not all of you are going to be able to awaken Innate with the same strength. That's because each of you are individuals on a unique spiritual path. Dear ones, I know who you are!

Old Souls of this planet, awaken! Awaken to a new process, and a new kind of life. You can double your lifespan ... and more! Don't be afraid of what you see around you. There will be those who don't agree with any of this, and the result will be that they can't do it. They don't understand it. Slowly, as you don't age as much, the differences between you and them may actually frighten them. It won't be forever, because there will come a time when all humanity will know what I'm teaching tonight is true.

Kryon live channelling "The Innate Revealed"
Enhanced by Lee Carroll for this book
Given in Portland, Oregon – November 22, 2014

Wow! What a gift Kryon has given us to help us move forward in our lives. Your Innate is ready and waiting to give you what you want. I am planning on breaking the bell-shaped curve and living beyond the average life expectancy in a body that remains healthy and active. What about you? It is never too late to start. Our bodies are very forgiving and there are countless examples of how humans have rid themselves of disease and sickness. Don't worry if you stumble and fall occasionally, the main thing is to pick yourself up and keep going. Remember: your Akashic lineage is God the Creator (smile).

Question for Kryon:

Can you give us more information about how to recognize what the body says to us? Can you describe this cycle?

Answer:

It's not a cycle. It happens all the time, and humans simply are not used to it. The Innate body uses several methods to get your attention, so that you will create good decisions.

The first is INTUITION: Intuition is given all the time as you move through life. It doesn't originate from the brain, and it uses an entirely different part of your anatomy to help you. It's illusive, not often seen as important, and usually discarded.

EMOTION: Do you suddenly react to something emotionally? Pay attention, for the body is telling you something.

UNEXPLAINED CHILLS: This is the body's best way of getting your attention. Chills are easy to create, and if you have them during certain situations, it's the body's way of saying "VALIDATION! - PAY ATTENTION."

Innate is always listening to you, and is ready to give you feedback.

Chapter Four

The Core Soul Group

This group is the most difficult to describe and explain because it is outside of 3D. The Human Soul Group and the Gaia Soul Group have attributes in which the effects are observable, such as muscle testing, using Innate and changes in the Magnetic Grid in response to Human consciousness (as discussed in previous chapters). But the Core Soul Group is predominantly experienced when we move beyond survival consciousness. Some people also experience attributes of the Core Soul Group during a past-life regression or a near death experience.

Within the Core Soul Group you have the Higher-Self, your Guides and something that is called your Soul-Split:

- The Higher-Self (which remains on the other side of the veil). This is the CORE self.
- Your Guides (helper energy). These are the parts of you that are barely outside of 3D, which are responsible for co-creation.
- Your Soul-Split (the piece that ALWAYS remains on the other side of the veil). Part of you is on Earth in 3D and part of you remains on the other side. This gives humanity "synchronicity." Your Soul on the other side sees the bigger picture, and together with the multi-dimensional soup of ALL Souls, is responsible for co-creation.

So the Core Soul Group is about co-creation and synchronicity. You create your own synchronicity with your Higher-Self, your Guides and your Soul-Split, along with other humans and their Higher-Selves, Guides and Soul-Splits.

The Higher-Self (The Core Self)

The Higher-Self in this group is what Kryon calls the Core Self. In 3D, we see the Higher-Self as the Divine self and sense it as *the God within.* But, there is also a part of your Higher-Self that remains on the other side of the veil. Within the Human Soul Group, the Higher-Self is the communicator, represented by the pineal and intuition. However, in the Core Soul Group, it is the CORE and represents the essence of God in your DNA. In Kryon Book Twelve, *The Twelve Layers of DNA*, the Higher-Self was identified in Layer Six – the "I am that I am" layer. When you open up to the sacred place within you, through prayer or meditation, you drop into the Core and feel the Creator inside.

This part of you, which is on the other side of the veil, has layers of existence that combine and meld when you start to open the portal to your Higher-Self. This helps your connection to that part of you which is sacred. Kryon often asks you to "drop into your Core." How do we drop into our Core? This question is difficult to answer, because each of us is so unique. The best I can do is to describe the sensation. When I feel my Core Self there is an overwhelming energy (beyond the strongest emotion), where I'm at total peace and no longer feel separated from anything. Lee Carroll describes his own experience in Chapter Three of Kryon Book 13, *The Recalibration of Humanity, 2013 and Beyond.* Every time Lee Carroll sits in the chair to channel, he says the feeling is the same. Below is a partial extract from Lee's book, in which he shares his experiences with us:

> "I sit in the chair and it's silent. It doesn't matter the number of people in the audience before me. I've done this in auditoriums filled with people and also in the wilderness within a circle of only a few. The feeling is that I'm about to cross the bridge, and there is always hesitation.
>
> I'm about to step into a mist of a reality that cannot be described. Oh, you can learn to channel, but nobody can teach

you what I'm about to feel and see. The mist is where the love is, and it's a place where you want to stay. The 3D mind is not prepared, and it took me over a decade to go to this purity, to this place, where I'm suspended between what I know in 3D and what I 'know' as a child of God.

How do I explain the dimensional shift of every cell being whispered to? While I'm in channel, my cellular structure changes – oh, that feeling! I keep my eyes shut, but suddenly I don't have eyes. Others can channel with their eyes open. I can't.

Spirit has removed the filters of 3D and has taken me out of my reality, but I'm still in my body. Nobody can teach this. There is no way to teach how to become pure and leave everything you have learned behind. You can't teach how to look back and only see one side of duality. You have left the shore and are looking back at the very essence of humanism, which you no longer are involved with.

Reader, sense quietness as you read this.

There is no sound where I am. There is the feeling of a breeze of some sort, a whispering wind. It has a message I can't decipher, and yet I can. It's a familiar voice in a language I know so well, but can't quite remember. I'm not channelling yet, or am I? There is no reference of time, and I feel the grandness of something more. What is it? What part of me am I about to meet?

'Who is there?'

The message to my cells is being delivered all at once and not through sound. Am I speaking in the chair yet? Does it matter? Will I return to my reality? Does it matter? Suddenly, I hear a voice and it's disconnected, but it's the voice of Lee. It sounds odd, since it's only one of many I have in me. My Akash rings with the truth of what is happening and the whispering voice grows louder.

'Greetings, dear ones, I am Kryon of Magnetic Service.'"

Lee's description helps convey what it is like to "drop into the Core." Many of you have experienced this when meditating. Some also experience it when they pray. Prayer and meditation are what humans use to communicate with God. Kryon has given a channelled message that describes the process of prayer and meditation, that further enhances our understanding about what is happening. Unfortunately, the word limit constraints for this book prevented me from including that information here, but I invite you to read this message as one of the free chapters available on my website: *www.monikamuranyi.com* under the "Extras" tab. Look for the chapter called "Prayer and Meditation."

An attribute of the Higher-Self, that can make it difficult to understand, is that it is everywhere at once. It is not found in any specific location. Many people view the Higher-Self as something that is higher (above us), but the reference relates to you "vibrating" at a higher level. This God part of you vibrates higher than anything else in your body, and it is found within your DNA. Kryon further explains where the Higher-Self exists:

The Higher-Self is in every molecule of your DNA. It is part of Innate. It doesn't reside in your heart or your brain. Instead, it is outside of you and inside of you. It permeates a body quantum field, which is what your sacredness creates. It's called the *Higher-Self* because it vibrates higher than your corporeal structure. Therefore, it is a part of you that is in a higher vibratory state, and one which creates a multi-dimensional reality. If you could only open the door between the *corporeal you* and the *quantum you,* called the Higher-Self, you would be complete. That is the study at the moment, is it not?

So here's what it comes down to: Do you have helpers? Yes. Are there guides and angels? As sensed by you – Yes. However, it's far more than that. They represent a soup of energy which is partially you, and partially the *higher you*, the *divine you*. All divine things are connected to the source, and the Creative Source of the Universe is part of you. The connection is always there. So, again, do you have help? Yes. Where is it really coming from? *Yes*. [Kryon smile] You cannot identify a place in a multi-dimensional reality.

"Why not Kryon? There is heaven, is there not? That is a place."

If you wish ... But is it one place, or in every air molecule? Is it in the life of nature? Does it permeate Gaia? Is it everything you see? Is it light? Yes. That means you're never alone. It also means that "Heaven" may be closer than you think.

Here's what the masters and the shamans know:

"Wherever I walk, I have help. My helpers all have my face, and they're beautiful. I'm a piece of God; I'm quantum; my guides provide endless help, and my intuition comes from The Creative Source. I have help from the air, the animals, the trees, and the dirt I walk on. Love permeates everything around me, and it is part of Innate. I do not ask *where*, for there is no *where*. I do not ask *who*, for the *who* is the one, and it is me."

These things may not make sense, because they don't represent the way you think in a 3D reality. But many of you can feel the beauty and the compassion which created it. Most of all, you can feel it inside you. Can you use it? That is the invitation.

What is the one thing an animal can feel, which is beyond food, nurturing, and shelter? It is love. Is it true or not true that animals can look in your eyes, and love you back? Indeed it is. It is a universal quantum energy that cannot be denied. It will tame the wild horse, and it's the only thing that will. It is palatable, beautiful, and it is quantum.

So why not apply this to yourself?

Say: "*I know I am connected to Spirit in a way that is eternal. I am that I am.*"

Kryon live channelling "Intuition, Guides and Angels"
Enhance by Lee Carroll for this book
Given in Sacramento, California – July 3, 2011

To conclude, the Higher-Self is found in each group of three, within the nine attributes of the Human Being. Your Higher-Self is the part of "you" directly involved in communication with God, and the part of you that's "connected" full-time to the family. You connect and communicate with the *God inside* when you "drop into your Core." In an older energy, humans would need to prepare to achieve this divine communication and it wasn't necessarily available to everyone.

However, in the new energy, Kryon has told us that we can have this divine communication all the time. It is available (through free choice) to every Human Being on the planet. Your Higher-Self is right there beside you (in every moment), no matter what you are doing.

Your Higher-Self is ready and waiting for you to claim your mastery, so that your daily walk is so loving, peaceful and different that you refuse to go into drama, anger, or worry, no matter what circumstances you are faced with. Every moment of every day, you are "connected to the family," as you walk in ordinary places. This is how the masters lived their lives, and they changed those around them because of it.

Perhaps you may feel this is impossible to achieve? Maybe some days are more challenging than others? Why not begin by asking for this connection in those moments when you are quiet and still? Devote some time to meditate and visualize this connection and tell your Higher-Self that you wish to initiate this connection and keep it going. Then, use the profundity of the emotional feeling that you have in those precious moments and keep them going! Come out of your meditation and walk this 3D world in a multi-dimensional bubble of love. You don't ever have to close the meditation and communication.

Questions for Kryon:

Most humans on the planet have DNA operating at around 33 percent. However, some Old Souls and the new ones being born, may be up to 40 percent. The masters who walked the planet had a very high percentage of DNA that was working. Their Merkabah (the energy field around them) affected those they came into contact with, often creating miraculous healings. Can you explain more about how this works? Is this why the Pleiadians don't visit us in their corporeal form, because their Merkabah would alter our DNA, and that defeats the purpose of self-awareness and removes free choice?

Answer:

This is new teaching: Human DNA is an "aware energy," and the field around the body, called the Merkabah, is also, therefore, always "aware." The entire reason why evolution happened in the time-frame it did, was due to this. We will refer to it as AE (aware energy). A channelling called "Evolution Revealed" was given about this in Sylvan Lake, Canada - January 24, 2015.

When one particular living system comes in contact with an evolved version of its own kind (Human with Human, for instance), it's aware of that, and tries to emulate it. Life didn't evolve through "natural selection" alone on the planet, but rather through a "fast-track" system of AE. Therefore, it was no accident of mutation that life evolved quickly. Instead, there was AE: Each time there was marked improvement, the entire group "knew" it, and would push new birth towards the new model. Remember, Innate is smart.

This is the "darkened room" metaphor we gave you more than twenty years ago: When many humans are in a very dark room, and one lights a match, they all can see better, not just the one with the match. All of them love the new sight awareness, and want to have it for themselves. Therefore, there are more and more with matches along the way.

The Masters of the planet had an evolved DNA, and many wanted to walk with them. Balance begat balance, and even nature reacted to their peaceful countenance. This is our best example of how balance and wisdom create attention and emulation. It's the staple of evolution. But indeed, it must happen by itself, and yes ... this is why evolved consciousness does not present itself to you in person, en masse. It would affect free choice.

But, be aware that this is one of the biggest "unseen" rules of nature that exists, and everything, including plants, have it.

Many Lightworkers have developed a good communication with their Higher-Selves. Sometimes a technique is used by Lightworkers in which they connect with the Higher-Self of other individuals to promote a benevolent outcome. For example, a Lightworker told me about a potentially difficult meeting at work. Prior to the meeting she meditated and visualized communication with the Higher-Selves of everyone who would be at the meeting and requested the most benevolent potential. The result was beyond her expectations, and everyone was talking about the positive outcome, instead of the expected drama and conflict. Can you tell us more about this process?

This is true, and is proof that pieces and parts of each Human are on the "other side," existing along with the 3D pieces here on Earth.

Think about it: if it's true that part of each Human Soul is also on the other side of the veil, it means that every Human has "angelic oversight," or the ability to have a bigger picture of reality. But, unless the individual Human can communicate with the portal of the Higher-Self, there is no way to work with this amazing gift.

Therefore, something happens that is truly compassionate and benevolent: Those few who can communicate with their Higher-Selves allow for ALL to benefit. In other words, there is a "party line" happening! The "meeting" that you describe could also be a "situation" in real life. Because *the one* got information about what to do, it's like the one got it for all. At some level, all the humans were helped through that meeting, or situation.

It requires consensus, and free choice to participate in such a thing, but quite often, even those who have no idea about a Higher-Self, still have their "Innate" (smart body) talking to them at intuitive levels, saying, "*good idea ... trust this person.*"

It explains a great deal, if you think about some of the mysteries of Human interaction, and why they work or don't work, so profoundly.

On numerous occasions, humans that are experiencing a profound connection with their Core Selves often weep uncontrollably. The emotions of this connection are overpowering. Can you explain why humans that feel this divine communication have no control over the weeping, especially as they do not feel sad?

This is easy: You can control your thoughts very easily, but not always your emotions. If your beloved dead mother or father suddenly wasn't dead, and came back to you, your body would not be able to control itself, and would sob in joy and wonder. Your heart would overflow, and there would be tears of celebration for days.

When the cellular Human Being finds the esoteric part of themselves, there is a reunion of the same kind, and the celebration often creates uncontrolled weeping, thanks, and joy. Remember, emotions don't really come from the brain.

This is often called the "awakening" of an individual to the Greater-Self. It can happen almost anywhere, for any reason ... not just in your ranks of Old Souls. Sometimes, it happens through emergencies, or profound personal experience, or just aging! There often comes a time when the person is ready to have an "aha" about the reality of who they are.

Your Guides

Your guides are vessels that contain the by-product of energy that is generated by your intent. It is part of the alchemy of energy, which is connected to the Cosmic Lattice. The mechanics of how our guides work provides an understanding about why every Human Being has the potential to change the planet when they change their life and experience spiritual epiphanies.

Role of the Guides

Let me tell you about something that happens with the alchemy of energy. There must always be a balance in all energy, including the spiritual. I'm here as the magnetic master to tell you that there is always a balance. Even within the center of your very atomic structures, within the atoms, all physicists have wondered why it is, that the nucleus is so small and the electron haze is so far away from it. You see, it doesn't make intuitive sense that the mass in the center would create such a physical situation of so much space. That's why we discussed the Cosmic Lattice, the power that surges - that's always balanced all around you. It is no different, dear ones, as you walk on this planet, with what you experience with your spirituality. For, when one energy changes to another, there is a balance shift. When you transmute one energy to another, spiritually there is a by-product. We're going to tell you what it is in spiritual terms, but not in terms that are mechanical or physical.

Your guides are vessels, and they contain the by-product of energy that is generated by your intent. This energy is carried by the guides. For those of you who have given intent to drop your old karma and move onto a new path, you are about to ascend a ladder of vibrational shift that contains transmutation after transmutation, alchemy after alchemy. You're taking what *was*, and turning it into what *will* be. Every time you do that, there is a by-product of energy, created out of nothing, through your *intent*. It is so great, dear friends, that another guide is often added to you in the process! That's why the third one comes on-line, which we spoke of almost ten years ago.

Energy Creation

Now you know. The guides exist, among other reasons, to facilitate the energy you are creating, seemingly out of nothing, which is all part of the balance of what happens when you make spiritual decisions. Let's talk about the first of three. It is only appropriate that we use three.

Intent

The first will not surprise anyone, for we are always speaking of it, and we're already there. *Intent* is the first. There is energy created with intent that transmutes karma. I don't think it's wasted on any of you to understand the energy behind the transmutation of karma. It is something profound, removed from you through intent, which transmutes into something else. We told you in other channellings what happens to it, for the potential of it has to go somewhere [for balance reasons]. The energy of potential karma represents an entire Human life potential! When you change it, what *was* the energy has to go somewhere in the transmutation process. As we've written, it goes to Gaia - to the very dirt of the Earth, and the planet absorbs that energy. Therefore, it transmutes itself from a spiritual aspect of the Human Being to a spiritual container that you call Earth. There it is. The by-product of that alchemy is Earth change. That is why the Earth moves as it does at this time, and that is why your oceans warm as they do. That is what is taking place, and we predicted that it would be so, if you care to look. The speeding up of your planet's weather systems and geological attributes are a direct result of humans taking their light.

Something else occurs when the intent of the Human to move forward is given. It creates a *new* energy. Seemingly out of nothing, there is another energy created - an energy that shakes hands with the Cosmic Lattice - an energy that is then stored by the guides of the individual that made the decision. This explains the *power* of intent, as we have discussed before. Pure intent draws from the Cosmic Lattice to create life change. In the process, this *new* energy is taken by the trinity within the Human, and the Human energy quotient is higher than before.

Other humans (especially seers) suddenly are aware of your increased vibration and power. Your aura changes, and your light shines like never before! Did you ever wonder what it is that is "seen" when you carry your light? Let me tell you what it is. It's the fact that, metaphorically, your guides are carrying "vessels of *new* energy," and those vessels of energy represent the NEW energy that was created when you made the decision to move forward spiritually with your life. There's a reason why those guides carry those vessels. Before this time between us is finished, we're going to tell you why - and what the mechanics are around it.

What if a Human makes no spiritual decisions during a lifetime? We have told you before, dear ones, that there is no judgment about this. The Human is honored for the journey - for being part of the play. And when the curtain comes down, the cast party celebrates - even the one who seems to have been the villain in the play - or who even died in the play. But there's much more to it than that. Those who give spiritual intent during this New Empowered Age create energy out of nothing. That's alchemy! That's where the action and life change is. That's where the "activeness of light" we have discussed before, *is*. That's when things start happening to a Human that lets co-creation take place. That's how a Human creates a new path - one where they are in charge of their future in a way that was not possible before. That's one of the three - intent.

The Physical

Let's talk about the physical. Some of you believe that there are many Earths with many futures and many roads. It's an esoteric thought - that there could be simultaneous realities existing together. "*What of it*," you might ask? You are not too far off. We have told other groups like this of the potentials that line up from the "snap-shots" of energy at a specific moment in your linear time. You see, these potentials of the planet are "recorded." It has to be this way, dear ones, because *we* are in the now. Your past and your future are all here *now*. The potential of this planet, therefore, is a snap-shot of *now*, and we can tell you what your future might be, based upon your decisions *now*, and the energy that is *now*. It's recorded, and it never goes away - never goes away. That's all part of the balance. This means that there's a multi-dimensional place where all those potentials are stored, like many simultaneous Earths - but only the potentials of measured energy at different linear times.

The physics of Earth is astounding. Your reality is changing, and your future continues to be a blank page. Almost monthly, it is revised by what you're doing here. The miracles of the physical body and the physical planet are examples of transmutation. There is no magic – it is spiritual wisdom and regular physics that make these things happen. You continue to draw on the Cosmic Lattice, and continue to create NEW energy for the planet, which changes your future potentials ...

... Oh but there's more. A few weeks ago [February 1998], your best scientists gave you information, based upon their best computers, that you would be hit by an asteroid not too many years hence. Don't you find it odd that the same scientists with the same computers two days later came back and said, "*Never mind, we made a mistake somehow, and it's not going to happen at all?*" Dear ones, did you ever consider that in two days, perhaps you (the planet) had moved on to another "track" of potential? The energy potential of Earth that was there five weeks ago now lives in some dark place called "The Future That Used to Be." To some, this may sound like fantasy. To the wise, it is so.

The math spoke for itself. Orbital mechanics are absolute, and yet, through some mystery, only a few days later, the numbers were done again and the answer had changed [according to scientists, they were not done correctly in the first place, but they were released anyway]. We're here to tell you, that this is an example of a miraculous transformation of energy, and it's caused by the *intent* of humanity, which we have called the critical mass. In the process of that alchemy, there was energy created that went from one place to another. It's still held in the planet, and it's still a potential, but the energy that was the by-product of the miracle is now held by the guides of every single Human who gave intent to change it – and everyone on the planet got to watch. This is not the first time you will see this kind of seeming "false alarm." *Intent* can change reality!

Emotional

Let me tell you about the third kind of alchemy – the most profound kind. You think the healing of the Human body and the balancing of the body is special? Let me tell you about the Human emotion. This is the miracle of miracles, you see. This is the one that takes worry and anxiety, and through the alchemy of intent transmutes it to peace. We have spoken about this over and over. Look at the energy it takes to create worry and anxiety - look at it. What happened to your body when you were in anxiety and worry? It changed - physiologically it changed. The cells - every single one - knew of the anxiety and the worry. You may have had weight loss, your skin may have changed - all of these things as a response to an emotion that you had. When you gave intent to vibrate at a higher level, through the knowledge and the preparation of what can be yours, you transmuted it into peace. There are some here that have done that very thing over and over - and there is so much love from Spirit sent to those who have learned how to do this!

I would like to ask you, "Do you know where the energy went?" Let me tell you this. There is just as much energy generated in a covert way creating peace for you as there was in the creation of anxiety and fear. But in the transference from the one area to the other, a new energy was created (which we call the "third" energy). It was spiritual - and the guides collected it like another color that spins into your Merkabah, for it was the color of victory. We have told you what happens when you walk through the bubbles of fear and face the tiger. Now you know what it is - the guides that capture that golden ring that was generated by the victory. They put it into their vat (metaphorically). Some of you have taken sorrow and grief and transmuted it into peace as well, and those who sit in this room (and read these words) know of what I speak. They have said, "*It is miraculous that I know how I felt before and I know how I feel now.*" The episode is still there, but the energy of grief or fear is gone. The transmutation is complete, and the energy of the victory was passed to the guides and held for you. That's why they're here, dear ones - that's why they're here.

Kryon live channelling, "Guides and Angels"
given in Coal Creek Canyon, Colorado – 1998

Hopefully, you now understand the purpose and role of your guides. Before I continue discussing information about your guides, I'd like to share an observation with you. Lee Carroll has been channelling the messages from Kryon for over twenty-five years. If you have followed the Kryon work since it began, or have read several books, you may have noticed that the channelled messages have evolved, and sometimes, information that seems conflicting may appear. This is the case with the information about your guides. The reason is because Kryon delivers messages that are commensurate with the consciousness of the group present, and given within the energy (vibratory rate) of the planet. There has been a significant demarcation between channels given pre-2012 in the old energy, and post-2013 in the new energy. Humanity is continually evolving spiritually, so it's appropriate the channelled messages evolve as well.

Over a decade ago, Kryon said we had three guides, but this was a metaphor. Kryon has since stated that you don't really have three guides. The *three* is only the numerological identification of helper energy. The number three becomes a "pointer" to another meaning. Some of the Kryon parables even presented guides in such a way that they seemed to be separate entities from us. However, your guides are actually a part of you. Understanding this attribute is incredibly difficult, because nobody wants to think they are their own guide. We prefer guides who are separate from us, that float around and give help and advice.

Often, our guides will appear to us as an individual with a unique personality. This guise is because our guides understand our psychology. A multi-dimensional soup of guide energy is difficult to perceive and communicate with, but a guide, who looks Human, dressed in specific clothes, with distinctive traits, is much more relatable. So if our guides are us, how does it work?

Let's talk about guides and helpers in a more specific and historical context. The channellings [scriptures] of the Ancients have gone along with your visualization of three guides. But you should be aware of this "three" number in this new perspective, because now I'm going to give you something that is different from 3D.

Twenty years ago, I simply went along with your perception of "three guides." It served you, and there was no wisdom to understand anything else. Now there is. I have news for you:

You don't have three guides. The *three* is only the numerological identification of helper energy. The number three becomes a "pointer" to another meaning.

I said earlier today [in an earlier channelling] that you all participate in a *third language* during my channellings. Some of you are not hearing what I'm doing with my partner at all [the channelling you are reading]. Instead, you've got your own personal messages happening and they're being transmitted right now. Therefore, what we call the "Third Language" is a catalytic, multi-dimensional language. It catalyzes the energy between you and me, and when you sit in front of me and you open that which is your third eye, the pineal is wide open. That's when the catalyst begins its work and you get intuitive, communicative messages.

The catalyst is between that energy you call Innate, or your Higher-Self, and this side of the veil where I am. This language is working with your intuition, giving you flashes, giving you instructions, holding your hand, giving you love. That's the Third Language.

You Don't Have Three Guides

Now it seems like you do have three guides, because there are three distinct energies that are divine that Spirit uses with humanity. The first Human to see them and publish this fact was Elisha, understudy of the prophet Elijah. When he watched Elijah ascend, it appeared to be three white horses carrying the chariot that Elijah rode up into the clouds with his voluntary ascension. He called this whole experience the *Merkabah*. This is a Hebrew word that means "to ride."

What Elisha was seeing were three energies that belonged to Elijah, and they weren't guides or angels that were apart from him. Instead, Elijah came in with them and he left with them. Dear ones, you come in with a divine energy that is so profound that part of it stands apart from you for life. You are bigger than you think. Your guides are part of you! They're not separate; they're not from other places; and they don't change. "*Uh oh. Kryon, in past books, you said they changed.*" Indeed, I did, and that was so you'd understand a simpler reality of divinity. Now you are graduates.

The Dark Night of the Soul – An Apparent Guide Change

Now I will give you something else you should hear. Many of you have had the situation where you believe your angels, your guides, whatever you call them, have gone away for a while. In the beginning of the Kryon work, we told you that for up to 90 days, you might experience what we now call *recalibration*. Back then, we called it "The Implant." It was "*the implantation of your permission to change.*" It would often be accompanied by a perception of the guides and angels leaving for up to 90 days.

Every single Human Being who recalibrates, no matter how many times they do it, will have a period of time where there is seemingly no help, and a time where Spirit has seemed to retreat from you. Now, I'm giving you this information, because some of you are going to go through it, and some of you have already gone through it, and it's not what you think. Now, I want you to listen to me, as I finally explain what is happening.

During this recalibration time, when you feel Spirit is not listening to you or your guides have gone, the best thing to do is simply read a good book. Don't try to figure it out. Don't make any decisions. Don't move your place of living. If you want to do something, why don't you sit in the chair and say, "*Thank you, God, that you cared enough for me that I'm going through this. Because when I come through this, I'm going to be different.*" You will be!

Human Beings recalibrate with intent and free choice to vibrate higher. With the recalibration comes more divine sight, more intuition, more light, and more of a revelation of who they are. When they re-emerge recalibrated, with the stair step of energy shift that they accomplished, seemingly, back come those guides! But I will tell you the truth. You think they've changed? Ha, ha. They haven't. The same set of energies are there that were always there, except now you *see them better!* Do you understand what I'm saying? However, in 3D, it looks like one set went away and another came in. The reality is that *you* shifted to such a degree that they just look different to you! That's how much you changed. You changed; they didn't.

Kryon live channelling "The Humanization of God"
given in Totowa, New Jersey – July 16, 2011

There is something else you need to know about your guides. When your loved ones die and transition from Earth, they become a part of you, as part of your guide set. This is difficult to comprehend, but it exists as part of the benevolent system for humans, and it all relates to your Merkabah. Kryon again emphasizes that your guides are not what you think:

I want to talk about guides. Now, my partner has told you that "you are your own guides." I know this is difficult for you to conceive, and I also know that you don't like the idea. However, I'm going to complicate it even more. He's right, but I want you to put it into another perception.

You have something that you have called the Merkabah. Loosely defined, this is your personal quantum energy field, which is about eight meters wide [26 feet]. It's a field created by the sum of the molecules of your DNA [which together are entangled at a biological level]. Every single Human Being has this field. DNA is unique, so each Merkabah is unique. The field of your Merkabah is not your Soul. It's not even your Higher-Self. It's you! The field of your DNA has a complete and totally different purpose than to interface with anything but your corporeal body; that's what it does. It interfaces with you and your consciousness.

This is complex, and difficult to explain. The Merkabah contains much about you, since it is the bridge with "Innate" [the smart part of your body]. It carries your divinity, your blueprint of life force, and even your Akash. Since your Akashic record is in your DNA, it is also part of the Merkabah. Therefore, you might say that you are always *broadcasting* your past through the field of your Merkabah. This, dear ones, is the reason many can read your past lives. The template of all you are is in the sacred patterns of your Merkabah.

The pieces and parts of what makes up your Akashic record are in the Merkabah and in your 3D. Some of them are perceived as your guides, but actually, they are *you with you*. But to your perception, it might be a *past you,* and so it has another face. Are you understanding this? There's more: To add to the complexity of this, there is a system of benevolence that is beautiful, and we have mentioned it before. The Akashic family that you come in with, which you call your corporeal mother and father, sister and brother, or what you would loosely call your family or loved ones here, are all part of your Akash in some way. In a quantum way, there is a reality to them that I cannot explain to you, because you're not aware of how this quantum soup works. I'll use the words *entangled state with your Soul* and you still won't understand it. It is complex, but here is the result. When you lose a loved one in your family, a part of their Soul energy (or their God part) goes into your Merkabah and is with you for life. Then, when you pass over, you'll do the same for your children, your brothers, sisters, mate, husband or wife. So let me tell you what that means. They are never gone! Do you hear me? They are never gone. Here is a system of benevolence you didn't expect.

It's real, dear ones. We are now starting to give you the complexity that you deserve to know about. Many of you won't understand it, but you can still get the concept. Every single part of this is part of a benevolent design to keep you peaceful and loved in the eyes of God.

Kryon live channelling "Demystifying the New Age – Part III"
given in Edmonton, Canada – January 25, 2014

One of the things I love about the Kryon channels is the "timelessness" they have. Kryon gave a channel in 2005 that expands the information about how our loved ones become our own guides:

Dear ones, if it is true that you are in some multi-dimensional space and are fragmented - that a part of you is helping those in the past that used to be your family before you reincarnated, then you might project right now those *who* are part of your own guide-set as well.

The ones whom you knew on this planet as family, who have passed over, are currently sitting on your shoulder. This is truth, dear ones. A piece and a part of them, whether they've reincarnated or not, is with you right now. "Out of space, out of time," you might say ... yet they are here. There is the mother, the father, the sister, the brother, and the child. They are all here. Do you ever wonder if the ones who departed that you loved so much, that you anguished so much over, could ever "look down from above" and see you? Well, they don't have to "look down." All they have to do is glance to the right! There is a piece and part of all of them with you now.

We invite some of you to feel this and understand what we're saying. It's part of the love of God that gives you this, so that you will not be alone ... ever. It's a part of the promise of family that we have never discussed with you before. It's never been transcribed before - part of the energy that you carry around with you are those who passed on in your own lifetime.

Now, whom do you think taps you on the shoulder to see the 11:11 and the 12:12 on the clocks? Why did you look at that particular moment? Why not when the clock was displaying 11:10? It's because you were tapped on the shoulder by those who love you and surround you, who wanted to say, "I want to show you something very unique and interesting. Look at the clock now!" The next time it happens to you, rather than feeling a wash of "What is this about?" or "Oh, isn't this interesting or odd?" we challenge you instead to say, "*I love you, too ... I love you, too.*" For that's what's going on. It's a tap on the shoulder. Your own loved ones are saying to you, "We're really here! Look at the clock - look at the clock! We're here, and if you don't believe it, we're going to have you do it again and again and again, until you understand that these things are not coincidental. We want you to know that we are proud, and that we love you."

Kryon live channelling "The Interdimensional Human – Part II" given in New Hampshire, USA – 2000, Kryon Book Nine

What a beautiful message – our guides are ALWAYS with us. This is something to remember on a daily basis, instead of thinking our guides are only there when we meditate or when we're in distress. Your guides are happy to hear from you, no matter what the circumstance. They are actively involved in creating the synchronicity you desire. The better the communication flow, the easier it becomes for your life to flow in a beautiful dance of synchronistic events.

Kryon tells us to begin a communication in whatever way works for you. Give your guides names and a personality if you wish. Talk out loud with them if you want. Call on them any hour of the day or night, and celebrate your life. Be prepared to "hear" new ideas, thoughts and loving energies throughout the day and when you least expect it. Be aware that your guides are with you in the ordinary moments of your everyday life, not just in your "spiritual moments."

Question for Kryon:

It's wonderful to know that our loved ones become our guides; however, it is extremely difficult to bypass grief. When someone we love so much dies and transitions from Earth, we miss them in the physical plane. At times it can feel unbearable to have to live without them. As our spiritual evolution continues, will this lessen our grief?

Answer:

No. Grief is often a catalyst for enlightenment, and is part of "compassionate personal learning." It is how the Human gets through the grief that will change. An evolved person will grieve just as much, but will "see through" the situation and work with Spirit to settle the emotions in a much more profound and mature way.

But the attribute of missing those who are gone will remain as one of the staples of Human Nature, and will always be part of your compassionate makeup. It needs to be that way.

Your Soul-Split

Your Soul-Split represents the part of you that is here on Earth, in 3D, and the part of you that remains on the other side of veil. This is the case for every Human Being, which means there is a collective pool of all the Soul-Splits that know the bigger picture, giving us the ability for synchronicity. Your Soul-Split is what actively "sees" the potentials, and then your guides give you the ability to take action on what your Soul-Split sees. The classic example that Lee Carroll and Kryon give to explain how this works is the parking angel. If you have never heard of the parking angel, I invite you read one of my free chapters, called "Co-creating Your Reality." Visit my website, *www.monikamuranyi.com*, and look for it under the "Extras" tab.

Using the example of the parking angel, your Soul-Split "sees" the parking spot that is twenty positions beyond your vision, while your guides are the ones who "tell" you to go to that place. This is the difference between synchronicity and co-creation. This is the link to the Human Soul Group, through Innate, the pineal, and intuition. They all work together as follows: The pineal and intuition activate the Soul-Split, which then sees the parking space; the guides go for it; and the Innate of your body allows it to happen. Are you beginning to see how the soup of energy works within the nine attributes? Each attribute has its unique qualities but all of them are engaged when we decide, with free choice, to get out of the 3D bubble of "survival consciousness."

Synchronicity and co-creation are part of the system of benevolent design, available for everyone. Most Lightworkers and Old Souls are more aware of it than others. I've heard numerous stories from other Lightworkers about their "synchronicity" experiences. You probably have dozens of examples in your own life. Examples of synchronicity are: When someone receives a phone call from a person they haven't seen for ten years, but they were just thinking about them; or when someone is looking for a new job, and before they even begin to look, they receive a job offer that is just perfect!

Synchronicity happens all the time, regardless of your belief system or your religious faith (if you have one). Synchronicity and co-creation with your guides, Soul-Split and Innate are part of a fast-track system to assist you in your life. It's simply a matter of being aware of the system and learning how to step out of linearity, so you can recognize when synchronicity comes your way. For many, using this system doesn't come naturally for many reasons, such as the beliefs imposed on us from childhood, the structure of our society and the dictates of how dreams and goals are achieved.

Let's take a look at two individuals, Claire and Alice, who both have the same desire to create a business, in which they own and manage a chocolate store.

Claire assesses her dream and writes a big list of all the things she needs to do in order to achieve her goal. She enrolls in a chocolate academy to become a fully qualified chocolatier. She attends courses in small business training and then invests her life savings into buying a chocolate business. Claire celebrates the realization of her dream. However, within the next three years she is out of business because a new department store opens next door, selling chocolates at a lower price. While the quality of Claire's chocolates is far superior to her competition, the consumers prefer the cheaper ones from the department store.

Alice, on the other hand, understands synchronicity. Alice creates a strong clear intention of wanting to create, own and manage a chocolate store. When chatting with friends, she is told about an old acquaintance that is the manager of a chocolate store. When she phones the store, she is told to come in for an interview to become an apprentice. Alice gets the job, and after three years, she understands everything there is to know about running a chocolate store. Although Alice hasn't realized her dream yet, she still holds her intention and waits for synchronicity, understanding that there is no time frame. After another two years, the manager retires, and Alice becomes the manager at the same time that a new owner has purchased the chocolate store. When Alice meets the new owner, there is chemistry in the air and sparks fly, as they both feel an electric jolt pass through their heart. After 6 months of dating, they become engaged and soon marry, whereby Alice's dream of owning and managing a chocolate store is realized!

Okay, I know I took some liberties in fabricating the story of the two individuals, and yes, I have a romantic streak in me, but I hope you didn't miss the differences between Claire and Alice. Claire tried to make it all happen using a logical, linear process. Alice pushed on doors and then waited for synchronicity to respond. Most people get fixated on what they desire, and then become busy in trying to figure it out! Your guides, Soul-Split and Innate already know exactly what you want. The moment you set your intention, it begins a process. The difficulty is, to let go of your ideas of "how" you think it will happen. In the above example, Claire thought she had to do everything herself and rushed ahead, without any thought beyond her goal. Alice, on the other hand, waited for synchronicity and trusted that her goal would be realized, but didn't try to figure out how, nor did she specify a time frame of when it had to happen. Alice could never have predicted that her manifested co-creation would also bring her the man of her dreams. There are numerous times when I've set an intention, placed my trust in Spirit and waited for synchronicity. The result has always been above and beyond anything I could have created by myself.

I want you to think back and remember your own synchronistic events. I'm absolutely sure you have had them. Do you remember how it felt? Do you remember how effortless and free of worry it was? When we trust that *Spirit has a plan* and relax and do things that give us a nice distraction, it speeds up the process. When we worry, we slow down the process and rob ourselves of joy. You are more powerful than you know, so relax and have confidence that all the divine pieces of you are constantly working on the other side of the veil to create the most benevolent outcome. Your Higher-Self, Your Guides, and Your Soul-Split all work together to achieve this, and Kryon explains how:

Human Being, you are not all here! [Laughter] Now you suspected that, didn't you? Listen: There are pieces and parts of you that are missing from what you consider to be the complete Human Being. In a four-dimensional space called "your reality," you have put skin on a creature, had it born into the Earth plane, given it a name, and called it the complete Human. But it isn't complete. It doesn't even begin to be complete within multiple dimensionality.

Here is information that some of you have always suspected. This explains how many things work, and it explains the tendrils and the strings that are magnetic between the pieces and the parts of who you are individually. Individually, you are not all here! There is a portion of every single Human Being in this room that is spread out into multi-dimensional space ... and the parts have many purposes.

(1) Let us speak of the first multi-dimensional one that inhabits your body. The divinity that you call the Higher-Self is not the end-all of the spiritual part of you. It's simply the one that stays with you in your body that you can sense. That Higher-Self is the part that you cling to. It's the magic; it's the spiritual part; it's the part you try to talk to and communicate with. But it's only a part of the name you call "yourself."

I want to give you the other parts, and I want to tell you where they are. I wish to tell you what they are doing, also. If, at the end of this, you say, *"This is unbelievable,"* I will have accomplished my goal. It is the love of God that has allowed such communication with The Third Language, and some will "see" it. Eventually, many will understand that all that is being spoken tonight from this stage is true – that you are so much larger, spiritually, than you think you are.

(2) There is a part and a piece of you that is on the other side of the veil right now as your guide. *"What? You mean to tell me, Kryon, I'm my own guide?"* Yes, a piece of you is. And we have described the guides before, and we're going to review this again. There is a piece of "you" that is part of the energy, which is what we call the "guide soup." Again, we tell you regarding guides and angels: You want to put numbers on them, give them skin and wings, name them, and say, *"There's three, there's four, there's eight."* Actually, they're infinite, yet they're one, like an ocean that is one ocean, but filled with millions of parts of water. Your guides and angels are forms of energy, not pieces of your 4D existence. We have told you this before: Part of you is in your own guide-set! What better advice could you have than a piece and a part of the angel that you are, sitting on the other side of the veil as a guide? It's a guide that is cemented to you wherever you walk on this planet,

but one who knows you intimately – who knows why you are here – knows the contracts, and knows the predispositions that you have. What better energy could there be for you, than *you*? Get used to it. That's the second part of you. Do you ever talk to yourself? Enough said. Long ago, we even described a possibility where your guides might retreat temporarily from you. When this happens, it's devastating for a moment! For *you* have left ... *you!*

(3) Let's talk about the third part of you. There is a part of you that is on the other side of the veil, which is in a planning session with all the rest of you! Now, how could that be? Think about it. Human Being, have you ever wondered how co-creation works? Have you ever wondered how synchronicity works? Are you aware that you cannot have synchronicity by yourself? It has to be in regard to those around you. Are you aware that you are also someone else's synchronicity? It has to be part of complex planning.

Co-creation is not done in a closet. It involves moving through life, giving intent, and an interface of energy with everyone you touch – everyone you come in contact with – those you shine your light around. What kind of planning do you think that takes? It's on a scale that has no time and yet all time. There is a planning part of you and also every other Human Being on the Earth, on the other side of the veil. Perhaps you had this idea that there was a planning session before you got here and now you're on your own? No. How does that make you feel, Human Being – angel – divine one? There is a piece and part of you on the other side of the veil that is coordinating with others for synchronicity, for co-creation, and for your intent. Did you think you were in a vacuum, and things around you just "happened?" No. There is guidance and planning still going on, and it's you and the others around you that are doing it – all of it – waiting for your search to take you to the place where you realize that the *ice* is not strange at all [Laughter].

We have told you about the challenge in your life being testing. We have told you that there is a golden plate that has your solutions as well as your challenges. We have told you that all is in balance, and in the past we have told you that you create your solutions at the same moment you create your challenges ... way before you get here. Now you know that the challenges are 4D, but the solutions are multiple D!

Now, how do you think that's facilitated for yourselves while you're here? What about the other Human Beings? Some of you feature 4D prayer: You get on your knees before Spirit and say, *"Please, God, make them change. Make the ones around me do this; make them do that."* Let me give you the multi-dimensional way: Instead of pleading with God to change others, start with yourself! Change yourself as much as you are asking the others to change. If you will show your light in this way, it begins a planning session for the others, too! I'll tell you what happens. Although it's through individual choice of the other Human Beings around you, your change creates energy. There are those in the planning sessions that see this and bring choice of intent to those around you. For you are creating a reality of your own through your divinity, the Higher-Self, the Guide-Selves, the Planning-Self, and every multi-dimensional Human Being around you is potentially affected. They are not changed, but rather they are given the energy of new choice, sometimes a challenge ... just because you changed yourself. This often creates search, compassion, and the beginning of real differences in all your lives.

And you want to put skin on the Human and give it a name and let it walk around the Earth alone? Hardly! That's not the way it works, dear ones. I haven't finished telling you the rest.

(4) This is going to sound odd, unbelievable, and very strange. Part of your contract here, as best as can be described in your linear fashion, is to be with those in your last Human

family on Earth, which you departed from before you incarnated in the body you have now. Did you know that? Simply put, you are part of the guide-sets of those you left in the last lifetime! You might say, "*Well now, Kryon, that does not make sense in timing.*" You're right. Get used to it. It does not make sense. In the NOW, all of these things are possible. *"Do you mean that I can be in two places at the same time in different time frames? I can be in the past and the future at the same time?"* Yes. And you will never understand that as long as you are a Human Being. At the level of The Third Language, however, it is the love of God that supplies this gift of understanding, and in a moment, you'll understand more of what the gift really is.

So, Human, you are busy someplace else helping family that existed in your past! Think of how profound that is! There will be those listening and reading who say, *"I still don't understand a thing he's saying."* But the language of the *three* presents to you what we are saying in a multi-dimensional way: You are doing work while you sit here, and you thought you were doing nothing. Perhaps you wondered when you were going to get on with what you came here for? You've been doing it all along in another place, in another time. Some of you have had dreams that showed you what you were doing. You cast them off as just so much fantasy, but now you know they were real. So often, the dream state is a multi-dimensional place where your brain disengages and free-floats. The energies of the *now* may come in, and you see them and feel them. That is why so many of the dreams that you have make no linear sense, do they? They are out of time, out of place, jerking around from costume to costume - have you noticed? You are closer to your actual reality when you're dreaming than when you're awake.

The "Longing for Connection"

I will give you another attribute. Here is an attribute that many of you have not thought of, and it's time it got presented.

We have just told you that the Human Being's structure is not all in the physical body – that part of it is on the other side of the veil, part in the guide-set, and part of it even in the past. Now, if you are that segmented – if you are truly that spread out, wouldn't you feel something? Yes. I would like to give you an attribute that Lightworkers are starting to hear and recognize and understand. Some of you have been watching, looking, and hoping that someday your "twin flame" would walk in. Someday the Soul mate whom you know is *out there* will "come back."

Oh, if you only knew what that meant! Here is the truth: You're not expecting another Human Being, dear ones; instead, you're asking for the return of those multi-dimensional parts and pieces of you to combine with the 4D self. You feel the longing and the love, and you want this so badly! We're here telling you that that's the longing for the pieces of *you* to come together!

Now ... what does that tell you about our teachings over the last 11 years? We have told you to discover self – that's where the magic is – that's where the love is! And now you are in the energy that promotes this reunion. It's a reunion that is so grand, that those pieces can touch one another in a multi-dimensional way. They can greet one another and say, "It's about time we found our self-worth. It's about time we fell in love with ourselves. It's about time we walked the Earth tall, sufficient, abundant, and proud that we are together." That's what that feeling is about. That's what it's always been about, and now in this energy we can give you this information. The longing for the love of your life is often the longing to connect with all the *you* parts that are spread out. Blessed is the Human Being who discovers self, for that Human will have internal love – not dependent, no longer longing, content in his/her life, and a grand lighthouse of energy.

*Kryon live channelling "The Interdimensional Human – Part II" given in New Hampshire, USA – 2000 Kryon Book Nine "The New Beginning"**

* Author's note: the original channel written above used "interdimensional" but this has been replaced by "multi-dimensional" in keeping with the evolution of the verbiage used in current messages channelled by Kryon.

There's another characteristic of your Core Soul Group that is important to understand. If you believe that part of your Soul is on the other side of the veil, what exactly is it doing? Your Soul is trying its best to steer you, through intuition, to be in the right place, at the right time. It's trying to orchestrate benevolence in your life. How do we recognize this benevolence? We recognize it through synchronicity. Your Soul (through synchronicity) wants you to meet the people you're supposed to meet, have the situations unfold that you're supposed to have, and have your life move faster because of it. It guides you to where you can manifest the reality you are co-creating.

What about those people who are completely unaware, don't know anything about these esoteric concepts (and don't even want to)? For example, let us hypothesize about a rapist and murderer that is imprisoned, who has a very high potential that they will never search for the divine within. Do they have a Higher-Self? Yes. What is it doing? Here is the answer, and some of you won't like it: It is looking for an open portal – anyone's! If your portal to your Higher-Self is open, even a little, the Higher-Self of every other Human Being (especially the Human Beings who have a closed portal and will never look for the Creator inside) will come through your portal in order to give you the highest level of benevolence possible, so that you can change the planet. Did you get that?

The Higher-Selves of all humanity are looking for one thing: Human Beings that have opened their portal to the Higher-Self, so that they can help you change this planet. The strength of help from the other side of the veil is exponential. It's not you with you, it's everybody with you, so that you'll be in the right place, to hear the right thing, to make the right changes, thereby changing this planet and moving all of us towards ascension. I think this is why Kryon often talks about how beautiful and elegant this system is, and I'm inclined to agree.

Questions for Kryon:

My own spiritual awakening was catalyzed by the sudden end in my marriage. I have often felt that my Soul planned this as a potential for me to awaken. I understand the decision to awaken was mine through

free choice. I also feel that if I didn't awaken during this opportunity, potentially there would be another time. Does every Human Being have these opportunities to awaken? Are Old Souls more likely to have these opportunities? There is also the promise that in our next incarnation, we will come in with our spiritual knowledge and hopefully, no longer require these "kick in the pants" catalytic times (smile). Can you tell us more about this Soul-planning aspect?

Answer:

You were astute when you asked if Old Souls had more opportunities for spiritual growth. Indeed they do, because they are in a more advanced learning cycle. Each Human has a chance to become an Old Soul, just like each Human has a chance to be a child, then grow into an adult. So there are no "privileged ones," just older ones.

Even though the Old Soul will have more of these opportunities, free choice remains the key to what happens. So, many times, even the oldest Soul will not learn anything, and simply go through these things and survive. Others will have life changes.

The more that Old Souls learn through these awakening experiences, the more mature the Akash becomes, so that the Soul will tend to "awaken" earlier the next time, with an Innate remembrance, or instinct of greater wisdom and maturity of Spirit. Here is a new thought for the Old Soul: Once learned, always known.

Is there a difference between the Lightworkers who died before 2012 and those of us living beyond 2013 and applying the new gifts and tools that are available in the new energy?

Yes. Be aware that there are some generic attributes in the new energy that apply to all humanity, and allow for more awareness and wisdom than times before

2012. But even so, let us also remind you that there is no "promise" of awakening the next time, only a greater potential to awaken. It's important that all who read this remember that they have a very honored choice, and they never have anything that will "happen automatically." There must be choice in all things.

There is a vast new energy developing on the planet since 2012. Humans who died in the older energy and have now come back, actually have an advantage. For they are exposed to this energy as "normal," and grow up within it.

Humans who have transitioned through it have a more difficult problem, since they are constantly trying to adjust to what they remember and grew up within. So you might say that the younger "Old Souls" just coming into the planet have the advantage.

Chapter Five

Soul Communication

The definition for communication, as given by the Merriam-Webster dictionary, is:

- the act or process of using words, sounds, signs, or behaviors to express or exchange information or to express your ideas, thoughts, feelings, etc., to someone else.

Source: http://www.merriam-webster.com/dictionary/communication

Traditionally, communication is understood as being verbal and nonverbal, where verbal communication is recognized by experts as comprising less than 10 percent of the overall communication! This means the rest of the information being communicated is nonverbal, which includes facial expressions, gestures, para-linguistics (such as tone of voice, loudness, inflection and pitch), body language and posture, eye gaze, and appearance.

One of the television series I enjoy watching is an American crime drama called *Lie to Me*. In the show, Dr. Cal Lightman is a world expert on body language and micro expressions (very brief facial expressions, lasting a fraction of a second). Dr. Lightman assists various public authorities in investigations to expose the truth behind the lies.

The show is actually inspired by Paul Ekman, Professor Emeritus of Psychology at the University of California San Francisco. Paul Ekman is recognized as the world's foremost expert on facial expressions. As a preeminent psychologist, he co-discovered micro expressions. Together with W. Friesen, Paul Ekman developed the Facial Action Coding System – a comprehensive tool for objectively measuring facial movement. Later, he began to study deception, starting with patients who falsely claimed not to be depressed in order to commit suicide when not under supervision.

Paul Ekman has authored several books, but his publication, *Telling Lies,* prompted national and regional law enforcement groups to ask for help. In 2009, he was named one of the 100 most influential people in the world by TIME Magazine. One of his recent projects is *Developing Global Compassion,* presented as Webisode Series on his website. In this series, Paul Ekman discusses compassion with the Dalai Lama. The webisodes can be viewed at the following website: *http://www.paulekman.com/webisodes/*

While Paul Ekman has undoubtedly advanced our knowledge and understanding, there are other types of nonverbal communication that are less understood, mostly because they are quantum. In the early years of my spiritual awakening, I studied the work of Peggy Phoenix Dubro, originator of the Electro Magnetic Field (EMF) Balancing Technique®. As an EMF practitioner, I worked with a system that exists within the Human energy anatomy – the Universal Calibration Lattice (UCL). Peggy teaches that every Human Being has a UCL, which is their personal connection with the unlimited universal energy source (Cosmic Lattice). In every moment, we are connected energetically to the Cosmic Lattice, and each other.

There are various other modalities that work with the Human energy anatomy. Before I moved beyond a survival consciousness, I had no idea that my energy field was continually broadcasting my words, thoughts and emotions, and yet, this is another type of nonverbal communication. Most of us are aware of the "energetic state" of the people around us. I can remember sensing when the people I sat next to were in a bad mood, even though they had a smile pasted on their face. I just wasn't aware that it was being broadcast from their energy field.

Every Human Being is continually sending nonverbal, quantum transmissions. Our DNA, Akash and Innate are also sending nonverbal communication. Kryon previously mentioned that the bridge to this communication is intuition, through the pineal. This explains how a medical intuitive receives the messages about a person's health. They sense the quantum energy within a person's field that Innate is broadcasting about their health, what's going on with their chemistry, and what might be developing.

There is something else that is always available – the energy of your Soul! Soul communication, therefore, happens when you connect with your Higher-Self. Think of your Soul as a radio receiver that is always receiving, and all you need to do is tune yourself to the right frequency. How do we tune into the right frequency? The answer is complex, but essentially, you must first *believe* that you have a Soul. Using *free choice*, when you give *intent* to connect with your Soul, your Higher-Self immediately becomes a conduit for this connection.

There are many individuals who, through free choice, have chosen to remain in duality and do not seek to connect with their Higher-Self. There are also many Lightworkers who have experienced (or are experiencing) a loss of their "former connection," which Kryon describes as part of the recalibration process. Kryon's advice is *don't despair,* for you haven't done anything wrong! Your connection is coming back, so do everything you can to stay out of fear, and allow yourself to relax. Kryon says your connection is coming back double! It's just that the recalibration process takes time, and all the cells in your body are involved in the rejuvenation process for a new consciousness to be imbued into your old energy body. This is why such a recalibration won't happen overnight – but it will happen (smile).

Connecting with our Higher-Self is done multi-dimensionally with quantum energy. Kryon describes this as non-linear communication. To understand Soul communication, we have to become more quantum. This allows us to receive and translate multi-dimensional messages. This is what Lee Carroll does every time he channels Kryon. Lee often talks about the early days of channelling. Kryon would give him everything at once, and Lee would have to try and remember it all and then deliver it as a succinct message. However, over the years with continual practice, Lee has learned to deliver Kryon's multi-dimensional messages as a linear communication – one word at a time, as a live transmission. If you are frustrated by not having a strong, clear connection with your Higher-Self, please be kind and patient with yourself.

It actually took Lee Carroll four years before he was able to channel the messages of Kryon. Lee describes his very first experience of Kryon as sitting in the chair and saying, "*Okay, Kryon, or whoever you are, if you are really there, then show me!*" The next moment Lee was overwhelmed with a pulsing love wash that had him weeping in the chair. It was the last thing he expected, and immediately he jumped up out of the chair and yelled, "*Don't ever do that again!*" Thank goodness that Lee's curiosity got the better of him and he continued to ask for the connection.

Like any skill, the more we practice, the better we become. Lee has learned to step aside and remove his Human filters and bias for singularity. This allows for a beautiful steady stream of communication from the Kryon entourage to impart loving messages, filled with profound love and teachings. Here is what Kryon has to say about the types of Soul Communication:

The Types of Soul Communication

Trying to describe communications to and from this "living physics" goes beyond the limits of any understood science. It challenges you to think differently about everything. There are basically two ways of thinking about Soul communication: (1) Communications from multi-dimensional sources *to you*, and (2) from the multi-dimensional parts of you *to them*. Right away, we acknowledge that you are capable of multi-dimensional communication, but you may not realize it.

There is a strong difference between linear and nonlinear communications. When I have said this in the past, not everyone understands it. So I am going to explain it the best I can, in a way I've not done before. I want you to consider for a moment that you have a very old typewriter. This is the kind of older machine with paper loaded into it and with a carbon ribbon that allows you to see the characters as you type on the page. As you strike the character keys, the machine creates a visible imprint through the ribbon onto the paper.

In this example, let's say you are typing along, and as you type, you see the characters on the page in a row, one after the another. Pretty soon you have letters turning into words, then sentences and then paragraphs, which form groups of similar thought. This is *linear communication*, and it's normal for you. In fact, it is how this very message is written to you, and it's how you are reading it – in a very linear fashion – words on a page in a row.

Now, whether you are reading or listening, you are perceiving one word after another in the structure of the language of my partner [English]. It is, therefore, linear – one word after the other, like the typewritten words on this page. That is linear communication. That is Human communication, and it's how your brain works.

Nonlinear communication would be as follows: Now pay attention, for this is going to be what my partner calls *a stretch to imagine*. Pretend that the typewriter is stuck in a way that you can type all day long, but it never advances the carriage to the left as you type. No matter how many characters you type, you are only going to get one unreadable single image – a big smudge, really. Every character is going to imprint itself over the last one. Now, what would you see on the page, dear ones, at the end of a long letter to a friend? It would be a single character smudge! All the characters would be piled up, inking over each other, and you would have no idea what the communication was. You'd look at it, and you'd be sorry that the typewriter failed and you hadn't noticed.

Now, consider for a moment that someone comes along who has full nonlinear communication skills. They could look at the smudge and see the whole message clearly! They're conceptual and nonlinear. They would see the thought that went into the message, and they would be able to *see within* the smudge. The characters and sentences are still there, dear ones. Remember? You typed all of them. But they're not there in a linear form. Instead, they're all together as a group [the single smudge].

A nonlinear communicator will see the smudge and perceive the entire message.

Now, there's an attribute about this that is difficult to describe to you. It's out of the logic that you are used to, so let me try to explain it. My partner, go slowly so this will be understood [speaking to Lee]. When the conceptual, nonlinear person is looking at the smudge, they are looking at something that exists already. A message has been typed. So they're not making something up or guessing. Instead, they are simply reading something that already exists in a nonlinear way. The message has been written and all the characters are there - oddly presented in one smudge - but it has been given in your real time.

There's an attribute of a nonlinear mind that you call autism that you should study. There are many autistic Human Beings who can tell you the day of the week for any year within any month. If you were to ask that person, "*What is the day of the week for the 15th of the month in May of 2035?*", many would know the day instantly. Most humans would gasp at what appears to be their computational efforts. But the truth is, that computation has nothing to do with it. You see, it's not a formula, and it's not math. The answer already exists, so it is *known*. You can go to almost any personal computer that is *calendar friendly* and find that information, because it already exists. It's a concept that has already been developed, produced, and stored.

The nonlinear mind works this way. Many with the autistic mind are able to interpret this information almost instantly, because they see the concept. They're not calculating anything. Now you know the difference between linear and nonlinear. The autistic mind is the forerunner of things to come and an anomaly of future Human development. These are the savants of the day, and many of their difficulties stem from their inability to work in a linear world.

How It Works – Nonlinear to Linear Communication

There's a lot of communication that wants to come to you from all manner of sources, so I'm going to start the list. Let's begin with channelling. Channelling is what you are hearing right now, and my partner has practiced it for 23 years. When he started, it was ugly [using his term], but it is fine now. But you should know that we're not speaking to him in a linear fashion. You hear it from him in a linear fashion, but that's not how we are giving it. You see, he is a *master interpreter of nonlinear concepts* coming through his pineal.

Right now, I'm giving this entire message all at once - *our smudge* - and he's interpreting it for you so it sounds like a flow of linear words. But it's a single thought group, and I keep giving it to him over and over. You see, we have practiced together, and we've both had to adjust.

When we first started, I gave him the concept, the entire channelling, in one smudge. [Lee makes the sound of a single syllable.] Like that! Then he had to remember all of it and give you the channelling. He wasn't very good at remembering, so then we tried something. If we kept giving him the same *smudge* over and over, he could interpret it in a linear fashion. By the way, I just gave you the secret to *mastering intuitive thought*. Ask for Spirit to repeat the intuitive message over and over. That should be your request to Spirit when you don't understand what the message was - repeat it! Have that intuitive thought repeated so that you can grasp it and see it for its beauty and its clarity. It may seem like this would be obvious, but remember that free will keeps us from doing anything for you unless you have asked. Spirit does not naturally repeat anything. Repetition is a fully *linear concept that you must ask for*.

We want to meet you in between the linear and the nonlinear, dear ones. Do you realize that this is why Spirit has talked to humanity through quatrains and in metaphors since the beginning? That's all we have - metaphors to help you see a message, since we deal in thought groups and *smudges*. However, the interpretation of these metaphors often become puzzles. People sometimes read scripture and they ask, *"Why can't you talk normally, Spirit?"* The answer is that we are not linear as you are, and we *are* talking "normally" for us. Even this very channelling is being given this way. As long as it takes to speak it, all of it is being given at the same time to my partner, a nonlinear smudge, over and over. He is then translating it to you in a linear way. Did you ever hear him tell you at the beginning of a channelling how many parts there would be? He does that many times. The only way he could do that is to already know the entire message, even when he begins it. Do you see? He is *reading* the smudge.

What is Channelling?

So we begin the teaching: What is this channelling? Channelling is the pineal of the Human opening up and giving communications from what you call *The Source*. Of course, it must also use the Human's culture and experiences, as he/she interprets them and then speaks or writes them to you. Any entity, energy or true communication through the pineal is from The Source. It can have many names or personalities to you, but it is all from The Source. The differences between channellers, therefore, is how they interpret and how clear the pineal is of *Human filters* [more on this in another channelling].

Channelling is a form of communication that is open to humanity, and you don't have to call it channelling. Instead, you might call it whatever you want to, but you should know that every single Human Being is open to learning it if they wish. Through free choice, many are simply not interested, but how about doing it just for yourself? It doesn't have to be an angelic energy or some entity. It can be your own Higher-Self. Many call it *automatic writing.*

This communication occurs through a multi-dimensional portal that opens through the pineal gland. This information does not come through the brain, as we've said before. This is *Soul communication* and it is multi-dimensional. It has nothing to do with synapse – nothing. Intuition is Soul communication, and it is not a brain function, and that's why it's hard to "pin down," for you are used to synaptic linear thought. It's how you are "wired."

Let us speak of the difficulty of this yet again. Anything I'm going to mention from now on in this section is about *others communicating to you in this nonlinear way.* This kind of communication from others must be interpreted in some way to make it linear. There are many attributes of this kind of communication, so I'm giving my partner a list and he can choose what he wants to talk about within the time that he has.

Personal. Let's talk about personal communications. How can you *hear* what Spirit or any other multi-dimensional source has for you, when it doesn't come to you in a linear fashion? This is hard! My partner gave some answers today, and the main answer is, through the *practice of recognizing intuitive thought* and understanding what is coming from your brain and what is not. It's difficult, at first. Humans want to analyze it or interpret it with intellect.

Dear one, do not let the synapse of your brain get in the way of God. Do I have to say that again? With intuition, you must learn to put linear logic aside and let the beauty of nonlinear ideas play on the stage of your consciousness. This may not suit your survival or what your friends think about what you are doing, but it will enhance your life. It's hard to change the way you think.

So, what is it that my partner had to learn, as the engineer, in order to channel? He wanted to analyze absolutely everything! It took years for him to discern the difference between pineal and brain, and then to *get out of the way of nonlinear intuitive thought.* At first he always wondered if he was "making it up!" Was it from his brain or was it bigger than that? Intuition is also responsible for what you call *creative thought* - painting, music, poetry and more. So it's no wonder that he asked this question! It's a valid inquiry. So for you personally, dear ones, this is what you have to do. Practice knowing the difference.

Now, there are many more sources other than channelling, which you call messages from God, that have messages to you in this nonlinear fashion [a nonlinear communication coming to you from intuition and not synapse]. It may surprise you what is next.

Animals. You love them, don't you? What do you know about animals, especially the ones you care for and love, the ones you call pets? They have personalities, don't they? They can *talk* to you! When they communicate, what does that sound like, dear ones? What do their voices sound like? *"Well, Kryon, you already know they don't have an actual voice."* Oh really? Then how do they "talk" to you? Now it gets good, doesn't it? They communicate through concepts. Their conceptual thought groups are available for you to *pick up*. So guess where you pick up these thoughts? It's through your pineal, which is the interpreter of multi-dimensional things in your body. It's not your brain, which is picking up their animal *broadcasts*, dear ones.

Now, some of you are good at this kind of communication. There are ones who are listening to this right now called *animal whisperers*, and they know exactly what I'm talking about. Why do they call it *whispering*? I give you my interpretation. It's because the communications are not linear, and they *whisper* to you through the pineal and not through brain synapse. It comes in thought groups, very softly and all at once, like the smudge. When you pick it up, you know what the dog or cat or horse or hamster or rabbit is trying to communicate. You know the requests they have, perhaps the distress they have, perhaps the celebration or the love they have.

Now, this kind of communication with animals is easy for you, because you all have felt this. I believe you know what I'm speaking about. So apply this lesson, for what I'm teaching today is no different and uses the same process you're going to use in real life and in meditation when you *listen* to God.

"Kryon, is it true that communicating with animals is Soul communication?" Yes, it is – *theirs to yours*, and if you're good at the interpretation of their thoughts, then why doubt yourself about the next step? Practice doing this communication with your own Higher-Self. Your Higher-Self is that part of yourself that vibrates higher than your cellular dimensionality, and it's part of your "Soul group." This "Soul group" is part of the nine attributes of the Human Being and is the core of you. It is the part that gives you information from the other side of the veil from that which you call God.

Actions are communication. My partner speaks of The Crystalline Grid and how it remembers Human action, such as what happened on a battlefield in the past. So the energy of the battle is still there, and it is transmitted to you and many can *feel* it. What do you think about the mechanics of this? This communication from what happened there in the past includes concepts of death, drama and fear. The energy is being transmitted by The Crystalline Grid right to your pineal and it's coming to you via concepts of emotion, not linear communication. Many can feel it and many cannot. Those who are used to feeling energy are the ones who understand and feel this first.

Some of you are good at this and you are proud of the fact that you can feel energy wherever you go. You can feel the energy of the group; you can feel the energy of the land and that which is The Crystalline Grid, and you can feel the energy of situations. But what is it that you are feeling? It is *Soul communication* at its best!

It is the grid talking to your *intuitive* self. It does not come from the brain, and it is not intellectual. This is physics. You are picking it up through the pineal, interpreting it, and receiving the information in a nonlinear form. In the case of the battlefield, something has happened on the ground where you are standing, and the energy may take you to your knees. That's communication! However, why is it that the communication that is so personal is the hardest to interpret? It's because the communication is *you with you*. This is what the teaching is about today - working to open up this concept.

Universal communication. When you walk into the forest and the trees talk to you, what is that about? Gaia speaks to you! What does that voice sound like? Am I getting through to you? Do you understand what I'm saying?

You are able to *hear* these things in your own way, but none of them are synaptic. Are the trees in trouble? Are they crying? Perhaps they are celebrating? All of this information is available to those who can *hear* it.

"Kryon, is it true that in the forest there are what you would call devas?" Here's my answer: Are you kidding? Of course! Yes! You are asking what they are. They are multi-dimensional aspects of Gaia. I love how humans deal with multi-dimensional energies. They "3D-ize" them. When Human Beings cannot understand a multi-dimensional energy, they make them entities, dress them [put outfits on them in their minds], give them names, and put them in Human movies. They're beautiful! You know they are, and they're everywhere. Go into the forest and they'll talk to you.

Sit down in the grass and let them communicate with you. They're part of the *energy soup that is Gaia*, which is Mother Nature, the personality that is the love of God in nature.

Dear ones, you're not going to receive bad things from a deva. You're not going to get bad information from hugging a tree. You know that, don't you? What does this tell you about how Gaia feels about you? These are just a few things when it comes to the subject of communication from others to you.

The Other Direction – Linear to Nonlinear Communications

A Human Being has a linear mind and linear communication. Because of this, you do not have the necessary tools for multi-dimensional communication. Now, you can develop these if you wish, and many of you have. But in general, as a Human, you've only got linear communication. So what about **you** with **Spirit**?

Dear ones, here is the truth: We don't have any trouble understanding you! This is because we are the master interpreters. We know exactly what you're saying and it doesn't matter if you're thinking it or saying it. We know what you are communicating because we're with you all the time. Your Higher-Self, which vibrates above the corporeal-self, knows the psyche of your mind. When you sit down to meditate, we know what you are going to do, because the potentials are there. You're already thinking about it before you do it, and that's what we see. Let me give you some hints about this communication with us. Stop giving us *lists* of what you want! We already know what you want. Instead, sit and say to us, *"Dear Spirit, tell me what it is you want me to know."*

Dear ones, we're already on board with everything in your life. Do I have to say that again? We're already on board with everything in your life! Come to us and let *us* talk to you. Just let us talk and try to interpret the thought groups that come first without analyzing anything. Get used to this. But as far as you talking to us, it doesn't matter how you do it.

Now, there will be those who will say, *"Well, Kryon, there have to be wrong ways of communicating with God."* No there aren't! *"Well, what do you think about religious groups who have to face a certain direction or have a prayer rug or they have to wear something special in order to worship correctly?"* Dear ones, let them do what their traditions tell them in their own culture, for it honors God! Is there anything better than that, to prepare them to talk to us? The same love goes into their communication as does your own. Cultural differences between humans do not matter to the other side of the veil, for we see a Human as a *corporeal representative of a piece of God*. All humans! It doesn't matter what you're wearing or what you're sitting on. Is that clear? There is no wrong way to speak to the Creative Source.

"Well Kryon, maybe there isn't, but I've had a few times where I was yelling at God. What about that? Isn't that the wrong way?" Dear one, we heard you, but we did not hear the yell. The yell was linear. This is hard to explain. What we heard was loving frustration. *Loving frustration*. We didn't see the anger. You weren't angry; you were frustrated, and that's the time when we want to surround you the most. The more you yell at God, the more angels are around you wanting to hold your hand! The next time you decide to yell at God, would you also open your heart and let us hold you in our arms for a while. Is that OK? In the moments of greatest frustration, when you have no answers at all and you can't figure it out, can you just be held? Is that alright? We're here for that. Old Soul, you've got to get used to this communication. It is so available!

Actions are an actual language. How you behave *talks* to The Crystalline Grid and *talks* to the Gaia grid. What you think talks to the magnetic grid, which we have called the *seat of Human consciousness*. Without you saying a thing, your actions are another way of communicating to everything and everyone around you. What you say out of your mouth in a linear fashion is heard by your corporeal body. How many self-help gurus have had to tell you that you're going to *bring to you* what you say out loud? Why is it that hypochondriacs bring to themselves the very diseases that they fear most and talk about? It's because the body hears them and gives them what they ask for.

The body is listening, the grids are listening, and even the Human Beings around you are listening. Do you spin in drama? Here we are again with this question. Do you think this is attractive to other Human Beings? Have you ever thought about that? What do you want to show someone about your belief system, your "God within?" Do you wish to show them how out of balance you are and that they should be the same? Think about it. How are you presenting your mastery to humanity? Old Soul, what have you learned through all of the ages that you bring to the party today? Is it *spinning* or is it love? *"Well Kryon, that's easier said than done. How do you stop spinning? How do I stop reacting to an unfair world?"* I just told you. If you'll open your heart and allow sacred communication, it's going to start a peaceful countenance for and with you. This is called *awakening to Spirit*. It's getting out of the old habits, the old fears, and starting to claim that part of your Old Soul that is *God in you*, available to you and to humanity and those around you.

Multi-dimensional communication. Those of you who are good at *speaking* to the animals have developed *thought group communication*. You're already on board for the best kind of Soul communication there is and you're starting to think outside of the box. You're looking into the animals' eyes and you're giving them pictures, aren't you? They're getting it, aren't they? It ought to show you that this works! Humans can develop multi-dimensional attributes and characteristics that are entirely consciousness driven, sent through the pineal gland to anywhere they want.

There are also helpers around you, and we've told you this. Do I have to list them again? There are benevolent entities and groups all around you. Some are from here [Earth] and some are not. Not just Pleiadians, Arcturians, the Hathors, or those from Orion and Sirius [to name some of the more popular ones]. They are endless! Do you know what they all have in common? Nonlinear thought communications. You can communicate with them the same way you do with animals.

Dear Human Being, we're going to open the door to full communication before we close this channelling. We wish to tell you that there is something we want you to know, to realize. Don't let our communication be mysterious! Don't make it strange. I've just given you the attributes of communication to Spirit and from Spirit. In the next channelling, I will continue with another subject:

What is it that blocks this communication? What are *filters*? What can you do to enhance communication?

Soul communication is part of what the Old Soul must learn in order to create balance on this planet and peace on the Earth. It begins here and now. It begins with understanding and demystifying the beauty of your relationship with Spirit. There is structure in these sacred things; there is a benevolent system in these things; and there is *spiritual common sense* in these things. We invite you to find it for yourself, for this communication will create spiritual evolution on this planet. It will be led by the very ones who are reading and listening right now. Family, that's the lesson for today. It's beautiful, isn't it? It's beautiful!

All we want to do is communicate, and it's time to get on with it. This channelling was to explain how it works. The suggestions today are how to make it better - even the very thing that you hear now, which is channelling. Demystifying what some have called spooky, unnatural and weird, is the task before you. Just because it isn't linear doesn't mean it's odd. The one that is the greatest of all is love. Can you explain it? Perhaps not. But you can emulate it. Go now and emulate the love of God within you to those around you.

Kryon live channelling "Soul Communication – Part I"
given in San Antonio, Texas – February 22, 2014

Kryon mentioned animal communication, something that attracts me greatly, due to my love of animals and being in nature. Allow me to introduce Anna Breytenbach, a professional animal communicator, who has been practicing for over twelve years in South Africa, Europe and the USA with domestic and wild animals. A video of Anna posted on YouTube has had over a million views. This video shows the incredible story of how a black leopard named Diablo became Spirit after an interaction with Anna. You can view this 13-minute video at the following website: *https://www.youtube.com/watch?v=gvwHHMEDdT0*

I have seen this video countless times, and yet each time, I am filled with emotion, as I witness the transformation of someone who does not believe in animal communication, to someone who claims his innate ability to talk with the animals he cares for. Details on the full documentary that this powerful 13-minute clip came from can be found under the Media & Articles section of Anna's website: *http://www.animalspirit.org*

Anna runs various workshops around the world that sell out fast. This highlights the huge desire for animal communication that is emerging within the world. There are numerous animal communicators who are devoted to helping us learn how to enhance our animal communication skills. Even without awareness of animal communication, numerous households across the world have pets. Nearly all pet owners experience a deep love and bond with their animals, through the unconditional love they give.

There are also numerous stories of how animals have rescued humans, as well as the healing quality animals have with humans. There are numerous types of programs, in which animals are used to assist in therapy, such as therapeutic horse riding, swimming with dolphins, and animals that visit nursing homes, hospitals, and children with disabilities. Animals can also send us their healing love just from watching their antics. Whenever I need a quick pick-me-up, I'm sure to find some footage of cats or dogs on YouTube that instantly brings me joy.

Perhaps a good place to start the process for communicating with your Soul is to have fun and connect with the animals. Talking with your Higher-Self needn't be serious and stressful in making sure you get it correct. Allow yourself to relax and trust that the connection is always there, available for you when you ask. Remember: Spirit sees you intent! If you receive a message that you weren't quite sure about, ask for it to be given again. In the following channel, Kryon reveals more about the process:

Soul Communication, Part Two

You've come here today to see how you can improve yourself spiritually, but the teaching goes beyond that. It may reveal things you didn't see before. Soul communication can also be defined as "you with you" and, therefore, the subject is also "getting in touch with your own divinity." Is it not true, dear ones, that the entire purpose of today's lesson is how to get in touch with the nonlinear parts of yourself? That is Soul communication.

Can you even conceive of the possibility that you are split into many multi-dimensional parts? As we have told you before, you are indeed in many places at once, but a significant part of *you* is really vibrating higher than your awareness and, therefore, is called your "Higher-Self." Balancing all this and becoming like the masters of the planet is really you getting in touch with the other parts of you that are sacred. That's Soul communication. So everything we say from this point on applies to that as well - you, communicating with the "higher you."

Spiritual Survival

Let me take you back a bit. How many lifetimes have you slogged through old energy? Slogged through it? You picked yourself up and the old energy of the planet knocked you back. This is a metaphor of the Old Soul awakening to the realization of divine purpose for itself and the planet, only to be ignored, or worse, to be "found out" and then feared.

Old Soul, it seemed that you just get started on a spiritual path and it kills you. You come back again and then you're enlisted in a war and it kills you again. You come back, you awaken; you become even shamanic, and it kills you for being enlightened. How many lifetimes has it been where all you can do is hold your own and try to survive in a world of very old, dark thinking? Survival becomes a word that means something completely different to the Old Soul. High consciousness in an old energy is like a square peg in a round hole, and this is what the Old Soul is used to.

Dear ones, this is ending - all of it - and this was the prophecy of the indigenous of the planet for this time. Here you are, ready for it. But the planet is not going to suddenly become higher in consciousness, dear ones. Instead, the systems around you and the energy around you are going to start getting easier, making it far easier to survive for those like you. There will be far less resistance and more openness of many people than ever before. This is the beginning of a very slow shift.

This also means that it's going to be easier for you to balance. We've used this "balance" word over and over. Many times, those in esoteric belief systems go into certain Human life categories, because it's pure survival. It's easy for you to be a hermit, speaking even to my partner. If you don't have to show your light, it's easier. In the past if you showed your light, you were hunted! You understand what I'm saying, don't you? For when you open the door and the light spills out, everybody looks at you because you are different. What's wrong with this picture? In the past, it has meant your demise. This is what is changing. But it's hard to forget it.

Non-interference

So in this energy, past the precession of the equinoxes, we've got some news: The first thing we would love to give you is what we call the "rules of the Creator." Now, these rules are not what you think. Let's get even more specific. We will call them *The Laws of God Toward Humanity*.

These laws are not breakable, nor would we want them to be. We absolutely would never violate them. Spirit is not like a Human. There is no consciousness that is linear, with rules or laws that must be obeyed or not. These are different kinds of laws. For instance, the laws of physics are absolute and they have to do with the way matter behaves in your reality. The laws of physics are not laws being obeyed by a consciousness; they're the laws of matter. In a similar fashion, there are laws of spirituality - the way God works.

So let me tell you about some of them. First of all, for all humanity they are honoring, beautiful and benevolent. Would you expect anything else from the Creative Source? Here is one law: We stand apart from you unless you invite us in. This is more than *free choice* for humanity; it is the law of the Creator. Do we like this part? Not really, for our love wants to shout that we are here, but we can't. It's our way of honoring the Human Being's free choice. If you really knew we were here, you would immediately change and there would be no test. No. The choice to find us must be yours and yours alone.

Dear ones, the old energy of this planet was difficult for all of us. You awakened and you were in survival mode, and within the old energy, the majority of humanity simply wasn't interested and didn't let us in. Can you imagine your children suddenly becoming different and not recognizing you? Can you imagine them wandering around and running into walls because they can't see? Imagine that you've got the only flashlight anywhere and they are in the darkness, afraid. But you can't use the flashlight unless they ask for it. They never call out for you because they don't even know your name! They don't remember who you are. You birthed them and you care about them, yet they don't know you exist. Can you imagine that? That's our law.

Another law: When you as a Human Being open your hand and your heart to a spiritual quest, things happen. Many of you even have a lineage of Akashic remembrance about how that feels (and perhaps the trouble it brings in an old energy). When you begin to answer that internal spiritual question, "Is there more?", you allow us in. At that moment, everything changes and we begin to communicate. That's our law. But when more and more of you do this, the law expands to other attributes around you also. Then they begin to change also. When enough humans begin this process, the very planet begins to shift. It's called fast-tracking.

Now, this is where it gets good. The shift also has to do with what you have called *the sensitivity of energy within the Human Being.* When you walk into a battlefield where The Crystalline Grid has *remembered* what happened there, you feel the drama of it. This is changing, and we told you about that. However, let's say you walk into that battlefield with another. You feel it, but they don't. The dialogue might go like this:

"What's wrong with you?"
You might say, *"Don't you feel the energy here?"*
"What energy? What do you mean?" they reply.
"Something happened here. Don't you feel it?"
"No, I don't."

That's when they look at you and think perhaps you're pretending, or that you want attention, or that you're "playing the role" of the oversensitive spiritual person. What is the difference between you and them? The answer is this: You're letting this awareness in and they're blocking it. We're going to talk about blocks in a moment.

Some of you will walk into the forest and you'll feel it. It surrounds you with its love and beauty. Gaia speaks to you. The trees are pushing out oxygen with a benevolent system of photosynthesis. The plants give you oxygen and you give them carbon dioxide. What a system! Look around. Science will say that system happened by accident - a random occurrence. Do you believe that? What a beautiful system! The trees themselves *know* who you are. You walk into the forest and you feel it hug you, but perhaps another is next to you who came with a chainsaw. They don't care and they don't feel it. To them, the forest is only a resource. What's the difference between the two of you? There's no judgment here, I'm just asking you. What do you think the difference is? The answer: You're letting multi-dimensional awareness in and they are not. You see, you are becoming more aware of multi-dimensional Soul communication. In this case, it's your enormous Soul energy communicating with the other parts of the planet who are also multi-dimensional.

When you make the decision that it's OK to feel this energy, it will be there. Most of humanity so far has not made that decision. They block it. The law is this - this communication will come to you only with your *allowance*. The moment you open the door of allowance, you may begin to feel it. Those are our *rules*.

It's not just allowance for communication from the Creative Source, but also from an amazing number of what we would call other *benevolent energies*. These others are represented by groups with names that you have given them. They also cannot get through to you unless you *allow* it. That's their rule as well. Your names for them are Pleiadians, Arcturians, Sirians, Hathors or those from Orion. There are many more, but unless you open to the possibility of them, they can't communicate either.

Most of humanity will stand next to you as you communicate and think you're not well. That's the way it looks to them. Listen, dear ones, the benevolent groups who represent your DNA essence [your seed biology], and who know who you are, are many.

The amount of help you have on this planet is staggering, yet the majority of humanity will not allow awareness of it or let the possibility into their reality.

The Old Soul

Now, that's where the Old Soul comes in. Dear ones, you're already tuned up! If you're hearing my voice or reading these words, you're *allowing* it. Let me tell you what's going on, dear ones, for there are various degrees of allowance. But the first one is to open the door - and it begins.

The energy of 2014 and beyond is going to start creating new paradigms on the planet. These new paradigms are for discovery, awakening, realization and for "a-ha" experiences. Not all of them will be spiritual. Science will discover many things that will pose new questions. Those questions and the answers will then open doors that won't immediately seem spiritual, but they will all lead in that one direction. The new discoveries of quantum physics and of consciousness that have been hiding will change the rules, forcing biology and physics together in an odd relationship. It will cause a rethinking of life itself and eventually lead to proof of a multi-dimensional reality of other consciousnesses around you.

New Discovery – New Reality

The doctor is operating on a patient. Chemically, the patient is out. Perhaps his heart has been removed and another is ready to be placed into a gaping cavity in his chest. A machine is keeping him alive by pumping his blood. His life essence is hovering above the operating table and somehow he is watching it all. Some patients have reported seeing things that only the doctors knew, and some have not. Those who went into that surgery with an allowance saw themselves on the table. That is "Soul communication." The multi-dimensional part of them watched it all.

There is so much here to look at, and some of it is very provable with time. When the studies begin in earnest, some of these things will start opening up. Humanity is going to have to give allowance to an entirely new set of concepts about life, and one of them will be this: Multi-dimensional life is eternal, completely separated from corporeal life. Consciousness is forever, and the Soul indeed comes back over and over. Can there ever be proof of that? Yes. But many will deny it. When more and more children begin to remember their last immediate deaths and can give facts that could not be known, it will start to be studied by those who are mainstream. More and more children will tell their stories, and you will know that a new chapter in spiritual awareness has begun on the planet. Many will deny what the findings show, for it won't fit their truth.

When the Earth starts to look at that, it will begin to turn the corner of all spiritual belief. How far away is that? Far, far away. Don't worry about it, dear ones, for you'll be there. Don't put a time limit on it. When it happens, you're going to be there. The next time you awaken in this [future] life, at many levels you're going to remember who you are. It will be, in a way, much grander than you did this time. It won't happen later in your life. Instead, it will happen when you are a child. You might be some of these example children!

Blocks and Filters to Soul Communication

Let me talk about blocks and filters. The main block to allowance, to you feeling these multi-dimensional things or believing them, is *tradition*. We use this word to mean, "what you've been taught." What you have been taught holds an energy over you that you don't really see as all that powerful, but it is. Changing the way you believe requires you to rethink something that has been sacred or precious to you because someone or some organization that you trusted taught it to you. Perhaps it was your parents, or your school, or others who you love, admire, and adore? Truth is the cognizing of concepts that you are taught. When that happens, your consciousness "owns them," and anything other than that truth is not seen by you as real. It's a commitment that you make, and it puts you in a box that you don't even know you are in.

How does a Human get through that incredible block? How can you change tradition? The answer is that you must suspend that which you have been taught and give allowance for something different. This is so difficult that some never get through it. They cannot, and it remains what we have called a permanent block. Professionals tend to have strong blocks, for they had the longest education to get them to where they are now. For them to allow information that challenges what they learned is difficult, if not impossible, for their reality, for it would create chaos in their intellectual survival.

Filter: Sometimes, Lightworkers can *allow* some information to become their truth, but not all of it. Let us say, for instance, that what you have been taught fights with one or two aspects of the esoteric system that Kryon teaches. You are open to some, but not to others. Is this a problem? No. Again, you have free choice to "clean the window" of your Soul to see whatever part you need to. Your Human psyche is compartmentalized in linear ways, so you may be wide open to one kind of thing, and yet with another, you're still undecided. That is called a filter, and we understand that the revelation of truth is an ongoing process for humans.

A filter keeps you from seeing the whole picture, but gives allowance for other things that are accurate. So you might say it skews what you do and how you do it. This is best observed in healers, psychics and channellers, who are mixing old energies with new ones.

Let's take a channeller, for instance. [Kryon smile] He may sit before you and he will feel that he has good and real information. However, his track record clearly shows that he is better in certain areas than others. He will give you predictions about the future, but then they won't happen. He will give you a time and date, and nothing happens. So what would you think about a channeller like that? You would think, *"Well, maybe he really isn't channelling?"* There are many like this who really are channelling, but who are still "cleaning the window" of how to interpret what they *see*.

They have a filter, and the filter might be that they have been taught that the future is going to be filled with doom. So that's what they *look* for when they are in a channelled state. It's hard for them to shake this, and they will indeed be channelling, but in the process they will go out and look at the potentials of what is going to happen on this planet and in the "soup of possibilities," and instead of seeing the strongest ones, they report the most dramatic ones – even if those are very remote potentials. You see? Their filter attracts them to the negative, no matter what.

For 25 years, I have been telling you, through my partner, that the strongest potentials for your planet are that you are slowly cleaning things up. The new energy is upon you, and you are headed towards a peaceful planet. I told you that there would be no problems at the millennium shift, and there were none. I told you that the Cold War would end, and it did. Against all odds and ancient prophecy, back in 1989, I told you that you would turn the corner, and you did. This remains the strongest potential of your future. Now I'm telling you that the old energy will fight back, and it is [look at your news]. It wants to pull you backwards, so it will remain in charge. But it can't.

Peace on Earth and higher overall consciousness remains the strongest potential, and that's why I'm here, dear ones. I hope you get that clear. But it doesn't mean there are no other potentials. There are some potentials that probably will not happen in a million years. They are also old potentials, but they're still "out there" and the channeller will see them through a dark filter and never see the bigger picture. Their filter is that doom is coming, so no matter what, they will come back and give you that message. That's a filter.

Another filter: What if I ask you a personal question right now? I know you, so I'm going to ask: "Do you believe this is real? Do you believe this channelling is the real thing?"

"Yes, I do," you say.

"Dear ones, do you believe you have an Akash that has multiple past lives represented within it and that you are an Old Soul?"

"Yes, I do."

That's good! You are doing well, and you're giving allowances, are you not? You're starting Soul communication. "Dear ones, are you ready to go to the next level?"

"Yes, I am."

Indeed! So then you proceed, and the first thing that starts to happen is that your pineal ramps up to give you intuitive thought.

You begin to have good communication but suddenly it stops. The filter is there.

The filter: You don't deserve this gift of communication. You are unworthy.

Why is it that humanity will look at a master's life and instead of listening to what the master taught them, they will decide that in order to worship and honor that master, they have to emulate the suffering that the master went through? That's a filter! Do you see it? So instead of absorbing the message, you absorb that you are unworthy, since you didn't go through what the master did.

Therefore - ready? - in order to receive the love of God or claim the divinity inside, you must suffer. That's a filter. This is not judgment, dear ones, it is simply revealing the way humans have made decisions in an older energy that did not have allowance. Humanity looks at certain things without the structure or the knowledge or the wisdom of what it really means. This filter, therefore, biases everything you do spiritually and pulls it to what you were taught. Do you know how many New Age processes are based on unworthiness? Many. Perhaps it's time to rethink some things and instead, start with this: You are magnificent! So get on with creating magnificent Soul communication. You deserve it!

Start over. Ask yourself, am I loved? Then let us take your hand and go from there. Feel the chills within the answer to that question, if you are really asking it with pure intent. Let's go to spiritual kindergarten and start from there, dear Old Soul, so the blocks and filters will start to disappear and the intellect will get out of the way.

In order to give you the message you hear today, my partner had to learn to cast off his filters, and they were strong. His filters told him, *"This is not the way it could possibly be. Scientifically, it doesn't make sense, and in 3D things don't work this way."* He said to himself in the early days, *"Lee, you're pretending to channel. You are making it up; it can't be happening."* Then his filters were slowly overpowered by the truth he saw. The biggest one - his lack of self-worth. My partner said, *"If I open my mouth, I'm going to make a fool of myself."* Well, he did! Then he got over it and it got better. Then he *allowed* us to come in and it got even better. You know how we got to him? We got to him through his heart, not his intellect. Then, and only then, he had to weigh the difference between his head and his heart and his heart won.

Dear ones, that is our invitation to you, now that you know the rules. We're here all the time. How much do you believe it? We are ready to help you in all things. How much do you believe it?

Now you know the blocks; it's tradition, past teaching and old energy thought. There is no judgment to what you *didn't* know, based upon an old energy that never let you know it. How can we ever be in judgment of any Human Being? How can we ever blame you for not seeing light when you were confined to a dark room? This is not a message where we are telling you that you were wrong and now you are right. This is a message to say that you were in the dark and now the light is being turned on! This is a message that says, it's time to start over in what you think you know, based on seeing new things that you didn't know were there!

Old Soul, you carry light. You may have to start over in what you think is truth. Healer, are you hearing this? I know who is here. So you want to know why things are not working as well? I know who's here reading this! It's because the old energy had you doing things that simply don't work now. Oh, you can continue it, but you are so powerful, and we want you to have results! Double it! Triple it! Your potential to help humanity is awesome!

Facilitator, listen to this and don't misinterpret it. You don't have to be poor to know God. Are you alright with that? You can earn a living and stand tall and say, *"I'm a healer; I'm a reader,"* and you can deserve to have an energy exchange. It can be barter or legal tender for your services, and it's appropriate. Who told you you couldn't? The answer: Tradition. If it's spiritual, it's supposed to be free. Have you heard that? If you offer a service, you can earn a living from it, and it won't violate any spiritual *rules*.

Let some spiritual common sense prevail. There are ways to balance the equation where you give away things that are not proprietary and charge for those that are. I told my partner years ago: Let the messages of Kryon be free! Let this energy be free. You are hearing and reading this for free, dear ones. That was the result. I told him it was appropriate for him to earn a living from the things he did as Lee, the Human. His teaching and his physical products were from his tools and his talent, but the messages of Kryon should be free to all. Do you see the integrity of this? Do you see the balance in this?

You don't have to suffer and you don't have to be poor. You can stand tall, Old Soul. It's time to be balanced with these things. Let others see the divine balance in you. Start to see and eliminate the blocks and filters that stand in the way of your magnificence. When you take the hand of Spirit, your Higher-Self starts to talk to you. When that happens, it is going to give you information that will help extend your life and your health. Dear ones, you won't have to worry about survival in an old energy if you stop the blocks and open the filters.

That's the message of today, but it's also the message of yesterday and tomorrow. There are so many of you and so many new to this work, and you need to hear it many times. Now, again, I know who's here, I know who listens, who reads and who watches. I know the stubbornness of the Human brain, so I'll say this to you, *"If not this lifetime, then the next. We're very patient and so is the Earth."*

There may be challenges along the way, dear ones, and there will be those of you who say, *"Civilization is going backwards."* I want you to use common sense. When you recalibrate an entire Earth and include the recalibration of Human consciousness, there will be a lot of those who go into frustration. There will be challenge. The old ways don't work anymore. You're going to see splits in everything, even the new age. I've told you that. This message will not sit well with those who are invested in old teaching and tradition. But it will be seen as a revelation to those who will *allow* it.

Refresh your truth!

Kryon live channelling "Soul Communication – Part II"
given in San Antonio, Texas – February 23, 2014

Questions for Kryon:

I understand that the best question to ask is "Dear Spirit, please tell me what I need to know," and then listen for the answers. How can we get better at listening? How can we improve the flow of communication?

Answer:

You have just asked a main question here: "How can I work with the new paradigm of humanism?"

The old paradigm has the Human Being existing the best they can, and working the puzzle through logic, prayer, meditation, and common sense. This would seem to be the ideal ... unless you knew what was coming. The truth is that the way the "New Human" will operate is to drop logic, pray and meditate differently, and learn to trust that illusive thing called *intuition*.

The New Human will stop the logic of *thinking things through*, will trust first intuitive thought, and "listen" to the Innate of the body, which will help create synchronicity. It's a far, far, different attitude, and one that requires far more courage.

Humans simply are not used to walking into the unknown. They wish to scope out everything first, and go prepared. But the new way depends on "Knowing" that you are cared for, and trusting the unseen. This is the whole meaning behind *"Dear Spirit, tell me what it is I need to know."*

Think of it as a two-pronged statement. (1) You are letting go of your own logic and puzzles. (2) You are clearing your mind to solutions and direction that will be coming less clearly (at first), and often in many pieces instead of all at once. The most frustrating thing for a Human to work and plan with, is incomplete information. Yet, reality is that way: It unfolds slowly around you as a multi-dimensional puzzle, as many make their free choices and

change the puzzle. Doesn't it make sense? Reality isn't a printed map.

As you metaphorically race toward the river, you have no idea where the new "multi-dimensional" bridge will be. In the new reality, the bridge is invisible until the last moment, and keeps changing its position on the river. It could be to the left or to the right, and keeps moving, as those around it change.

Still, you race toward it, knowing that if you make the wrong turn, you will have a problem. Most humans want to stop and consult a 3D map to see where the bridge is ... pre-planning, and attention to general preparation is a staple of good mature thinking. Faster! ... those around you think you gone mad and are illogical!

As you round the corner approaching the river, the bridge is still on the move, changing every minute or so as the reality around it moves. Suddenly there is a flash of intuition that says, "The Bridge is to the right." You steer there, and move right to it, as it reveals itself to you. You cross it just in time to see it behind you ... moving yet again.

Blessed is the Human who realized what this all means. You can no longer plan ahead. If you are joining the ranks of those who wish to be in the new energy and "closer to the Creative Source," you must *be in the moment.* Plan what you need to, and be ready to change it all, if asked. Then breathe and relax through it all, in the arms of the Creator.

Our bias in singularity means that we tend to think of our Soul separately to our Higher-Self, our Akash and our Innate. They each have different roles, but all work together. There are numerous channellers on the planet giving messages from different entities, yet they also all work together. What is the process used for the number of humans chosen to deliver the messages and will the birth of a new consciousness see new entities delivering messages?

First, let's start a new idea. Kryon and others are not "entities." Just like the Human likes to separate and compartmentalize things, they do the same for Spirit. We are in the "soup of God," and it's impossible for us to split apart into pieces called "entities." But the Human doesn't know anything different. So, "Who are you?" is asked, no matter what. Humans see anything with a personality as separate, just as they are.

Let me ask you: When you think of Gaia, or "Mother Nature," how many "Mother Natures" are there? Most would answer that there is just one, yet it presents itself in many forms. Why are we different? The answer is that we are not. It just seems that way.

Angels, entities, and what you call "master guides" are all from the same source, and are actually one personality with many sides. What makes us seem different to you is that every one of us is channelled by a Human. So it's the Human who personalizes the energy from our side of the veil.

So why then, do we have different names? And why then do we announce ourselves with these names? The reason is that we announce our purpose, or our specialty of benevolence – not our personalities or identities. (*Kryon of Magnetic Service* is a full description of purpose, not a name.) But humans actually want personalities, like having personal friends. So we cooperate with this, to make it comfortable for all.

The ones "chosen" to give the messages are the ones who agreed to it. Simple. When you look at the grand picture, there is no life and death and life and death. It's just a normal process of single Souls transitioning through rejuvenation, and a system of refreshing biology. In that process, there is much happening on this side of the veil, which is beautiful and loving.

The man who is channelling this now, understands that he asked for it, and he had the years behind him as an Old Soul, and also the planetary experience in other areas. He awoke early to spiritual thinking, but not channelling. But his common sense and experience eventually led him to this task, which he knew of before he was born. He also now recognizes how pure this has to be in this post-2012 energy. Many humans who channel, do not see the service they give, and instead, they mix their Human personality with the information to make it seem more attractive to other humans. There is no issue with this, and no judgment. However, the information may not coordinate with others of purer heart, and will appear simpler, and driven more by the biases of the individual channeller's true purpose.

This entire process of channelling will leave soon. For instance, my partner's next life will have no channelling in it. Instead, he will help lead a new government by intuition alone, and his wisdom and ideas will be seen as profound. It's "the new channelling," and will be seen by others through the results of his action, and not through information passed in trance. He will simply have it happen through the new process of "Dear Spirit, tell me what I need to know." It will come in a stream of consciousness, like it will for so many others. He will have a group around him who has the same.

Sometimes humans meeting each other for the first time feel an instant connection, suggesting a profound or immediate past life together. Other times humans have an irrational dislike for someone, no matter how hard they try to overcome it, again suggesting a profound or immediate past life together. Then there are times when humans interact with someone that may have been their mother/father/sister/brother in a past life, yet they never feel the connection. What accounts for these differences? Are there filters in place as part of the set-up we create for ourselves during the planning process done on the other side of the veil?

This is almost entirely driven by planetary experience and time. The things you speak of are attributes of Old Souls. The newer Souls on the planet do not have this, and will not for a long time. So not everyone is aware of it, and others are very aware of it. Experience on the planet drives it.

I told you very early that the incarnation process often happens in groups. Some call it "group Karma," but that's an old name. Today, let's call it "Akashic Family." What I wish you to understand is that since this is so, we have a more concentrated grouping of Old Souls than not. It's not random, where Old Souls are mixed in with new ones. Instead, they tend to group together through family (birth) or synchronicity, which seems accidental. It's not. Indeed, they may marry newer Souls and therefore mix it up, but often the contracts do not work.

What this Old Soul grouping process does, by default, is to group *newer* Souls together as well. This often makes it harder for the newer ones to exist, because the more experienced ones are often in another social group. The reason for creating this is to fast-track learning for the younger ones. Greater challenge often creates a faster wisdom factor. For instance, if you pay for your son to go to school, he may not do well. But later, if he pays for school himself, he will do much better. There is something about "self-investment" that propels learning at a faster rate.

So, very often, the less experienced will have to go through more, in order to get up to speed. This is by design and agreement. *"Is this fair?"* you ask. It's growth and learning, just like you have experienced in school. The Souls who are older and have more learning, will be the ones who receive more mature tasks. The younger ones will learn survival and will slowly know what the Old Soul knows. The system is a good one, for grouping Old Souls together is a catalyst for planetary change.

Adults did not accompany you on the playground, watching out for the bullies. They didn't stand there

and warn you about peer pressure that was obviously affecting you. NO. You had to learn it yourself.

So, dear ones, when you experience someone who you either instinctively like or don't like, this process is at work. You are sensing your Akash, and it is giving you direction that is unmistakeable. "Don't go there" ... or instead, "go there." It's your Innate, telling you what you need to know.

Chapter Six

Soul Journeying

There are numerous books available that describe the journey of Souls. Perhaps you have even read some of them? There are also many books that discuss what happens to us in the afterlife. This chapter is probably very different from anything else you have read. Even the title, "Soul Journeying," doesn't accurately convey the concepts presented by Kryon, but it's the best substitute. The reason why the title is misleading is because the Soul isn't actually journeying anywhere. It simply "is" and so what this chapter is really about is the *Human Journey to Meet the Soul.*

As mentioned in the first chapter, there is no such thing as a Human Soul. The Soul is something that belongs to the Human only because it's Human right now. The Soul is a piece of God, Spirit, the Creator, or whatever term you would like to use, and was existing before the Earth existed. It's the piece of God that is you, visiting your corporeal body right now. When you take your last breath, your Soul is still there. When you next incarnate on Earth, your Soul is there. Your Soul is not singular and does not have anything to learn. This concept is very difficult to understand.

During March 2014, Kryon delivered two very profound channelled messages on Soul Journeying in front of an Australian audience. Lee, a former audio engineer, is incredibly meticulous about recording the live Kryon channels, which he later posts on his website for free. On rare occasions, "unseen forces" will interfere and stop the recording (smile). This is what happened in Australia, but Kryon repeated the information the next weekend in New Zealand, and enhanced the original channel. Lee has said this sometimes happens when something new is being presented, so that he gets another chance to refine his understanding and improve the delivery of the message. This is what sometimes happens when we receive intuitive information. It comes in so fast that we doubt it ever occurred. The next time this happens to you, ask for the message to be repeated! Just like Lee Carroll, you may understand more the second time around (smile).

As you read the channelled messages on Soul Journeying, you will discover that Kryon has given us information that may be controversial to many. Who is right and who is wrong? To answer that question, I think it is important that we review the process of channelling, particularly in the context of an old energy compared to the new. There is nothing new or mysterious about channelling. When artists paint, composers write music, and sculptors create statues, they are channelling. The sacred scriptures of the planet, regardless of what religion, were all channelled. The definition of channelling is: the divine, inspired words (or energy) of God, as imparted to humans by humans.

In an older energy, communication to the other side of the veil was different from what it is today. There was ceremony, ritual and certain kinds of preparation, developed in order to fight the old energy, in order to survive. There were also processes, procedures and rules, in order to give alignments to the body, in order to achieve a certain balance to work with an old energy. However, that old energy is no longer here, and past traditions are no longer needed. When Lee Carroll channels Kryon, he simply sits in the chair, takes a moment to clear his mind and begins the message.

Another attribute of the old energy is that divine messages received from the other side of the veil were seen, metaphorically, through an opaque lens, sometimes distorting the view. With a new consciousness and new energy on the planet, the lens has started to become clearer, bringing with it new insights and understandings. Can you also see

how the bias of singularity would present a challenge to the concept of a multi-dimensional Soul that is not singular?

This is where your own personal discernment comes in. Does the information make spiritual common sense? What is your intuition telling you? My intuition tells me that the information from Lee Carroll and Kryon, delivered in a new energy, through a pure filter, is expanding what we know and giving us new concepts. Perhaps the answer to the question, "Who is right and who is wrong?" can be replaced with the question, "Is it possible that our previous understandings have been limited?" If so, then there isn't necessarily a wrong answer, merely one that was incomplete.

As you ponder these questions, it is a good time to ask you, what do you know about Soul journeying, walk-ins, Soul mates and Soul inheritance? My own knowledge and understanding on these topics has been limited. However, a search on the Internet revealed plenty of information about these subjects. I was fascinated to learn that a "walk-in" is an ancient concept, described in Hinduism. The traditional concept of a Soul walk-in is a person whose original Soul departed and who then received a new Soul. Does this sound linear to you? Again, this demonstrates our bias for singularity. Kryon often uses the expression "the soup of God." It also applies to our Soul. So, think about the soup of your Soul. Imagine your Soul has the flavor of chicken soup. When your chicken soup Soul encounters a walk-in from a coconut milk soup Soul, you essentially become a chicken coconut milk soup Soul! The Souls blend together because they are from the same source (but different flavoring, such as what comes from your Akash). Sound confusing? Perhaps Kryon can unravel the puzzle in a way you can understand:

Some of the teachings in the new energy are an expansive consciousness, where you are seeing more of who you really are. In that expansive consciousness, it's not just about discovery of a new biology or new inventions, but rather, it's a realization of the *who*, when it comes to *who* is in you. The Creator is imbued in every molecule of DNA. It's there in a way you cannot itemize and you cannot count. So, dear ones, neither can you count Souls on the planet, because they are not singular or ready to be counted.

The *soup* of energy, which is God, becomes your *Soul*, and this is the hard part. Before I'm done today, if you think this is confusing, just wait. What I have to reveal is not something that you can cognize easily, and it's not something that you are really ready to fully understand. But I want to tell you that even within your confusion, I want you to see the grandness of what is here.

The grandest thing is that you are a part of the Creative Source. When the restraints of humanism are lifted from you, dear Human Being, the God within begins to show. You're not a part of God, you *are* God! This is because the soup of God does not compartmentalize itself and slip into Human bodies with names and personalities – and that is what I want to tell you about.

Souls Are Not Singular

This is controversial to your intellect! The Souls that you claim as "yours" are not singular, but rather, they are part of the whole. That's easy to say, but hard to grasp. When you look at another Human Being and you say, "Namaste," you are honoring the God in you, greeting the God in them. Did you ever think they might represent the same Soul? Are they the same God? Then they have to be the same Soul! But you don't think that way. You have your Soul and they have theirs. That's what you think, and it's the best you can do, because if you combine them together, there are logic problems with your linear mind.

The mind that is linear sees your Soul as yours alone, and this itself will keep you from understanding this message. What I'm going to tell you is that, when you cross your own *bridge of understanding*, you'll see that it amplifies perspective. It does not subtract from the magnificence of your Soul in any way.

There's no such thing as a singular Soul, for it is always connected to the whole. The soup of God is always in a soup. You might call it a *collective* if you wish, for it does not separate itself from the whole. The pieces and parts of it, if you wish to call it that, inhabit Human consciousness and you identify these parts as your own, but they are greater than that. My partner's teaching this year will be about the nine attributes of the Human Being. Three of those attributes are from the *Soul group*, and he talks

about the *core*. The core is what you feel when you get into a deep meditative state. You touch the core and you think it's you. Well, it isn't! It's everyone! That's why it feels so magnificent. I don't want you to think this is a foreign entity inside you, either. It is *you*, but the bigger you. You are God.

The Soul Is Not Limited to Humans – and It Isn't "Learning"

I'm going to break some paradigms that you've been taught. The Human Soul, as you call it, does not belong to humans. It's part of creation in all parts of the Universe. Therefore, other spiritual biological entities also have Souls just like yours. Not all intelligent life in your galaxy have Souls, only the ones "seeded" from a spiritual source. We will leave this for another time. Just understand that the very nomenclature "Human Soul" is incorrect.

There is no such thing as a Soul in a "learning capacity." Souls don't learn. Humans do. Yet you are told that Souls come and go in order to learn something. You are told that some are wiser than others. My partner uses the words *Old Soul*, which may be confusing. You're all old, it's just that some of you have been humans longer than others. The actual term *Old Soul* doesn't even make sense, because there's no *time* for a Soul. Souls always were and always will be a part of God. So really, *Old Soul* is not a correct label, but humans will continue to use it, because it means something different when you are in a 3D reality. It's a descriptive of a Human who has lived many, many lives.

Listen, there's no such thing as Souls who are in a learning capacity in order to be better Souls. They are not eventually going someplace else where they might be *graduate Souls*. This is all in the bias of the mind of the Human Being who is attached to Human reality. Humans learn; humans graduate; a Human moves from one level to another. Souls do not, dear ones. You simply have placed your reality onto another system, not understanding that it's not like you. So get used to this, and other things about Souls. A Soul does not have a Human reality. A Soul has God reality.

What if I told you that your Soul is identical in its magnificence to every Soul on this planet? Get ready: Who is the worst

Human Being you can think of? In history, alive now, dead – who is the worst one? Guess what? He or she has the same Soul you do – a perfect piece of God that allows discovery or not. That tells you a great deal about free choice. It tells you that this specific magnificent piece of God is available, at full strength, to any Human who wishes to look.

We gave you a channel once before that explained what the *rules* were of Spirit. The main one was that we cannot interfere with free choice. We can watch you make mistakes, watch you turn your back on the magnificence inside you, but we can't interfere or even give you signals. We can watch you develop evil and nurture it. We can watch you kill and do horrendous things, sometimes even in the name of God, and we can't do anything. It has to be you who makes the choice. Those who have been Human longer on this planet make far better choices. They are aware of the God inside at some level. That's just one attribute that I want to demystify. There is no "level" of learning with Souls.

There Are No Soul Levels or Advancement

This one is similar to the last one: There is no advancement of Souls from one level to the next. There is an idea that Human Beings have that a Soul might start as an animal and then graduate to a Human. In this thinking, somehow the Soul goes through certain incarnations where it is a lesser Human Being or perhaps an animal in order to graduate to a wise, Old Soul. This is simply not the way of it.

Again, dear ones, Human reality, logic and your basic Human nature create levels of advancement for yourselves. Then you place this system upon God and then even teach these things. Did you know that this diminishes the Creative Source? *"Kryon, do you mean that animals don't have Souls?"* I didn't say that. Animals have a different kind of what you might call a Soul, and yes, certain ones reincarnate. We have told you that before. But listen: The system never crosses the barrier of animal to Human – ever.

The energy of the Creator that you carry is precious and it's sacred. It only belongs to entities in this galaxy who have been seeded for spirituality and are given the free choice to expand to an ascended state. That is what is inside you, Human Being, and it's not in a dolphin, a dog or a horse. It belongs to your spiritual Human DNA, and it's part of a grand plan. It didn't start as an animal. There are those who actually believe the lower the animal, the lower the Soul. There is the thought that you start as a hamster and become a dolphin someday and eventually a Human. By the way, this is still taught in certain places on Earth. I want to tell you that's not the way of it at all, and it is simply humanism carried into a mythological state and does not honor who you are or what is inside you.

So there is no learning, there are no levels of advancement, and there's no hierarchy. *"Wait a minute, Kryon, what about archangels and lesser angels?"* We've given that discussion before. All of the categorizing of Spirit is your own Human organization. It's where you put them in *your* importance and what *you* name them. That is a Human attribute, dear ones, and it is not God. There's no management system or flow charts with God. There's no hierarchy of who is in charge of whom with God. Instead, it is a system that is known by all who are on my side of the veil. It is beautiful, sacred and perfect. There is a "oneness" here.

There are scientists who have looked out into the Universe and are starting to realize it could not have happened by accident. Humans are taught that things happen randomly and that this leads to evolution. Some scientists are now struggling with what they see, because it is outside of the reality of the evolution of life being chance. The odds are staggering that it was a benevolent system of design.

It's true: Your galaxy was designed this way. It was created for life and postured in a way that allows for what is happening in this moment - allowing you to sit on this Earth and hear these words. It's all about you and free choice to find the God part, the Soul within you. It really is. Everything revolves around the Human Being on this planet and many of the animals know it at some level. However, getting *you* to realize it has been slow. So right now, the task is to better understand the spiritual system that supports you.

It's Not You Against the World

You are not *bucking the system* when you go outside and you look at the things that you don't think you can control. Things happen to you; sometimes the weather seems to be your enemy, and sometimes you're just bounced around from place to place. Many feel it's *you against everything around you*. Is this how you feel? Did you know that all of these things are invitations for you to change? Perhaps you know humans who have had very unfortunate lives? Everything bad has happened to them at every single juncture! Dear Human Being, that particular Human has actually had a grand opportunity to be brought to zero and to take the hand of God, perhaps over and over! But instead, they took the role of victim and eventually they claimed it! That's who they are, and so it will continue happening. With free choice, many have turned their backs on the idea they might be able to control their lives better, and this kind of decision often creates more randomness of events and no control over life. That's a path they willingly have taken. Some will wallow in the grief of life and some will take the hand of God and move forward.

These are the decision points that we give to humanity over and over. Dear ones, learning is not always through grief! Do you understand? Sometimes we get your attention through joy and celebration. It depends upon who you are, what you believe, and what might get your attention. Did you know that "random" things are only the beginning blueprint of your reality? Did you know that "average" is only a state of reality that exists if no other energy is involved in changing it? I want you to think about that one – and perhaps we will teach more about that later.

Your Soul is forever. It's unchangeable. It's perfect and beautiful. What do you call it? *Higher-Self*? That's a good name. That is the *self* that vibrates higher than you do – a part of God. But you still want this *self* to have your name on it, don't you? Did you know that the Soul has no personality? There are no attributes of humanism at all in the Soul. Oh, if I could only give you the big picture! I would love you to see it! There is a perfection of the Universe that you share with every other Human Being on the planet. It's inside, ready to be developed. Do you know what enhanced Human consciousness really is? It's building the bridge to connectivity with the Soul. It's when you start to understand that, really, you're all the same.

Will Religion on the Planet Survive the New Energy?

We have spoken in the past about the evolution of spiritual systems [religion] on the planet. We have discussed what to expect, and we have told you to look at how organized religion will shift. In fact, it's already happening - a very slow understanding that your systems simply reflect the concept of branches of the same tree, and they are not opposed to each other, but simply different. We describe it again, for it shows how the collective Soul plays a part in awareness.

The question has arisen, *"Will religion survive?"* and the answer is yes. We told you before, that it doesn't matter how humans find God. It really doesn't matter! There will be many levels of Human awareness represented by many ways to worship and grow. Cultures don't need to meld into one group to become enlightened. It's important that all of the various processes remain, so that Human Beings just starting out can go through whatever spiritual processes they wish and have enough time to honor their own timing of learning. The search for God is unique to each Human Being.

So what about organized religion? How is it going to change? It's going to start seeing connectivity, and this is what we teach. When the religions of this planet join together in dialogue and they eventually realize they are unique, but have much the same compassionate purpose, they will relax. When they see it's fine to worship the way they wish, yet at the same time, acknowledge the others' right to worship the way they wish, wisdom will expand. You will see an expansion of this planet's spiritual awareness, with increased knowledge and understanding and compassion. But as long as they separate into groups, where each one claims to be "right" and they don't talk to each other, there can be no growth. But you knew that, didn't you?

Religion is not going to diminish or go away. In fact, it's going to get bigger! Look for better understanding between belief systems. When you see separation and radicalism, it will look alarming to you – yet it has been there all along. In the very new energy, it will start showing itself as being lower consciousness and not of God. Change is everywhere.

Isn't it interesting that on your planet, there is a full realization of a monotheistic God? There is one God, a theme expressed by most of the humans on Earth. Most of the Earth also believes there is an afterlife [something beyond death]. Yet you segment yourself into thousands of "doctrinal pieces," deciding who gets to worship the *one God* in the correct fashion. Those who do not somehow will be left behind. This attitude is what will change. It's about connectivity and compassion for another's process.

Walk-ins/Soul Sharing

Now, what I'm about to give you will challenge your perception of connectivity to the max. We bring up the subject of Soul sharing. You're not going to like this, dear ones, because it breaks the paradigm of your traditional thought.

We'll start simple, then we'll get complex. Soul sharing: Have you heard of a walk-in? Many have. Let's speak about what it is, what you think it is, what you're taught it is, and then the problems of logic and singularity that exist because of it. Here is what you're often told: A Human Being will pass in death and then come back. But in order to come back quickly and skip over an often seven- to 15-year growing-up period, they become "walk-ins." In order to accomplish spiritual things quicker, they will *Soul share* by agreement, and will "pop in" to another existing Human's life at the approximate age of eight to 13. That's a walk-in as you see it. So now, supposedly, you have two Souls in one body. Follow me so far?

Now, the walk-in has an attribute that you have to ask about. *"What happens to the first Soul? Does it take a subservient position? If the first Human's name is Sally and the second Soul comes in and that used to be Henry, how does that work?"* It's confusing. *"What does Henry think about it, being in another gender with Sally? Can they exist together? Does one take a back seat? Does one go forward? Does one simply give up and go back? What is the process of this?"*

Human Beings who are esoteric wring their hands and have discussions where they argue and say, *"How can this be, and what do we make of it?"* And we sit by and we look at it and we say to you, what are you talking about? What is the issue?

You have a 3D argument going on, and all of the machinations of your logic reveal your singular bias. Henry and Sally are just fine with it all! You see, what you don't know, and what you haven't figured out yet, is that there are not two Souls in that body! There is only one, and it's called God. The Henry and the Sally separation is only what you made out of it. One Soul joining another and Soul sharing is like God with God. It's you with you. You just got bigger. One soup joined another, and now there is a larger soup.

There will be arguments like, *"Well, what attributes of the Akash belong to Sally and what attributes of the Akash belong to Henry?"* What if I told you they combined them? What if I told you things just got bigger with the walk-in? Would that be alright? What if I told you that the whole purpose of the walk-in is the combined Akash? This is so the experiences of many lifetimes can combine to another Human Being as one. Now that's confusing, since you want them to only be one. You see, it's bigger than you think.

There are no puzzles to figure out with the majesty of God. Walk-ins are very common, especially with an Old Soul passing and coming back quickly into one who has already grown biologically. It is a system of benevolence and a fast-tracking system that allows things to happen better than they would have otherwise, and also take less time. Now, that was easy. But these explanations are going to get more confusing if you're confused already.

Soul Mates/Soul Sharing

The next subject is Soul mates. It's not always what you think. Here is an example: One person meets another person and they have a connection. It doesn't matter if it's outside of romance, although that's there, too, to really confuse things. It may be from a past life as a brother, sister, mother or dad, but they *know* each other. They think like one person. They can have conversations just looking in each other's eyes and they are amazed. They must have spent lifetimes together in order to have this similarity of thought and thinking of ideas and passions. There's an attraction to be with that person, to just stay with that person, because they represent something that is so special - and you call it *Soul mate*.

What if I told you that you just met a portion of yourself? I told you, dear ones, it gets spooky. What if Soul sharing is simply an attribute where you meet a piece of yourself in another Human Being? This is where many will put this information down, walk out of the room, and say, *"This is not for me. This can't be for me."* Dear Human, I want you to use your discernment right now and spiritual logic. If God is not singular and you are a piece of the whole, and everybody is in you and you are in everybody, then why is this so spooky? When you see a piece of yourself in another Human Being, why should that be so unusual? It's simply part of the way Soul sharing works. Instead of seeing God in that person, you're seeing *you* in them! That's how it feels, doesn't it? Perhaps you have been together as a walk-in during the past, sharing one Human body? Now you are in two bodies again. That's what a Soul mate is. No wonder you're attracted to them and they're attracted to you!

Soul sharing cannot be explained satisfactorily to any single-digit dimensional Human Being, and everything that I'm doing now will simply complicate it by a huge factor.

Reincarnation/Soul Sharing

Let me tell you the most complicated one, and then I want to give you an example. I have told you that there is a system of reincarnation that honors the family and that at the very least, the system has one generation skipped for reincarnation within a family. Most of the time it's two generations, but often it's every other generation. This allows for new Souls coming in to learn and for Old Souls to be their children and their parents. It mixes it up and it's helpful for both. For instance, Old Soul, your children are probably not Old Souls, but your grandchildren are (or will be). Skipping every other generation, or two generations, is the most common. It's very common to see your parents in the eyes of these children.

Some of you know what I mean, for in general, you say that you know your children best, but when your grandchildren came in, you saw something in them that you recognized as unusual. Now, I want to make this very clear, yet I cannot easily. All this talk about reincarnation and skipping generations is very understandable to you and it's fine, as long as the grandparents are gone. But if they're still alive, there's a problem. How can your living parents be your grandchildren if they are still alive? What do you think of that? You look in the eyes of the kids and you know who they are, but they can't be! Or can they?

The answer is that they can be and it's Soul sharing. It's not complicated if your parents have passed, but very complicated if they are still around. Do you understand this is a Human linearity puzzle? It's not a puzzle for God. Have you heard that in quantum physics, light can be in two places at the same time? Welcome to a new reality! It's not that complicated when you take it out of your 3D box.

There is more, and I'll talk about inheritance that is different between Akashic and chemical tomorrow. We are really going to mix it all up. So now that I have put a stick into what you have been told and stirred it up, who are you? Is it possible, the more you get to know each other, the more you see the same God in all of you? The connectivity is what solves the problems of Human variety - of you not getting along for centuries.

There will come a day, dear ones, if you follow the same progressions as those before you on other planets have, there will come a time when you acknowledge the similar God in all humans first, and then the personality differences in you second. This is the secret to peace on Earth.

Looking at other humans and recognizing that their desires are the same as yours is a type of compassion. This eventually creates generosity, not bullying and conquering. You start to look at what you have in common and not your differences. Many will observe you and will observe your graciousness and maturity in how you live day by day. That's the only vehicle through which you have, to teach other Human Beings about God. Let them see the attributes of God in you.

The Story of Evelyn, the Everlasting Tree

Let me give you a little story and then we'll close. I want to talk about Evelyn, the everlasting tree. You know, sometimes parables don't make a lot of sense. Because they are allegories, you have to forgive some of the 3D logic and just listen. Evelyn doesn't really exist in nature, but it's a story that comes close enough to what nature does that you'll understand.

Evelyn had an essence about her as a tree. The essence of Gaia was there and she knew that she was Evelyn the tree. She had a consciousness of the grand plant that she was. Her purpose, her sole purpose, was to grow as much as she could, as tall as she could, to supply her share of oxygen to the planet for humanity.

Evelyn put down roots as trees do, and she could feel her roots go down deep. Then they would absorb the nutrients that she needed for her growth, the resources of the soil of the Earth. She grew even taller. As she grew taller, her roots spread out more and more, in order to anchor the size that she was and the majesty she represented in her forest.

Now, Evelyn wasn't really aware of the roots any more than you are aware of each Human hair. There were so many of them! But one in particular, a great distance away, found its way back to the surface and began to grow upwards. It sprouted and grew, and this sprout then became another tree. This little sprout also became aware of Gaia and started growing just like Evelyn had. It also had a name - Martha.

Evelyn is now aware of her neighboring tree, since it's now big. Evelyn is watching Martha grow up. But Martha is Evelyn's root. In fact, they are still attached! Over a period of time, Martha put down some roots and the same thing happened with her. At the same time, Evelyn had other sprouts going on the surface in the other direction. They were all Evelyn's roots, still attached to Evelyn, but sprouting as other trees with other names. You see where I'm going with this?

Eventually there became a forest and all the roots were connected, all connected. The life-force of the nutrients of the planet are surging through all of them. There is no end or beginning of any root, since they are all connected with each other and all have individual names and "tree consciousness."

Now, let's interview Evelyn. *"Evelyn, who are you? As you look around the forest, are you Evelyn or are you also Martha and George and Sally? Who are you?"* Evelyn would have to stand tall and say, *"I am all of them, and they are all of me, for our roots are combined together from the same source."*

I want you to look at this story and understand that it is a metaphor for who you are. In nature, you look at these kinds of things and say, "*How unique.*" You don't see it as you do yourselves, with individual personalities and lives to live as Human individuals. But the story of Evelyn is more true to humans than you think. Connectivity, and the realization and *oneness* of it all, is going to be the salvation of humanity. But it has to start, literally start, with you understanding that the Soul inside you is bigger than anything you ever thought.

Now, I told you a moment ago that Soul has no personality, not like you think. But it does have attributes. It has perfection, love and benevolence. That's what you feel when you are in touch with the core. The hand of the Soul, which is God, is always open to you, always. From the moment you're born, the invitation is to discover who you are, and take that hand and begin changing your reality. Move into a position where you can change the planet by living a sacred reality of awareness. You know I'm right, because you wouldn't be reading this message otherwise.

Finally, a word of advice: These decisions must be with your free choice and your intent and your full understanding. *"That's what I want to do,"* is what you hear yourself saying. Don't do anything because you *should* or because you came to a meeting and heard a channel that compelled you to do something. Don't do that. I want you to sit by yourself, alone in the chair, and ask your body, *"Is there more?"* Be honest and listen for an answer. It will shiver in response [chills] and the first thing it's going to say back to you is, *"What took you so long to ask?"* It will say, *"Yes!"* And that is the beginning of discovery.

That's really the unspoken invitation, dear ones, of every single Human Being on the planet. If you relax and talk to that which is the Innate of your body and let it help guide you to the truth, you'll get it. Don't listen to me or a Human Being to do this. I want you to start listening to *you*. Is this channelling real or is it not? Use your discretion and discernment and discern the energy of this message through the God in you.

This time has passed tonight for me to give you a message of love, coming from that Source that is within all of you. You ought to recognize a small voice, not the Human voice, but the other one that's been talking to you in the third language all this time. It has been whispering, *"Listen, listen, listen, this is what you came for."* It really is! Dear Old Soul, you are the hope of the planet. Whoever is listening to this and cognizes the truth of it will understand that this is your time. Get on with it.

Kryon live channelling "Soul Journeying – Part I"
given in Auckland, New Zealand – March 22, 2014

I'm going to continue the teaching of last night about the Soul. I only have a couple of more things to say about it, and you may have heard some of it before. My partner speaks of these things when he teaches, but I want you to hear it from me. So this becomes part two of what we call *Soul journeying*.

Now, just for clarity, the Soul isn't journeying anywhere. The theme here is about you, who are journeying to meet it. It's about your cognizing what it is. Basically, it's you journeying to meet yourself. We have named it this way for a reason. It's not linear. You have to look at it backwards in order to understand the profundity of it ...

What Is The Human Soul?

I want to continue discussion of your journey to knowledge of the Human Soul. First of all, and most controversial, it's not a *Human* Soul! We call it a *Human Soul* because we're on Earth with you and because that's what you call it. The Soul *is* the Creator. We've told you this before. Long before this Earth was even cool enough to walk on, the Soul existed. It would eventually be a part of you. It's eternal in both directions [past and future]. Think about it: Before humans existed in any form, you had a Soul. So with your 3D logic, do you understand why it can't be called a *Human* Soul? Let me take you on a journey. We ask this: Where have you been – the core you – the Soul? Who are you?

Before the Pleiadians did what they did for this planet, where were you? Did you have anything to do with what came before life on this planet? Many spiritual leaders – experts in spiritual things of your Earth – will tell you that everything started when you arrived. Really? That's funny! Let me ask you, did God arrive when humanity did or was God here already? If your Soul was part of God then, indeed, you were here during creation!

I want to give you some information that may make things bigger than anything you have been told. There have been many worlds before yours that have gone through what you're going through. The Pleiadians are the most immediately connected to you and they are your spiritual parents. They did the work, and they continue to watch over you like parents would watch a child who has total and complete free choice of action, without knowledge of their parents. There is benevolence, love and caring. There's an awakening on this planet, and you've passed the precession of the equinoxes, which was the spiritual calendar set up for this test. You're currently in an energy that I foresaw and that I told you about 23 years ago, and here we sit.

There's celebration in certain parts of the galaxy because of what is happening to planet Earth. Is that too big for you? Oh, don't look at your news today, for your struggle with old energy during the transition is not what we're talking about. I'm talking about world events, but not *world* as you would think of it in your news, but rather *world* that represents the Earth from its creation to now – a *world* representing all the things that have taken place in your history and what you've done with it. You're sitting at the precipice of massive change. You have free will, as you always have had and always will, but we've seen this before. Dear ones, we've seen this before! Here's what I want to tell you: So have you. Did you realize that?

Your Soul Has Been Everywhere!

Your Soul has been involved in other places, on other planets and in other constellations. It has experienced life that is ancient in this galaxy, dear ones, compared to yours on Earth. So old! Life can fully start and build itself structure within a few million years, when a planet is ripe and ready and begins properly and accelerates in the right way. It's not that unusual or difficult. Listen science, this is a prediction: When you eventually find any kind of life in other places that are not related to this planet, it will have the same kind of biological DNA structure as you are used to. These DNA structures are common to the galaxy, and it is how life develops. Oh, there will be some variations, but you will see a structural commonality that will give you a larger question: Is there a galactic biological system? Yes! It will tell you something: What you have on the planet is not unique. Hardly!

When you look out at the stars and ask yourself, *"Is there life?"* it's like standing on a beautiful beach on the planet and asking if there's another beach anywhere else. Just because you can't see it, doesn't mean it doesn't exist. The processes that would create multiple beaches on your planet are the same processes that would create multiple planets that would have life.

So you have been part of many of these places - not the corporeal you, but the Soul you, the part of the collective that is the Soul. This begs the question, "Who are you?" The best and most profound way to answer that is through the pineal. You can start a communication through your cellular structure that, at first, you won't feel. But this opens a door and keeps it open. Then very, very slowly, the energy seeps in and you realize you are changing in a very benevolent and sweet way. It doesn't surprise you or shock you or make you afraid. Instead, you wake up one day and you realize you are not alone. You realize that there's help, and that you're more peaceful and healthier. That's when you start realizing that it's working. So, what is the discovery? It's that your Soul isn't a Human Soul. It's the God part of you, and has been part of the development of life in this galaxy for eons. Now, that's an OLD SOUL!

Just so we don't frighten and we don't startle you, we go slowly. Humans are slow to cognize things that they haven't seen before or never imagined before, so we go slowly. There's nothing more beautiful than watching awakening Human Beings who are finding what has been missing in their lives, but which has really been there all along. We have told you that you are "eternal in both directions," meaning you always were and always will be. So, does this give you a hint as to where your Soul might have been in the past, before the Earth?

Your Seed-grandparents

You have been part of the bigger plan all along and have been a Soul of the Pleiadians as well. Does this shock you? The Pleiadians had a full million years or so of life on their worlds, as life was just beginning on Earth. They also had a planet that seeded theirs, a much older one, in another constellation in this galaxy. That makes the older group your "seed-grandparents," and their name is Arcturian. Orion was even before that! If you're working with these groups, dear ones, you already know that they are here to help – the way grandparents help. But you were there, too! You really are "star children" in the grandest sense!

Lifting the Veil Is Not Automatic

Now, I wish to let you know that in this new energy, the veil between us is lifting slightly, because you have *pulled* on it. It's from a brute force of consciousness and spiritual awakening. This is what will pull upon the veil that separates us. It doesn't get thinner by itself. It just stays there waiting for you to pull on it with your consciousness. That is the arrangement you have at the moment.

Let me put it in better terms. If you are going to awaken to who is around you and who is multi-dimensional, it is going to be on your terms, not ours. That's always the way it has been, dear ones. It is the Human who has to search if God is to be found. God is not going to present a situation to you that is going to give you positive proof of who you are or what is on the other side of the veil. This is the big puzzle for you to figure out. It has to be that way, and it's fair and honors free choice. Every single planet that has gone through this has figured it out in this fashion. So here's what I want to tell you and here's how it applies to today's teaching: You were there. You were there! Again, you are your own ancestors and you are your own seeds. Let me ask you: Do you think some of this information you carry in your Akash might someday awaken when it's needed? [Hint]

Does this galactic ancestry carry over into your Akash? Some of it does, but not as much as your experience on Earth does. Now, we're going to tell you a little more about that in a moment, but right now, I want to tell you that there are two things I wish to remind you of. We've given them before, but now we're talking about Souls in general, so it's even more profound.

Two issues need to be worked on to move into graduation. The first is this: Even though yesterday [the first channelling] we told you that you cannot place Human attributes on God and that it's a mistake to think that the Creator of the Universe has Human ways, there's still one issue that you always seem to develop on your own. It's an old energy concept that's going to have to disappear before anything happens of significance on this planet and that is the *concept of judgment*.

Judgment is a Human attribute and an old energy one at that. It's a separatist attribute coming from one Human looking at another, or one civilization looking at another, and deciding that the other one is not doing something right or is somehow interfering with the status quo. It's a survival attribute, not a balanced attribute. Judgment is everywhere, all over the planet, and it always has been. Did you ever watch your children go through their phases of maturity? One of the phases is, *"You're doing it wrong!"* Then they separate from that other "wrong" child and cling to those who are "doing it right." It's a growth issue.

Judgment creates wars and increased separation. However, when you built your religious structures, you decided that it belonged to God as well. It does not. It belongs completely to humans. But because it was so ingrained into your consciousness, you naturally assigned it to the highest power that is. You needed God to have the ability to be separatist also – separating humans

into the ones who make it and the ones who don't. God does not judge or separate pieces of itself!

The second is this: You're walking around feeling small. Why is that? Why do you humble yourself before God? Now, I just got in trouble, didn't I? You are told that being humble before God is a good thing! However, if you are a *piece of God*, why are you humbling yourself before yourself? Does this information make sense to you? It's time to use evolving *spiritual common sense*. If you are a piece of creation, you don't have to bow to yourself.

What if instead you said, *"It's time to stand up from my humbling position and take the power that's mine! I take my power with benevolence, courtesy, generosity and integrity – not humbleness."* What good is it going to do to grovel before God? How is that helping the planet? The reason I'm in trouble with this message is because the *"grovel message"* is what you've been given since day one! Remember this past message? *"God is great and you're not. Therefore, you should bow before the almighty."* But there is something wrong with this picture. The masters told you of your magnificence, not of your unworthiness! If you apply my teachings of yesterday and today, you start to realize that you are a piece of the very majesty that is God itself! The "almighty" is within you. It's in every single molecule of the trillions of DNA molecules. This represents the Higher-Self of each Human, and this Higher-Self has a very peaceful and patient consciousness, waiting for you to discover what is really there. Do you really think your Higher-Self wants to be worshipped? The answer is no.

I want you to start thinking differently about God, and about the Soul, and about what you have inside. You deserve to awaken to your magnificence. How about that statement? Also know this: Human magnificence doesn't show itself in egotism. You don't stand and beat your chest and tell everyone how good you are. No master has ever done that. Instead, you awaken to the wisdom within and the maturity of mastery. People will see it in you!

What is one of the chief attributes of mastery? Silence. You knew that. We have taught you, "Be still and know you are God." It's silence. When you are silent, there is an internal *knowing*. You're wise beyond words, because in history you've *been there and done that*. Perhaps you don't know the details, but just sit there for a moment and be quiet. Don't you feel who you are? Is this too far removed from your Human intellectual pursuit? Is this too far removed from your 3D logic to think that there was more to life than what you've been told?

Stop humanizing God. Stop creating attributes of situations that are Human and then applying them to God. How many times have you heard there are trapped Souls in some places? You are told that they may be trapped between one place and another, then humans decide what those places are. This is all *Human made*. You know this, don't you? How can the parts of the Creator of the Universe be trapped? There is no individual Soul energy. It's not in 3D and it's not singular. It's all part of the whole. It is a collective, which is part of you.

How can you have part of God trapped between some Human-created levels? You can't. It's mythology at its best, dear ones, so the next time somebody looks at whatever it is that they're looking at and says, *"That's the result of a Soul being trapped,"* I want you to know better. You don't have to correct anyone, dear ones. It's good enough that YOU know better. I want you to see the real system that exists, the one that is beautiful. Listen: With Souls, there are no Earth problems and no purgatory. All that is Human structure applied to God. There's no Soul that goes some place in preparation for something else, as we told you that yesterday. There are no levels of Soul-dom. Your Soul is part of God, and God is the Creator of this Universe. The awesome energy of God is not segmented or trapped - ever! It's beyond that, way beyond that. It represents an energy of something I can't even describe to you. But for now, all you have to know is that this energy of God loves you beyond measure and that everything that is there for you is benevolent. You don't have to jump hurdles, dear ones. You don't have to prove yourself one way or the other. Instead, let the essence of God in you become self-evident.

Soul Sharing

When you expire corporeally [in death] and move on to the next energy, the Soul is collected from your body and becomes

part of the whole again. Now, when you sense somebody who has departed and who is singular [you might know their name], it's real and very singular. *"Joe died, and I feel his presence."*

However, remember what we've told you in the past? Pieces and parts of your loved ones who have passed over become a part of you [your Soul] for life. That's *Soul sharing,* dear ones. It's important you understand how this works. If your Soul is not singular, there is room to believe that within it are complexities of existence. How can your Soul be all your past lives, too? Do you see what I'm saying? You are a magnificent system of humanity and not singular. *"Joe's body died, and the magnificent part that was bigger than the cells of Joe lives on. I sense his eternalness."* Start seeing yourself as a collection of God's best.

Worship

We say it again: If you wish to go to your knees to honor God in any way - when you pray or when you meditate - we are there. There's really only one request you should consider asking your Higher-Self. The question is, *"Dear God, tell me what I need to know."* It's the best one. Again, the reasoning is this: All of the other things that you could possibly ask are subservient to that one request. *"Tell me what it is that I need to know, dear Spirit, in order to solve the problem to get from A to B."* You know who you are. You didn't come here to suffer, dear ones. It's time to work through that concept as well. Someone needed to hear that. Suffering was not the plan. Whatever has happened is now *water under the bridge.* You have complete control over your own cellular structure and it wants to hear from you.

Soul Inheritance

I want to bring up the final one, and this one is difficult. We always save the best till last - the ones that are harder to understand and concepts that are perhaps things you haven't pondered much. You will now.

This attribute has to do with what we will call *Soul inheritance.* When you look at inheritance as you perceive it, it's mostly cellular and in three dimensions [your reality]. Inheritance of this kind is what we would call *chemical inheritance*, but the confusing part is that you, as a Human Being who is aware of your spiritual complement, are dealing with an oxymoron – two kinds of inheritance at the same time.

All this happens in one *single body*. Chemical inheritance is that which you are taught in school. It carries over with it a great deal of what your parents had and what your grandparents had [genealogy]. You look like them, have attributes in cellular structure like them, and within your DNA, there are things that pass forward to you through birth. These would be certain talents, instincts, allergies and predispositions for disease or health. Some of you can even look at your hands and you will recognize your parent's hands. That's chemical inheritance and it's powerful.

The oxymoron: The man who sits in the chair in front of you right now [Lee] has a chemical inheritance. His chemistry is Irish, and if he tracks back his lineage, he will find that it's not too many generations removed before he finds his relatives in Ireland. There, he can track his name [Carroll], which is very Irish, right back to a family who is there today. Some day he may even visit his heritage. That is his *chemical* inheritance.

However, we have exposed lately that his immediate past life was not Irish! It was *across the ditch* in Australia! [an expression used in New Zealand] Say what? How can that work? Who is he? Is he Irish or is he Australian? The answer is that he has one path that is Akashic and one path that is chemical. So, therefore, he is a combination – a unique Human Being who has an entirely different past when you look at the Akashic family compared to the chemical one. The fact is that they are both accurate. Is that confusing or what? But most of you have this identical attribute!

It doesn't have to be confusing when you look at The Parable of Evelyn the Everlasting Tree that we gave you before. I'm giving you things that mean something to those of you who were here last night. Human, you stand in the forest and you all have the same roots from one tree in the center. Do you have the lineage of who you think you are in the trees around you or the master tree? You have both.

The chemistry you have, you can track backwards chemically and you will know your 3D lineage. This is your corporeal lineage, which can easily co-exist with a different Akashic lineage. However, the most powerful lineage is the past life and is Akashic. This is the one that will give you the most difficulty and also the most reward. What is confusing is this: How can there be two paths that are so different? As a linear thinker, you want to separate them in your mind and ask, "*Which one is accurate?*" But they both are.

Look at it this way. Let's say you are a car. Your car Soul came from a lineage of cars that drive on the left-hand side of the road. That is your karmic car lineage. When you incarnate, however, you are a Ford. That doesn't change the side of the road you were used to, or the side you now have to learn to get used to. You are just doing it now as a Ford. So your chemistry is the Ford, but your Akash is what side you drive on.

Take my partner: He knows that he's part of the chemistry of his parents, his grandparents and their parents. He has the chemistry of all of them. But he also knows that the part of him that is God knows the lives he lived with other chemistry, from other parents and other grandparents. The instructions we have are these, dear ones: Don't over-analyze it! I want you to look at yourself and celebrate how this has come together to create who you are. You are a unique Human Being - absolutely unique. The corporeal complications and the puzzle are beyond anything you can imagine. I have just disentangled a puzzle that some will listen to, and they'll start to realize the puzzle has always been there. It's going to unravel in each of you some things that you didn't understand, like how an Akashic reader can take you on a whole different path than what your parents did.

Don't try to figure it out! Instead, I want you to only see the beauty of how it has created *you*. Is that good enough? That's all you have to look at. You are unique in every single way. Perhaps you've got the strength of the chemistry that you need and the Akashic lives that you need in order to build an *Old Soul* who can make a difference on this planet today? Did you think of that? Everything that you've gone through had a purpose. But now you're done *going to school* and you're done just *surviving*. Now it's time to come out of the cave, see who you are, check out the magnificence around you, and stand tall and feel the light of a benevolent God. Claim your mastery!

Simple? No. But you will always start with small steps, and they will always turn into bigger ones. So now it's time to start. That's the message of the day. It will get more complicated. I promise. [Kryon laugh]

Kryon live channelling "Soul Journeying – Part II"
given in Auckland, New Zealand – March 23, 2014

What do you think about what you just read? Is your head reeling with information? Do you now have more questions than what was just answered in the above messages? I'm guessing that yes, you have lots of questions. Me too! Lee Carroll's website has an entire page that lists various questions that have been answered by Lee or Kryon. You may also be interested in the pay-for-view series of question and answer videos that Lee has done, available from his website, *www.kryon.com*, for a reasonable fee. In the meantime, I have included four questions below from Lee's website, in addition to a few questions of my own. They relate directly to the Human Journey to meet the Soul.

Dear Kryon: Talk to me about walk-ins. I believe I am one, and if so, do I go home?

Answer: A true walk-in is a difficult thing to understand, for you have to begin to understand something else we've taught about the fact that *you* are not singular. You have many parts and pieces to your spiritual body, and sometimes they even involve a meld with another energy. On this side of the veil you're "singular." So this doesn't make sense. On the "home" side of the veil, you're multiple, which is your natural state. This involves many more dimensions than you can see or are ready to understand at the moment.

For reasons that you can't comprehend, sometimes a part of you comes into the Earth plane and grows up. Then later, usually

through some kind of traumatic experience, the other part joins *you*. Some have "seen" this as two different entities, where one kind of warms up the place for the other, then leaves. [Smile]

There are really two different kinds of walk-in experiences. One is just like I mentioned, where two actual entities are involved by agreement, and one comes in to start, then the other steps in and *takes over* when it's time. Then the original takes a back seat, melds, and becomes a part of the whole of the experience for life. This is what we've told you in the past about walk-ins. Now there's something even more to know, since you're now at a point where advanced information is possible.

The second kind of walk-in experience is where there's an "enhancement" of the first Human consciousness to such a degree that it appears that another Human arrived! Actually, it's just the other part. The reasoning is about timing, and also about life purpose. Many times, a walk-in is one who suddenly has a purpose after the experience. That's accurate, but the purpose is due to the fact that now all the parts are together, and are aware of what to do. Sometimes it's so dramatic that even the walk-in individual sees the past as another person! Sometimes they even change their names. The logistics and "rules" behind walk-ins are not list-able, since they're infinitely variable. Sometimes the other part never arrives if the timing isn't right. Sometimes it arrives so strong that it's scary!

As to the question, "Do I go home?" ... you might be misunderstanding something. A true walk-in, after the experience, *is* home! The whole reason for a walk-in experience is a time enhancement. There's no entity who "held a place" for another. Instead, it's a Human entity who may now be "multiple," who now gets to have *the rest of the story*. Any walk-in has great purpose for the Earth and is needed in its entirety (a full complement of parts, including the one that started the process at birth).

Dear Kryon: Does the walk-in theory have anything to do with dissociative identity (multiple personality) disorders?

Answer: No, it does not. Walk-ins are those who have a contract with others to share the space of what you would call a Soul, in a balanced manner that does not show itself to anyone. One of them spends the time growing up, and the other comes in quickly when it's time. This is a system which allows a very quick return of a Soul, much quicker than the process of reincarnation. Conducting a walk-in is an extremely efficient way to return to Earth, eliminating the time usually necessary to grow up when a Soul reincarnates. Normally walk-ins have a specific task or work to continue. This system is very beneficial to all of you.

Dear Kryon: Can you explain the difference between the terms Soul mate and twin flame?

Answer: These represent different energies, but similar attributes. Both indicate a partnership. A Soul mate is a partner for life. It does *not* have to be a romantic one. It can be mother and daughter, or two unrelated people who team up for whatever reason. And yes, it can also be romantic. Therefore, it is a partnership energy.

The energy of a twin flame is one that's your mirror-image energy. A twin flame is one who finds the "other half" of what it is seeking in purpose. Twin-flame energy isn't necessarily a partnership issue like a Soul mate is. It's more about coming together to fulfill a wholeness that's missing in potential or purpose.

A Soul mate might be a partnership that's good for life, but it may not result in anything else. A twin flame has purpose behind it, driving toward a goal. Let me give you real-world examples. A past leader, Ronald Regan, has a Soul mate called Nancy. But the discovers of the DNA structure, Watson and Crick, were twin flames.

Sometimes, twin flames are also together in love, but even if they are, that's convenient for the bigger picture ... something to be accomplished together. Soul mates exist together for joy and life extension. Twin flames exist together to accomplish something that neither could do alone. They also can be both! When that happens, it's really obvious.

(**From Lee:** Please see Kryon Book Six, page 333, for a similar discussion. Also, Kryon gives references to St. Germain's work regarding twin-flame energy.)

Dear Kryon: My two sisters and I are triplets. We've been told that we are one Soul in three bodies. I was under the belief that each body houses a separate Soul. I think my ego is upset that I'm not an "individual," if this is true. Can you enlighten me on this?

Answer: The most difficult thing to explain to a Human is the concept of how something singular in appearance can be many things in reality. You appear to be one Soul because you have one body. When angels are drawn in your books and paintings, even though they are multi-dimensional beings, you give them skin and wings and call them one name!

So you continue to believe in "one body, one Soul." The reality is that every Human alive is multi-dimensional and is in many places at one time. Even as you sit there reading this, parts and pieces of you are in other places doing other things. Is that, then, one Soul in many places, or many Souls? The answer is both. Your single-digit dimensionality limits your concept of how this is, since everything before your reality is singular.

So the very premise of your question can't be answered, since nobody on the face of the Earth has one Soul. A better question would be, "Do your sisters share a singular purpose with you?" The answer, as your intuition told you, is no. They may have the same astrological aspects, but each Human is a separate piece of God, multi-dimensional and, therefore, not singular. Each is a different piece of God, on Earth in lesson to be independent.

The confusing part in all of this is what you do share with your sisters. You all share a common thread of divinity that might actually look like "one Soul" to a reader (in 4D). This thread is your karmic bond, and why you all came in together the way you did. This has to do with potentials, past energies, and your current expression of lesson. But it's not the "same Soul."

Again, we liken this to a bowl of soup. It is singular in appearance, yet fluid inside. You can't ask how many soups there are in the bowl. It's different for all, but each bowl is singular. The soup is the divinity. Don't ever let the container fool you. It may be the same size and color, but the soup in each is diverse and tastes different. It's composed of many parts that make up what it is. It might be nourishing or poisonous. Only the soup can decide what vibration it will be.

Celebrate this with me! Isn't it a wonderful situation that you have? The connection to your sisters is unique to humanity. Only twins and other multiple-birth humans have it. This is why you will always be "connected" as long as you live. When one of you leaves, finally, watch what happens: You will still be connected! Multi-dimensional things are like that.

Questions for Kryon:

In a previous question, you said that walk-ins have nothing to do with those who suffer from dissociative identity (multiple personality) disorder. However, can you tell us about humans who suffer from bipolar, schizophrenia and dissociative identity disorder? Where does this imbalance come from, and as the planet starts to balance the masculine and feminine, will these cases diminish?

Answer:

The actual truth is that the disorders you have discussed will increase. The real reason these are taking place at this moment is due to the clash of old and new, within the playing field of Human transition. The duality is increasing in intensity.

Did you notice the increase of Autism? It's not the drugs or the water or the designed food, dear ones. It's simple. It's a recalibration of where the Human Being on Earth is going. In the process of all great shifts, there will be both fore-runners of the new energy, and mixtures of old and new who are not developed yet. They are either savants who regular humans can't deal with, or dysfunctional due to mixtures of energy.

Any evolution has this, and your own biologists can see it in the social structure of animals who have new,

unexpected shifts and changes in their environments. It's the same with humans in their new *energy* environment. For some, it creates confusion, and for others, it's a blessing.

These things will eventually balance so that those who suffer from these symptoms will be fewer. But they are almost entirely due to the shift of energy on the planet, so expect more of this.

Now ... something new: There is a propensity to see someone who "has this or that," or who was born with "this or that," to be labelled for life. This is now going to change. Instead of being "something for life," as the new energy becomes more common, the ones who did poorly in the old energy ... will get better! The Autistic will suddenly find themselves in a world which actually seems kinder and less disruptive. To you, they just "got better." To them, things just started to make more sense and they could finally communicate.

Bi-polar and even schizophrenia may also improve. Think of it, dear ones, as mind confusion between the old and the new. A Bi-polar Human is one living in both energies, and a schizophrenic has come in with personalities from both the past and the future ... all caused by the recalibration of the planet's energy.

Stepping out of the Human bias of singularity is difficult, especially as it relates to concepts such as Soul sharing. Using the metaphor of Evelyn the Everlasting Tree, my Soul, unique to me, is also a piece of several other humans that are alive right now. This would also mean that I have the Soul of others, like my grandmother. Each of us is, therefore, a blend of many Souls in one corporeal body. However, Akashic attributes, such as personality, fears, phobias and talents are unique for each Human. Our Akash is linked to our Soul, but if we are a blend of Souls, how does it work in terms of our life expression, our karma, and our life lessons?

Think of it this way: Your SOUL has a *universal* Akash, and your cellular structure has a *personal planetary* Akash. You are all connected at a beautiful esoteric level, where the family is first, and you share common purpose to be on Earth, and to help the galaxy. Although the "oneness" of your Soul is wonderful to think about, the personal Akash drives your planetary experience.

Evelyn, the Everlasting Tree, has the roots of many, and she is part of the many. Because of this, Evelyn has the attributes of her *type* of tree. The others do too. She will look a certain way, grow a certain way, and be nourished and reproduce a certain way. So will all her family, which she is connected to. She is indeed "one" with all of the others, and shares their attributes.

However, Evelyn may have pests that bother only her, and a river next to her that she has to deal with, since it is eroding her massive roots. She also has a man who wants to cut her down to make space for a cabin! Do you see how this is? She is "one" with the others, but separate in her own space.

It's the same with humans, only with greater purpose and a more complex interaction of energies. You are all "one" with Spirit, and sharing this via your Soul, but you are unique within free choice and your Akashic experience.

Taking the previous question further, my Soul is potentially also on Earth in several other corporeal bodies. It's incredibly challenging to think of this possibility, again because of our bias in singularity. Would this explain why I have feelings and emotions from my Akash that would suggest I was living concurrently in different places with different circumstances?

Just to be clear: Your "oneness" Soul could be shared by many, but the individual that you are is only YOU. The others also have their own individual Akashic experiences, age, and life's purpose. Yes, it's a bias to share a Soul, until you understand what that means.

Think of you sharing your "God part" with many others, who are also aware of the beautiful connection to Spirit, just like you are. Therefore, you are sharing the "energy of creative benevolence" that is your core, and the "oneness" of everything. You are NOT sharing your personality, and there is only really ONE of the unique you.

The *ocean* is Mother Nature, but so are the *mountains*. They are entirely different, yet some may gaze upon them both and say ... *"Isn't Gaia beautiful!"* People may also gaze upon a group of you and say, *"Isn't Spirit wonderful!"* It's the same. You have the same "Soul group," but you also have individual attributes for your unique lives.

Do not let this confuse you, since it is not the puzzle you think.

During a channel given at a Lemurian Sisterhood event, led by Dr. Amber Wolf, it was revealed that the Pleiadians were able to birth children without pain. However, they chose, instead, to experience the full spectrum of energy that happens during childbirth, including pain. This was because it created such a unique experience that enhanced motherhood. The cause of death in humans varies greatly. Some die peacefully in their sleep, others die slowly with great pain from a terminal illness and some others experience horrific trauma and terrible violence. Will this variation and attribute change as our planet ascends? What was it like for the Pleiadians?

The evolution of the Human Being will eventually create great wisdom. It will be greater even than the wisdom of the masters. You will not evolve biologically only, for this new energy will create DNA efficiency that is mainly seen in how you act and think, rather than the way you physically change.

As life progresses and evolves, you will have far greater control over your own cells. Those who wish to pass quickly can "will" themselves to go in peace. Greater healing will be possible, and your Innate will be your friend. You will "know" what is happening inside, and be able to work with it.

The Pleiadians eventually had control of physics with their mind. This is no different than some of the masters of Earth showed you. It's not magic, but common-sense-evolution. With that came common-sense-wisdom, and the thing you spoke of regarding birth. However, let me complete this circle of knowledge for you:

When DNA is working at greater than 80 percent, you live a very long time. So long can you live, that many never think about death. Death comes when it comes, but sometimes greater than 1000 of your years. The basic reason for this is that the cellular rejuvenation system works far better than it does for you right now. A body that rejuvenates at 80 percent will have an immense life span. Some will be able to actually put themselves in a non-corporeal state, knowing they can't reverse this, in order to live indefinitely. It's a very different culture indeed, when you stop the need for the reincarnation process, and where all of you are Old Souls, and some can void death itself.

So put yourself in this unique place if you can. There is no need for birth, and no survival chemistry for the race to have children. Children are still born, of course, but not near as many. The race needs to replenish the bloodline, when indeed some pass on. Long ago they created less than zero population growth through their collective wisdom. There are no "rules" of who can have children, and no "rules" of how many. Instead, the collective wisdom of the many, know what to do intuitively. There is no chemical birth control. The women "will" their cells to produce the fertile eggs only when they want children. The evolved body has control over itself, and complete Innate communication. Note: It's the women who choose how the population will grow or not.

Children are born naturally, in order to honor the natural process. The pain of birth is seen as a badge of honor, and is desired and celebrated. It is also only available for the women to do, and the men celebrate something they can't do, even if they wanted to. It's hard to describe the difference between the way it is with you, and the way it is with a totally evolved race.

Wisdom is like that. Looking at an evolved wisdom from a place that doesn't have it, is often like looking at the ocean. Past the barrier of the surface, there are tremendous processes, an awesome abundance of life, systems that you don't know about, and a depth that is not measurable by your sight. Yet, it seems to be just a calm water surface ... and you can't see what you can't see.

IN CLOSING

Thank you for taking this journey with me to unravel the mysteries from beyond about our Soul. I hope that your perception has altered and that you are aware of your eternal existence. As I was contemplating how I would summarize all of the information about our Soul, I received a phone call from Lee. He was preparing for the last meeting of 2014 in San Rafael, California, and wanted to know if there was anything that Kryon might help with for the book! "Are you kidding?" I said. He assured me he wasn't, and immediately I expressed that I would dearly love Kryon to tell us how all the nine attributes of the Human Being, Soul Communication and Soul Journeying fit in together. I think you will be delighted with the elegance and beauty of what Kryon said in closing to this book:

Let us review what we have said about the Human Soul: The Soul is not part of that which is corporeal, yet it resides in you at a corporeal level. So, it's not chemistry; it's not synapse (brain created); and it's not intuition. It's none of the things that you've studied. It is something you can't understand yet, since it doesn't fit into any box you have created for yourself within your 3D science. It's a piece of the Creator – the Creative Source, which is responsible for "all that is."

Long ago, the Creative Source built a beautiful benevolent system, and it needed a Universe in order to accomplish it. Now you have galaxies and planets, and life. All of those were put together over time, accomplished properly, and not accidentally.

The Creative Source that built the planet still surrounds you. The galaxy that you are within is inside you too, in certain ways, and it hides. It hides because it's part of the test on the planet for you to discover, with free choice, what is there. To make it hide even more, there's only a certain percentage of information you can handle, so you're not even aware that you don't know everything. You're not aware of its grandness or what it is, but you are aware of it intuitively, for intuitively, each Human "feels" that there is something more.

Dear Human Being, as far back as you can look at your history, you came onto the planet and you looked for the Creator. It was an intuition, inside. This is because the Pleiadians came and gave you altered DNA, and the knowledge of light and dark. This is the creation story, and this awareness makes you search for the source of all things.

The Human Soul permeates everything about you. It is not *locatable,* and is pure multi-dimensional energy - sacred energy beyond anything you can ever measure. It's not in a scale that you've ever seen. You don't have a word for it. You don't have colors for it, either, since it's too far above any sensory perception that any Human will ever have. But it is the love part that you feel and sense. You can't explain that at all. It's conceptually beyond your thinking. You simply can't explain your Soul, and you can't explain the Creator. But you know it's there.

Your Soul has no gender. It's generic and beautiful and filled with splendor - and it's inside everyone. Dear ones, it's inside me. I am not a Human, yet it's inside me! I speak to you from a position of honor and gratitude. I've never been a Human, and sometimes I can't believe what you go through. Astonishing to me is that you would have signed up for this! But the Soul is bigger than anything you can imagine. It's the engine of compassion for the Universe.

The DNA Connection

Is the Soul part of your DNA? Yes, of course. Your DNA allows Soul energy to be carried in a certain way, with each Human. I've identified the layers it resides in, but that's not all. It's in every

chemical in your body. It resides in the energy of your consciousness in ways you don't know. It's accessible in ways you don't know, and it loves you beyond measure. I cannot tell you what it is because, again, you don't have the concepts to understand it. But if you could think for a moment of the most beautiful colors you've ever seen, that would be the wrapping it comes in. The most benevolent force you ever felt, that would be the door to the Soul. The most love you've ever had for anyone or from anyone would be the opening words it would speak to you. It surpasses anything you've ever experienced on the planet, and the Pleiadians knew and understood this. With permission from Creative Source, they gave it to you a long time ago. Your DNA was altered, and you now have 23 chromosomes because of it.

Dear ones, the things I give you today will sound outlandish, beyond weird and strange to many. We're prepared for that, but many of you have to hear these things. I'm talking to Old Souls, both listeners and in person. Not all of you will relate, but many can feel the truth. I want to tell you who you are, and if I haven't given you this information before in this way, you need to hear it now.

The Beginning

When humanity was ready to be seeded by the Pleiadians, you were simply part of the animals on the planet, designed to be at the evolutionary stage you were. You were indeed the top of the evolutionary ladder. You were way beyond that of cave men, and you were ready. You looked like you do now, and acted like you do now. But according to plan, you were ready. In the scheme of evolution, it really wasn't that long ago. You were a Human Being, ready to receive something that only a few planets have had, and you had 24 chromosomes (as the apes do, right below you on the scale of evolution).

The beginning of this process was two hundred thousand years ago. One hundred thousand of them were just getting the process ready, so that you would arrive at only *one kind* of Human instead of many kinds, like the other animals have. Even your science asks this question, on why there are no Human varieties, as nature produces with everything else. But esoterically, here is the question: When it was time to build Lemuria, and the seeding took place as it did, who do you think was here to receive the seeds? Do you think it was just regular humans who had come up through Earth's biological evolutionary process? Was it just another animal, by chance, to become the *Adam and Eve* of the planet? The answer is no. It was *you*, and you incarnated from the Pleiades for this moment!

I want to tell you something: When it comes to reincarnation, it's not limited to this planet. You were aware of that, were you not? You had to come from somewhere. When you have exponential growth of humanity, where do you think the pool of Souls comes from? The answer has to be, *other places*. Spiritual life does not emerge from nowhere. Souls are waiting and ready to be part of this planet.

Reincarnation has been happening for millions of years with other planets, long before two hundred thousand years ago. You came from the Pleiadians! You agreed to drop that which you had evolved to, come back into a form that was basic, and receive the seeds. This was because you had to be of a certain kind of chemical readiness called Soul remembrance. All these things you've never heard of, had to be correct for the seeds to take. For the fusing of the DNA into the 23 chromosomes had to work for you and come into a biological body that would not be overwhelmed by it.

The Creation Story

As we say, this is your creation story. So let's put it in simple terms so you can relate to the mythology of your time. Adam and Eve were special; they were you. They had arrived (incarnated) fresh from another place, ready to receive the knowledge of light and dark. This process wasn't random, and your scriptures have told you that. That's who you were. You're not just Old Souls. You're very special Old Souls. You've come from the Pleiades, a system of stars you wouldn't believe. You came from everything, to almost nothing, and you did it because you saw the potential of today. How many lifetimes have you lived within the last

hundred thousand years? What have you been through to get to today? It's vast.

I want to tell you where it's going, and the potential of where it can go. Then I want to paint some timeframes for you, and I don't want to scare you with how long it's going to take. However, I want to show you the potentials of what can happen, and this is where it gets odd.

Life in the Galaxy

Do you believe there is other life in your galaxy? If you are one who's waiting for proof, then you should stop reading, for it's going to be a while before you get the proof you need. However, some things are self-evident. When you were young, and went to the beach, did you postulate if there were other beaches on the planet? If so, did you therefore say, *"There are none until I prove it, and go see them all?"* No. You figured out that it's simply the way the ocean works ... everywhere. There are tens of thousands of beaches, even though you only see one - it's common sense. Well, life is that way within the galaxy ... everywhere. It happened just like it did on Earth, with the same process. The thought of you being the only ones who have lived is absolutely against all common sense. Even still, you might say, *"I still have trouble with the whole idea."* If so, then you are one of the humans who has been programmed to accept the mythology of creation above scientific probability. There is no judgment with this, but it may delay the grandness of your self-realization.

When I say *Pleiadian*, who do you think about? What do you picture? Perhaps a creature with humanoid form, only a bit taller and very wise? Perhaps they come here in vehicles, or (gulp), instantly without vehicles? If they come instantly (as they indeed do), what might that tell you about what they have, that you don't?

The Seven Sisters

Let me paint a picture about your seed parents: The Pleiadian stars, the Seven Sisters Constellation, are actually made up of nine suns. Of the nine, there are three main habitable planets (all settled by Pleiadians eventually). They have been a society of enlightened humanoids for two million years. Think for a moment – you've got two hundred thousand years, and one hundred thousand of it where you actually seeded properly. Fifty thousand years ago is really where it all began in Lemuria and other related places. Yet, I just told you that the Pleiadians have been at it for two million years!

Therefore, you're looking at a society that is eight times older than yours – eight times! They went through what you did, almost to the tee! They grew up and matured the way you did, and there was a timeframe for them too. They went into *graduate status*, like you are now doing, and everything changed for them. Two million years they have been around, and a large portion of that, about ten thousand years, were spent killing each other. Sound familiar? Killing each other! Indeed, they were in the *playground of consciousness* casting stones and calling names, without any elegance of maturity while in the dark. These are the very same issues you have been through. They passed the marker and they began to receive information, just like you.

The Attributes of the Pleiadians

Dear ones, their DNA is structured like yours; only the chemical count is different. You probably knew that. You're going to find this all over the galaxy, for the principles that created it here, have created it everywhere. It is the basic galactic building block of life. It exists even in your solar system, and you're going to see it someday when you are able to go to all the places you are observing. You will find DNA! Then the "aha!" You're going to start understanding that it's a naturally occurring life process everywhere.

As they matured and grew up, the Pleiadian DNA started to become more viable. The percentage of its efficiency began to increase ... 44%, 54%, 55%, 66%, 77%, 88%. Let me tell you what happens at 88%. At that point, you actually start to meld with the Soul. You're designed to be divine! Did you know that? I want to tell you something. You're designed to live forever. Your design is that of renewable biology. Every cell keeps going and going, especially

the divinity in you. When it starts becoming more efficient, cellular rejuvenation creates new ones from the stem blueprints, not copies as it does now. This cellular structure never really gets old. You never get old! *"Kryon, this sounds nice, but what are you going to do with overpopulation when a civilization never gets old?"* Let me give you a hint: The Pleiadians have got three planets. Does that tell you something? You learn to move around, and you learn about the Universe. It's not an issue and it's not a problem. It becomes a beautiful, easy choice. In addition, there is divine wisdom not to reproduce - ultimate free choice to control population freely and with collective wisdom.

A Pleiadian is the closest thing you'll ever see to an angel in your life. They're working at 88%. They have control over physics, and it's natural, not done with devices. They've entangled themselves with anything they want to be entangled with [entanglement used as a physics term here]. The Human Soul is divine, physics at its core, with wise control over everything. The Creator is in the Soul. The Creative Source is the master physicist of the Universe. If you are at 88% of that, you've got control over everything. That's the seed that you have inside. Does this sound familiar? What did some of the masters of the planet do that was so remarkable? Use common sense - it was their control over physics. Miracles? Perhaps master-like abilities are just DNA working at 88%.

The Pleiadians were seeded by others. We've talked about Orion and Arcturus. These names are your seed grandparents. There's even one before those names, which you've never even heard of. Think of the time scale and it should make sense. Your planet is more than four billion years old. Where have you been? You're the new kid on the block here! You're really new. Imagine what was going on in your galaxy while the Earth cooled. Do you know how long a billion years is? Imagine what went on, and the life that was going through its own cycles. This is common sense, and involves good probability thinking from those who call themselves scientists.

This is the only planet of free choice in this galaxy at this moment, dear ones, and each selected planet has this attribute

– one at a time. You have just passed a major marker, and all the life in this galaxy that has divine DNA knows about you. The signal was sent in December 2012. I want to tell you what that does. It brings celebration, hope, visitors, and help. The real system of maturity begins. This wasn't a "given" in your probability. In fact, you pulled this out at the last moment.

Spiritual Evolution

My partner has spent the day talking to you about spiritual evolution within the cellular structure of your body. This evolution begins to create a symbiotic relationship between your DNA, your Akash, and your intuition. All of these things he covered, but he never really talked about the Soul. The reason is because we haven't given this to him yet. The system of spiritual evolution comes through the Soul, period. It doesn't come through the pineal or the brain. The pineal senses the Higher-Self. Intuition senses the Higher-Self. But the Soul is the energy that delivers the information. The Soul is connected to the grids. Your Human Soul is the catalyst, and always was, for the graduation energy that you are now ready to receive. This ascension energy does not come in through the Human portion of cellular structure. It cannot. Many planets fail, and destroy themselves, since an entire civilization "growing up" and maturing is a process of free choice through non-cellular systems.

Different Kinds of "Remembrance"

The time capsules* that are opening, which the Pleiadians have activated, are going to be "seen" by several parts of you. Some, through the grids, but some are seen by the *Soul* part of you. The Soul part of you is only engageable as you approach 44% (of the efficiency of your DNA). This is the signal for it to fully unfold. Spiritual evolution is going to be an increase in something that we've never talked about, but which you are starting to feel. We're going to call it *Soul remembrance.* You are starting to remember things beyond Earth!

Your main Akash only features experiences from Earth. Let me tell you something about that. We gave you information a

long time ago about what happens to your Akashic remembrance when you pass over the veil. It stays here on Earth. It's in the Cave of Creation, in a crystalline substance that *remembers* or stores everything. It's like you have your own crystal, and it stays on the planet. When your Soul comes back, it picks up the information, puts it into your DNA, and off you go into another reincarnate adventure. In other words, your Akash stays here on the planet.

So let me ask you this: If this is so, why then are some of you remembering who you were on another planet? The answer is that some of you are remembering the Pleiadian energy. Some of you are remembering that you actually went through this before! For some, it's giving you hope, because you know what happened. You got to see 88% within your DNA a long time ago, and that's why you're here. The chance of that happening here actually needs this remembrance, and you're not going to miss it! Who knows how long it's going to take? It doesn't matter, because you're going to be here the whole time. This is *Soul remembrance*, not cellular DNA Akash remembrance. Soul remembrance deals with all life, everywhere. Eventually, you may even remember that you are eternal.

Who were you five million years ago? This is going to occur to you, as well. Do you want to really know where your Souls are coming from? The answer is from *all the planets of free choice, which have graduated*. They're not coming from the sky in some Soul-well from the Creative Source. They are coming from other places that have gone through this, dear ones. That's who you are. However, the ones in the room and the ones listening and reading wouldn't be here, unless you had a certain attribute of Soul remembrance that is already at work.

The Pull of the Future

This attribute of spiritual maturity is so attractive, dear ones, that you can't leave it alone. You KNOW what it feels like to come to a place where you're one with God. You've been there and you've done that, and you were the first on the planet to receive the seed. Now you begin to awaken and remember a little of what it was like – just a little. You struggle with the conflicts of being a

Human, but at the same time, you know what might be ahead, and what you can do. Frustration happens, and sometimes, chemical imbalance. In the last two years, many have even died. Maybe some of these have been friends of yours? You weren't ready for it. Maybe they've been partners? I want to tell you something, if you haven't heard it before: They're back! The reason they left was to have a new blank slate now, at the refresh of the energy. They had to leave in order to pave the way for your return, dear ones, because of what happened in 2012. They were scheduled to leave early, to pave the way for your coming back.

You see, there is a grand system here that is beyond benevolence. There is a system here that reeks with the greatest love of the Creative Source, and you can't imagine it. It is dripping with honor for you, waiting for you to become one with God. Even beyond that, as you increase the percentage of efficiency of your DNA, your Soul brings in more creative energy from the Central Source. That's the evolvement of the Human spirit. It's way beyond biology, way beyond consciousness, as you handshake with the Creative Source of the Universe.

Timing: Always the Issue

I complete this simple story of the Soul. Now you know what's happening. You might want to review the words, "How long will it take?" Too long. [Smile] Dear ones, this is just the beginning. You're in year two [2013 was the year of recalibration; year 2014 was year one]. Now you will slowly start to see humans mature in spirit. We have said it over and over. The things that are so out of balance today in humanity will start to be balanced and mature with time. Eventually, you'll see change everywhere in every aspect - even politics.

Balance, compassion and wisdom will start to be seen. When you reincarnate next time, you're going to remember who you are, that's my promise. You may not remember your name, or what Human you were, but you will remember that you were here, and you are back. You're going to pick up where you left off. You'll be a wise old child beyond any children you know today, and you're not going to make the mistakes you did this time around - none of them.

This is new wisdom, and it comes in with you. Much more than the normal Akash, Soul remembrance will keep you safe and your children will carry what you carry. That's the way it's going to work. Basic Soul remembrance will propel it forward past *peace on Earth* into graduation! Is this too esoteric for you? It's okay. I've got time for you to understand it. Check in with me - in about a million years.

And so it is.

Kryon live channelling "The Human Soul Revealed"
given in San Rafael, California – December 13, 2014

The above channel highlights that, despite a long period of history, humanity hadn't learned anything other than war, kill and conquer. Something either had to change, or the much predicted Armageddon would destroy humanity. Something did happen, we changed and we have passed the 2012 marker. As a result, the Soul is now taking the load for spiritual evolution and pushing us to learn more about what the Soul really is, and this will propel us into peace on Earth and beyond. What Kryon has revealed to us is that the Human Soul is going to be the major player in the next stage of spiritual evolution, whereas it has not previously been this way. History shows that we never evolved **wisdom**. The "conquer and kill" cycle kept repeating. We now have the ability to begin integrating the Soul with our consciousness – we have Soul Maturity. The new gift and tool we have available to us is: ***The ability to integrate the Soul*** in a way that we never could before we passed the marker.

Congratulations, Old Soul, for your magnificence and your grandness, and the part you now play in creating a history that will be unlike any other on Earth! We are indeed all awakening and the Soul is ready to begin this new journey with you.

Namaste!

---

* *http://www.kryon.com/CHAN%202013/k_channel13_saltlake.html*

ABOUT THE AUTHOR

Monika Muranyi has always had a deep affinity and connection with our planet Earth. She has a Bachelor of Applied Science degree with Honors obtained at Southern Cross University, New South Wales, Australia. Monika has worked in various national parks within Australia and New Zealand for over fifteen years. She is an accredited Electro Magnetic Field (EMF) Balancing TechniqueTM Practitioner (Phases I to XIII). Her passion also includes photography. Many of her photographs can be seen on Lee Carroll's website, as well as her own:

www.kryon.com and *www.monikamuranyi.com*

Monika has carefully researched the information within this book, and travelled to many places during the process of discovering and understanding her own Akash. Some of the places where she has travelled include Australia, New Zealand, United States, Chile, Argentina, Brazil, Uruguay, Bolivia, Peru, Ecuador, Colombia, Venezuela, Mexico, Hawaii, Russia, Ukraine, Poland, Bulgaria, Hungary, Germany, Switzerland, Spain, Italy and Portugal.

The inspiration to write and produce this book is a result of Monika's desire to share the wisdom and teachings of Kryon, so that others can understand the magnificence of who they are and reconnect with their Soul essence, that Golden Angel that lives within each one of us.

PREVIOUS TITLES

Have you ever wondered about Earth energies, ley lines, portals, sacred sites, and the conscious relation between Gaia and humanity? If so, then this is definitely the book for you.

Have you ever wondered where your personality comes from? What about your fears and phobias? What creates a child prodigy? Is it possible that you have lived before? The answer to these questions and more is the purpose of this book.